THE
National ◆SABR◆ Pastime

New York, New York
Baseball in the Big Apple

Edited by Cecilia M. Tan

 **Published by The Society for American Baseball Research**

THE NATIONAL PASTIME

Editor: Cecilia Tan
Design and Production: Lisa Hochstein
Cover Design: Lisa Hochstein
Fact Checker: Clifford Blau
Proofreader: Norman L. Macht

Front cover photo credits:
National Baseball Hall of Fame: *New Yankee Stadium, Ebbets Field, Polo Grounds, Shea Stadium, Tom Seaver, Casey Stengel.* Keith Allison: *Derek Jeter.* Leslie Jones, Boston Public Library: *Jackie Robinson.* Library of Congress Bain Collection: *John McGraw.* Major League Baseball: *Yoenis Cespedes.* US Department of the Interior: *Yankee Stadium 1920s.* Wikimedia Commons, Richie K: *Citi Field.*

ISBN 978-1-943816-47-7 print edition
ISBN 978-1-943816-46-0 ebook edition

"New York's First Base Ball Club" by John Thorn previously appeared in slightly different form as "New York Base Ball Club (a.k.a. Washington BBC, Gotham BBC)" in *Base Ball Founders*, edited by Peter Morris et. al., McFarland & Company, 2013.

Society for American Baseball Research, Inc.
Cronkite School at ASU
555 N. Central Ave. #416
Phoenix, AZ 85004

Web: www.sabr.org
Phone: (602) 496–1460

Contents

The Making of Legends

Francis Kinlaw

Before King George took over the Bronx,
Before the Dodgers and Giants flew west;
Baseball stars sparkled in New York
During seasons that ranked with the best.

Terry Cashman recited many of their names
While singing *Willie, Mickey and the Duke*;
Players who excelled on lustrous green grass,
Gaining glory, but few piles of loot.

But much of that excellence might not have
 been noted
Without descriptions from radio and print,
As reporters of news brought light to the sport
And expanded baseball's big tent.

Men in booths spoke through eastern airways—
Shining stars of New York radio;
Their voices were heard in neighborhood streets
Recounting a pitch, hit, or heave-ho!

There was a Barber (not Sal), and a Hodges
 (not Gil)
And others of broadcasting fame:
Mel Allen and Harwell, Gowdy and Gleeson,
Vin Scully on the road to acclaim.

Dizzy Dean and "The Scooter" entertained after
 playing,
Joe E. Brown arrived from movie screens;
Connie Desmond and Doggett, Bob Delaney and
 Helfer,
Bill Crowley and Jim Woods could set scenes.

Andre Baruch sat among the Flatbush crew,
Nat Albright gave studio re-creations:
From his sound effects and imagination
Came ballpark sounds, even ovations.

Men with typewriters, meanwhile, fed bits
 and bites
To a public hungry for every phrase;
Morning and evening papers brought vivid accounts,
Further igniting a national craze.

The *Herald Tribune*, the *Daily News*,
The World-Telegram and the *Times*;
Competition reigned, and you could buy all four,
For only a couple of dimes.

The *Journal American*, the *Daily Mirror*,
Morning Telegraph and *New York Post*;
Topics affecting three major league teams
Kept readers absolutely engrossed.

To writers like Dan Daniel, and Drebinger,
Ken Smith and Roger Kahn;
Joe King, Kremenko, Murray and Gross of
 the *Post*,
Sports fans were habitually drawn.

Ed Sinclair, Joe Trimble, and Ben Epstein
Had loyal readers, too;
Rosenthal and Effrat, along with a host of their
 peers,
Shared quotes or an interview.

Willard Mullin attracted readers in a different way
As cartoonist for the *World-Telegram* and *Sun*;
By depicting characters from the New York scene—
Most notably his "Brooklyn Bum."

All of which fed the fame of those men
Who were praised in Cashman's great song;
A fame dependent upon, in an obvious way,
The cast that kept tagging along.

Sources

Databases maintained by SABR's Baseball and the Media Research Committee.
Marc Okkonen, *Baseball Memories 1950–1959* (New York: Sterling Publishing Company, 1993)
Stuart Shea (Gary Gillette, Executive Editor), *Calling the Game: Baseball Broadcasting from 1920 to the Present* (SABR, 2015)
Curt Smith, *Voices of the Game* (New York: Simon & Schuster, 1987)

New York's First Base Ball Club

John Thorn

Recent study has revealed the claim of the Knickerbocker Base Ball Club of New York to pioneer status, as well as that of Alexander Cartwright to be the game's inventor, to be suspect if not altogether baseless. I have taken up the latter claim at length in *Baseball in the Garden of Eden* and will not do so here, except to reiterate my view that baseball was not invented but instead evolved. All the same, however, it had many fathers—prime among them William Rufus Wheaton, Daniel Lucius "Doc" Adams, and Louis F. Wadsworth—each of whom may be credited with specific innovations that were previously credited to Cartwright.[1]

Adams played ball as early as 1839, the year he came to New York after earning his M.D. at Harvard.[2] As he declared to an interviewer in 1896, when he was eighty-one:

> I was always interested in athletics while in college and afterward and soon after going to New York I began to play base ball just for exercise, with a number of other young medical men. Before that [i.e., before 1839] there had been a club called the New York Base Ball Club, but it had no very definite organization and did not last long. Some of the younger members of that club got together and formed the Knickerbocker Base Ball Club, September 24, 1845 [actually September 23].... About a month after the organization of this club, several of us medical fellows joined it, myself among the number.[3]

Wheaton testified to an interviewer in 1887, when he was seventy-three, that he had written the rules for that New York Base Ball Club in 1837.[4] And Wadsworth, who in 1857 gave to baseball the key features of nine innings and nine men to the side, began to play baseball with the Gotham Club, successor to the New Yorks, in 1852 or 1853.[5]

While the Knickerbocker was the most enduringly influential of the baseball clubs that sprang up prior to the Civil War, it was not the first to play the game,

or the first to be organized, or the first to play a "match game" (one contested between two distinct clubs), or the first to play by written rules which we might regard as governing the "New York Game." This regional variant, in which we may detect the seeds of baseball as we know it today, was distinct from the Massachusetts or New England Game, also called round ball or, with justice, simply "base ball," a descriptive name that applies, in my view, to all games of bat and ball with bases that are run in the round—and thus not only to the New York Game but also to the versions played in Massachusetts, Philadelphia, and elsewhere.

If the Knickerbockers were not the first to play the New York Game, what clubs preceded them? Perhaps it was the Gymnastics and the Sons of Diagoras, clubs associated with Columbia College, who played a game of "Bace" in 1805, which the former won by a score of 41–34.[6] Perhaps it was the unnamed clubs that contested at Jones's Retreat in New York's Greenwich Village in 1823.[7] It may have been the men of the Eagle Ball Club, organized in 1840 to play by rules similar if not identical to those of the KBBC.[8] Or it may have been the Magnolia Ball Club or the New York Club, each of which played baseball among themselves at the Elysian Fields of Hoboken in the autumn of 1843 and, like Doc Adams's medical fellows, had played in New York City before then.

So, it must be said, had many other men who would become Knickerbockers. They were playing ball at Madison Square and Murray Hill in the early 1840s. Charles A. Peverelly, in his *Book of American Pastimes* (1866), wrote:

> At a preliminary meeting, it was suggested that as it was apparent they would soon be driven from Murray Hill, some suitable place should be obtained in New Jersey, where their stay could be permanent; accordingly, a day or two afterwards, enough to make a game assembled at Barclay street ferry, crossed over, marched up the road, prospecting for ground on each side, until they reached the Elysian Fields, where they

"settled." Thus it occurred that a party of gentlemen formed an organization, combining together health, recreation, and social enjoyment, which was the nucleus of the now great American game of Base Ball so popular in all parts of the United States, than which there is none more manly or more health-giving.[9]

The Knickerbocker party of course did not wander about northern New Jersey looking for a place to play. They had been preceded by other clubs, both baseball and cricket, in selecting the Elysian Fields; proprietor Edwin Augustus Stevens (in conjunction with his brothers) had already donated the use of his grounds to the New York Cricket Club and the New York Yacht Club, and had offered liberal lease terms to the Magnolia and New York baseball clubs.[10]

In this support of sport, Stevens was of course encouraging traffic to the Elysian Fields: he controlled the ferries as well as the resort, which included the Beacon Course, a horseracing track opened in 1834. By encouraging play (and gambling) on his turf and along his waters, he created a long-standing model for "traction magnates" to own baseball clubs. Of less interest to scholars have been the naming precedents from clubs in sports that captured the public fancy earlier than baseball, but these provide archaeological hints at how baseball developed within pre-established models.

Both the Knickerbocker and New York names were attached to boating clubs in the early years of the century. Rowing was America's first modern sport, in that competitions were marked by record keeping, prizes, and wagers, yet also provided spectator interest for those with no pecuniary interest. The first boat club to be organized in the United States was named the Knickerbocker, in 1811.[11] As reported in the *New-York Mirror* of July 15, 1837, by boating veteran "Jacob Faithful," who borrowed his *nom de plume* from an 1834 novel by Frederick Marryat:

This club suffered a suspension during the war [that of 1812], and for many years subsequently the boat which bore its name was hung up in the New-York Museum, as a model of the finest race-boat ever launched in this port. Subsequent attempts to revive the association fell through; and though many exertions to form new ones were made, yet the first effort that succeeded in establishing the clubs upon their present footing—viz., building their own boats, wearing a regular uniform, and observing rigid navy discipline, was made in the year 1830, by the

owners of the barge Sea-drift, a club consisting of one hundred persons, which could boast of one no less distinguished in aquatick and sporting matters than Robert L. Stevens for its first president, with Ogden Hoffman, Charles L. Livingston, Robert Emmet, John Stevens, and other good men and true for his successors. To this club the rudder of the old Knickerbocker was bequeathed, with the archives thereto pertaining: nor was anything spared by the members, during the first years of their existence as a club, to give spirit to its doings.[12]

Baseball historians take note. Jacob Faithful was attempting to counter a recent assertion in the *New York Evening Star* that the Wave Club had been the first "to introduce the amusement." The new organization of 1830 referenced above was named the "New York Boat Club."[13] The Knickerbocker Boat Club—whose very existence had already, by 1837, been cast into oblivion—did not disappear immediately after the War of 1812. It was still conducting boat races and theatrical benefits in 1820. For its celebrated race of November 1820 against the British-born boat builder John Chambers' *American Star*, the Knickerbocker Club's John Baptis built a replacement for his dry-docked Knickerbocker rowboat of 1811 and called it the *New York*. The *New York* was characterized in the press as "having the real Knickerbocker [i.e., American] stamp."[14]

Boat racing was nothing short of a craze in the 1820s and '30s, as recalled by Colonel Thomas Picton in *Spirit of the Times*, July 7, 1883:

After them [the *New York* and *American Star*] came the *Atalanta*, manned by dry-goods clerks; the *Seadrift*, by bakers; the *Neptune*, by Fulton Market butchers; the *Fairy*, by law students; the *Columbia* and the *Halcyon*, by city collegians; the *Water Witch*, by engine runners; the *Red Rover*, by Ninth Ward firemen, and so on to the end of a miraculous chapter, utterly exhausting the catalogue of sea-gods, nereids and hamadryads deified in pagan mythology. Boat-builders toiled night and day in the production of racing novelties, and one fair of the American Institute, appropriately held at Castle Garden, was almost entirely consecrated to specimens of their art, painted in all the colors of the rainbow, and in others, emanating from overtaxed imaginations, any man inventing a previously-unknown hue being tolerably certain of immediate canonization.

To my eyes, the boating craze, with its attachment of clubs to specific occupations and classes, parallels intriguingly the baseball craze of the 1850s and '60s.

The New York Cricket Club that has come down in history was organized at McCarty's Hotel (the Colonnade) in Hoboken on October 11, 1843, as an American-based answer to the St. George Cricket Club, which filled its playing ranks with English nationals. The first twelve members of the NYCC were drawn from the staff of William T. Porter's *Spirit of the Times*, with elected members coming from the sporting set that swirled about that weekly journal, including Edward Clark, a lawyer; William Tylee Ranney, a celebrated painter who lived in Hoboken; and James F. Cuppaidge, an accountant who played as "Cuyp the bowler."[15] Some have speculated on a connection between the New York Cricket Club and the New York Base Ball Club, founded in the same year, but firm evidence has not yet emerged. Picton, the NYCC secretary, wrote in the *Clipper*: "The New York, with commendable fore-sight…established their grounds at Hoboken, to the rear of the Elysian Fields. For a couple of years they played upon a section of the domain of Mr. Edwin A. Stevens but subsequently they removed to a more spacious and accessible locality [the Fox Hill Cricket Ground], just beyond the upper end of the old race track [the Beacon, which closed after the 1845 season]."[16]

The NYCC continued until 1873, but it had stood on the shoulders of earlier cricket clubs bearing the same name. A club of that name had formed in 1837, the same year as the Gotham or New York Base Ball

New York Yacht Club clubhouse in ruin, ca. 1900; designed by A.J. Davis in 1844.

Club, as referenced in the Wheaton reminiscences below. In 1838 it played a match with the Long Island Cricket Club for $500. One year later it played an anniversary match at its grounds on 42nd Street, near the Bloomingdale Road (today's Broadway). Coexisting with the St. George Cricket Club for a while, ultimately the NYCC merged with it under the latter's name, a move that inspired Porter to a nationalistic response in 1843.[17]

According to Chadwick, a "New York Cricket Club" had been founded in 1808 at the Old Shakespeare in Nassau Street; it lasted but one year. But another one predated that by at least six years, meeting at the Bunch of Grapes, at No. 11 Nassau (corner of Cedar and Pine) in 1802.[18] A bit of newspaper digging for this essay has revealed an even earlier New York Cricket Club, going back to 1788.[19]

A New York Sporting Club for the preservation of game within city limits had been created in 1806.[20] Members of the Hoboken Turtle Club—New York's first club, founded at Fraunces Tavern at the corner of Broad and Pearl streets in 1796—were called to order in June 1820 for "Spoon Exercise." In sum, the notion of a New York Club devoted to *baseball* did not arise from nothing.

Accordingly, a series of questions confronts us. If baseball was played by organized clubs prior to the Knickerbockers, which of these might lay fair claim to being the true first—that is, first to organize, first to draft rules for play, and first not only to play a match game but also to endure long enough to influence the game's development? Reflect that the Knickerbockers are credited with playing the first match game, on June 19, 1846…yet history has not accorded an equivalent laurel to their opponents, the New Yorks, who defeated the "pioneers" by a score of 23–1. If the Knicks could not defeat them on the field, however, they were more successful in eradicating them from the historical record, dismissing the victors as unfairly advantaged "cricketers" or, even worse, "disorganized," a slap at any purposeful aggregation in the rising age of system.

Peverelly offered this capsule portrait of the New York Nine: "It appears that this was not an organized club, but merely a party of gentlemen who played together frequently, and styled themselves the New York Club."[21] Henry Chadwick, who may have fed Peverelly his line, had written in the *Beadle Guide* in 1860, "We shall not be far wrong if we award to the [Knickerbockers] the honor of being the pioneer of the present game of Base Ball."[22]

In fact, the New York Club not only preceded the Knickerbocker in every innovation cited above, but was also its progenitor. The process by which they became two separate clubs may not have been an altogether amicable split. The understanding of veteran baseball players at the turn of the twentieth century was exceedingly hazy as to who had been a Knickerbocker and who a member of the New Yorks. A widely syndicated article by Albert G. Spalding (it appeared in the *Akron Beacon Journal* on April 1, 1905) announced the formation of an investigative body to examine the origins of baseball; this has come to be known as the Mills Commission. (This article was read by Abner Graves, who responded to the editor of the newspaper and lifted Abner Doubleday to inventor status.) Extracting from the materials he had received from Chadwick, Spalding named eleven men as Knickerbocker Base Ball Club founders, including: "Colonel James Lee, Dr. Ransom, Abraham Tucker, James Fisher, W. Vail, Alexander J. Cartwright, William R. Wheaton, Duncan F. Curry, E. R. Dupignac Jr., William H. Tucker, and Daniel L. Adams." The first four of these played with the New York or Gotham club, as did Wheaton and Tucker. The last named, Adams, did not join the Knickerbocker until one month after its founding.

Known as the New York or Gotham or Washington from the 1830s through the 1860s, these clubs were lineally the same, and appear to have gone by several names at the same time. The murky relationship between the original Gothams of 1837, the Washingtons, the New Yorks, the Knickerbockers, and the later Gothams may be summarized below.

Because they regarded themselves as the first organized club, the Gotham Club was also called the Washington. A matter of custom, this practice was said to denote that they were, like the father of our country, first. Another explanation, personally alluring but not yet proven, is that the Gotham's alternative name referred to its origins with the influential merchant class—mostly butchers and produce brokers—of Washington Market, founded in 1812. Some of these men organized in 1818 as New York City's first target company (for archery and riflery), which they named the Washington Market Chowder Club.[23] It survived all the way through the Mexican War into the next decade. The *Tribune* reported on November 29, 1850:

> Washington Market Chowder Club. A company bearing the above name, composed, we understand of the butchers of Washington Market, passed our office yesterday morning on a target excursion, accompanied by Dodsworth's Band. They were very numerous, and fine looking body of men. And it would be indeed surprising that any company composed of butchers should be anything else than fine looking; that occupation embraces the most robust and hardy men in the city.

Many in the meat trade went on to become political wheeler-dealers and sporting men (not sportsmen), from Bill "the Butcher" Poole—whose father had been a Washington Market butcher before him, with his stand occupying the same place—to James McCloud, the butcher and pool-seller who facilitated the Louisville game-fixing scandal of 1877.

The weekly *New York Illustrated* offered a colorful capsule of the Washington Market in 1870:

St. George Cricket Club at Hoboken, New Jersey, 1861. Note the child prodigy George Wright, standing at center.

Flour, meal, butter, eggs, cheese, meats, poultry, fish, cram the tall warehouses and rude sheds, teeming at the water's edge, to their fullest capacity. Fruit-famed, vegetable-renowned Jersey pours four-fifths of its products into this lap of distributive commerce; the river-hugging counties above contribute their share, and car-loads come trundling in from the West to feed this perpetually hungry maw of the Empire City. The concentration of this great and stirring trade is to be met with at Washington Market. This vast wooden structure, with its numerous out-buildings and sheds, is an irregular and unsightly one, but presents a most novel and interesting scene within and without. The sheds are mainly devoted to smaller stands and smaller sales. Women with baskets of fish and tubs of tripe on their heads, lusty butcher-boys lugging halves and quarters of beef or mutton into their carts, pedlars of every description, etc., tend to amuse and bewilder at the same time. Some of the produce dealers and brokers, who occupy the little box-like shanties facing the market from the river, do a business almost as large as any of the neighboring merchants boasting their five-story warehouses.[24]

At some point in the early 1840s the Gotham club was renamed the New York Ball Club, retaining most if not all of its Gotham members. The New Yorks then spun off the Knickerbockers, as Wheaton relates in the 1887 interview offered verbatim below. The Gotham, meanwhile, continued to play ball among themselves from 1845 to 1849, just as the Knickerbocker and Eagle clubs appear to have done. In 1850 those Gotham and New York members who had not attached to the Knickerbockers in Hoboken reconstituted themselves as, yet again, the Washingtons, playing at the Red House Grounds ("a most comfortable 'asylum for distressed husbands,'" offered *Spirit of the Times*) at Second Avenue and 105th Street in New York.

In 1851 this Washington Base Ball Club challenged the Knickerbockers to match games that have been preserved in the historical record. In 1852 the club reverted to its old name of Gothams, "consolidating with" the Washingtons.[25]

Admittedly, this is a serpentine path. Let me now bring in William Rufus Wheaton to help fill in the story. Born in 1814, Wheaton attended New York's Union Hall Academy, at the corner of Prince and Oliver streets, near Chatham Square and the racket court and handball alley at Allen Street, which he appears to have frequented. He read law with the notable attorney John Leveridge, passed the bar in 1836, was active in the New York 7th Regiment, and in 1841 was admitted to practice in the Court of Chancery and the Supreme Court of New York. His legal training, more than that of any other original Knick mentioned as a "father of baseball," equipped him to codify the venerable if still anecdotal playing rules.

Wheaton was a solid cricketer as well as a base-ballist. He umpired two baseball games played between the New York and Brooklyn clubs on October 21 and 24, 1845, both of which were played eight to the side and reported in the press, with accompanying box scores. He recruited members for the Knickerbocker Base Ball Club, as Peverelly noted. He was the club's first vice president. Although paired with the tobacconist William H. Tucker as the entirety of the Knickerbocker Committee on By-Laws, Wheaton appears to have been the one who truly wrote the rules that were formalized on September 23, 1845. Before that, by his own account, he drew up the rules for the Gotham club of the 1830s, which the Knickerbockers adopted with little change aside from repealing the Gotham provision for an out to be recorded by a catch on the fly.

By the spring of 1846, however, barely six months after the founding of the Knickerbocker Club, Wheaton resigned. We do not know the circumstances. On June 5 of that year, the Knickerbockers, not yet one year old, elected their first honorary members, forty-nine-year-old James Lee and fifty-three-year-old Abraham Tucker, both of whom had been Gothams. Wheaton was not accorded such an honor.[26] He left the Knickerbockers and returned to active play at cricket, going on to win a trophy bat for highest score in a match of the New York Cricket Club in October 1848.[27]

On January 28, 1849, a month before Alexander Cartwright's departure from New York, Wheaton embarked for California in a speculative venture called the New York Mining Company, in which he was one of a hundred gold-besotted souls who purchased and outfitted a ship, the *Strafford*, for what would be a 213-day journey to San Francisco around Cape Horn. Although he returned east upon occasion, he made his substantial business and political career in the West.

On Sunday, November 27, 1887, an "interesting history" appeared on page fourteen of the *San Francisco Examiner*. It was entitled "How Baseball Began—a Member of the Gotham Club of Fifty Years Ago Tells About It." This interview with an unnamed "old pioneer," undoubtedly Wheaton, lay buried in the microfilm archives until 2004, when Randall Brown published extensive excerpts from it in his landmark article, "How Baseball Began," in SABR's *National Pastime*.[28] Here is the entirety of the *Examiner* piece, with variant spellings and styles intact:

HOW BASEBALL BEGAN
A Member of the Gotham Club of Fifty Years Ago Tells About It.

PLAYED FOR FUN THEN.
The Game Was the Outgrowth of Three-Cornered Cat, Which Had Become Too Tame.

Baseball to-day is not by any means the game from which it sprang. Old men can recollect the time when the only characteristic American ball sport was three-cornered cat, played with a yarn ball and flat paddles.

The game had an humble beginning. An old pioneer, formerly a well-known lawyer and politician, now living in Oakland, related the following interesting history of how it originated to an EXAMINER reporter:

"In the thirties I lived at the corner of Rutgers street and East Broadway in New York. I was admitted to the bar in '36, and was very fond of physical exercise. In fact we all were in those days, and we sought it wherever it could be found. There were at that time two cricket clubs in New York city, the St. George and the New York, and one in Brooklyn called the 'Star,' of which Alexander Campbell, who afterwards became well known as a criminal lawyer in 'Frisco, was a member. There was a racket club in Allen street with an inclosed court. [A note in the Clipper on October 23, 1880, evokes the period: "In olden times Chatham square used to be an open meadow or common, and was the play-ground of the boys of this city. Baseball was the favorite game played on the square, but it was then a simple pastime, with flat sticks or axe-handles for bats, and yarn balls. Occasionally a boy, more lucky than the rest, would bring on the ground a ball made of a sturgeon's nose, procured from the racket court in Allen street, where it had been driven over the wall by a rash blow."]

["]Myself and intimates, young merchants, lawyers and physicians, found cricket to[o] slow and lazy a game. We couldn't get enough exercise out of it. Only the bowler and the batter had anything to do, and the rest of the players might stand around all the afternoon without getting a chance to stretch their legs. Racket was lively enough, but it was expensive and not in an open field where we could have full swing and plenty of fresh air with a chance to roll on the grass. Three-cornered cat was a boy's game, and did well enough for slight youngsters, but it was a dangerous game for powerful men, because the ball was thrown to put out a man between bases, and it had to hit the runner to put him out. The ball was made of a hard rubber center, tightly wrapped with yarn, and in the hands of a strong-armed man it was a terrible missile, and sometimes had fatal results when it came in contact with a delicate part of the player's anatomy."

THE GOTHAM BASEBALL CLUB.
"We had to have a good outdoor game, and as the games then in vogue didn't suit us we decided to remodel three-cornered cat and make a new game. We first organized what we called the Gotham Baseball Club. This was the first ball organization in the United States, and it was completed in 1837. Among the members were Dr. John Miller, a popular physician of that day; John Murphy, a well-known hotel-keeper; and James Lee, President of the New York Chamber of Commerce. To show the difference between times then and now, it is enough to say that you would as soon expect to find a Bishop or Chief Justice playing ball as the present President of the Chamber of Commerce. Yet in old times everybody was fond of outdoor exercise, and sober merchants and practitioners played ball till their joints got so stiff with age they couldn't run. It is to the oft-repeated and vigorous open-air exercise of my early manhood that I owe my vigor at the age of 73.

"The first step we took in making baseball was to abolish the rule of throwing the ball at the runner and order that it should be thrown to the baseman instead, who had to touch the runner with it before he reached the base. During the regime of three-cornered cat there were no regular bases, but only such permanent objects as a bedded boulder or an old stump, and often the diamond looked strangely like an irregular polygon. We laid out the ground at Madison square in the form of an accurate diamond, with home-plate and sand-bags for bases. You must remember that what is now called Madison square, opposite the Fifth Avenue Hotel, in the thirties was out in the country, far from the city limits. We had no short-stop, and often played with only six or seven men on a side. The scorer kept the game in a book we had made for that purpose, and it was he who decided all disputed points. The modern umpire and his tribulations were unknown to us."

HOW THEY PLAYED THEN.
"We played for fun and health, and won every time. The pitcher really pitched the ball and underhand throwing was forbidden. Moreover he pitched the ball so the batsman could strike it and give some work to the fielders. The men outside the diamond always placed themselves where they could do the most good and take part in the game. Nowadays the game seems to be played almost entirely by the pitcher and catcher. The pitcher sends his ball purposely in a baffling way, so that the batsman half the time can't get a strike [meaning "a hit"] or reach a base. After the Gotham club had been in existence a few months it was found necessary to reduce the rules of the new game to writing. This work fell to my hands, and the code I then formulated is substantially that in use to-day. We abandoned the old rule of putting out on the first bound and confined it to fly catching. The Gothams played a game of ball with the Star Cricket Club of Brooklyn and beat the Englishmen out of sight, of course. That game and the return were the only two matches [i.e., games with other clubs] ever played by the first baseball club. [NOTE: These undoubtedly refer to the contests of October 1845.]

"The new game quickly became very popular with New Yorkers, and the numbers of the club soon swelled beyond the fastidious notions of some of us, and we decided to withdraw and found a new organization, which we called the Knickerbocker. For a playground we chose the Elysian fields of Hoboken, just across the Hudson river. And those fields were truly Elysian to us in those days. There was a broad, firm, greensward, fringed with fine shady trees, where we could recline during intervals, when waiting for a strike [i.e., a turn at bat], and take a refreshing rest."

LOTS OF EXERCISE AND FUN.
"We played no exhibition or match games, but often our families would come over and look on with much enjoyment. Then we used to have dinner in the middle of the day, and twice a week we would spend the whole afternoon in ball play. We were all mature men and in business, but we didn't have too much of it as they do nowadays. There was none of that hurry and worry so characteristic of the present New York. We enjoyed life and didn't wear out so fast. In the old game when a man struck out[,] those of his side who happened to be on the bases had to come in and lose that chance of making a run. We changed that and made the rule which holds good now. The difference between cricket and baseball illustrates the difference between our lively people and the phlegmatic English. Before the new game was made we all played cricket, and I was so proficient as to win the prize bat and ball with a score of 60 in a match cricket game in New York of 1848, the year before I came to this Coast. But I never liked cricket as well as our game. When I saw the game between the Unions and the Bohemians the other day, I said to myself if some of my old playmates who have been dead forty years could arise and see this game they would declare it was the same old game we used to play in the Elysian Fields, with the exception of the short-stop, the umpire, and such slight variations as the swift underhand throw, the masked catcher and the uniforms of the players. We started out to make a game simply for safe and healthy recreation. Now, it seems, baseball is played for money and has become a regular business, and, doubtless, the hope of beholding a head or limb broken is no small part of the attraction to many onlookers."

* * *

The scorebook that Wheaton referenced, along with the Gotham by-laws and playing rules, was not a figment of his aged imagination. Gotham shortstop Charles C. Commerford wrote to Henry Chadwick in 1905 that the first baseball game he saw (he played in the 1840s and 1850s) was played by the New York Club, which "had its grounds on a field bounded by 23rd and 24th streets and 5th and 6th avenues." Commerford would have seen this game just prior to the fall of 1843, when the New York Ball Club moved its playing grounds to Hoboken. "There was a roadside resort nearby [the Madison Cottage] and a trotting track in the locality. I remember very well that the constitution and by-laws of the old Gotham club, of which I became a member in 1849, stated that the Gotham Club was the successor of the old New York City Club."[29]

Commerford added, in a 1911 letter to the New York World: "There was always some little contention between the Knickerbocker Club and the Gotham Club as to the date of organization. The Knickerbockers claimed

that they were the first to organize and the Gothams claimed priority, as the New York Club was merged into the Gotham and the former (New York) always insisted that they were the first to organize as such."[30]

To provide additional gloss on Wheaton's reminiscence, the games cited above, in which the Gothams "beat the Englishmen out of sight," were the very same games recorded in the press as pitting New York against Brooklyn in late October 1845. These were the last two of three games played between representatives of the two cities in that month, although we cannot say for certain that the first game was played by the same clubs as the latter two, as no box score survives to identify its contestants.

The Knickerbockers played *their* first recorded game, an intrasquad contest, in that month as well. On October 6, seven Knicks won by a count of 11–8 over seven of their fellows in three innings. Wheaton was the umpire. William H. Tucker scored three of the losing squad's eight runs.[31] Like Wheaton and other Knickerbockers, he had been a player with the New York Base Ball Club and maintained his tie to them, indeed playing in the two formal matches of the New Yorks with the Brooklyn Club on October 21 and 24 of 1845, a month after he had helped to form the Knicks. In *The Tented Field: A History of Cricket in America*, author Tom Melville pointed to an even earlier contest between Brooklyn and New York clubs, played on October 10 and reported in the *New York Morning News*.[32] Research more than a decade later has revealed a somewhat fuller account in the obscure and short-lived newspaper the *True Sun*:

> The Base Ball match between eight Brooklyn players, and eight players of New York, came off on Friday on the grounds of the Union Star Cricket Club. The Yorkers were singularly unfortunate in scoring but one run in their three innings. Brooklyn scored 22 and of course came off winners.[33]

Many of the early New York baseballists had cut their teeth on cricket, and this was true of the Brooklyn players as well. In the game of October 21, conducted at the Elysian Fields, the eight players of the New York club won handily. They did so again in the game three days later, played at the grounds of the Union Star Cricket Club, opposite Sharp's Hotel, at the corner of Myrtle and Portland Avenues near Fort Greene. The scores were, respectively, 24–4 and 37–19. On both these occasions the Brooklyn baseballists included established cricketers John Hines, William Gilmore, John

Hardy, William H. Sharp, and Theodore Forman.[34] Their lineup appears to have been identical for the two games, as the Ayers in the October 21 box score and the Meyers of October 24 may be alternative renderings of the same individual. The other seven Brooklynites match up.

For me, the New York Base Ball Club second anniversary game of November 10, 1845, reported in the *New York Herald* on the following day, has much in common with the purported "first match game" of June 19, 1846, while the games of October 1845, particularly the latter two, seem to be true match games between wholly differentiated clubs. It could be argued—I certainly would—that the Knickerbockers played no match games until they met the Washington club on June 3, 1851, a game the Knicks won by a count of 21–11. Look at the cast of characters in the *Herald*'s account of the anniversary game.

NEW YORK BASE BALL CLUB: The second Anniversary of this Club came off yesterday, on the ground in the Elysian fields. The game was as follows:

Runs		Runs	
Murphy	4	Winslow	4
Johnson	4	Case	4
Lyon	3	Granger	1
Wheaton	3	Lalor	3
Sweet	3	Cone	1
Seaman	1	Sweet	4
Venn	2	Harold	3
Gilmore	1	Clair	2
Tucker	3	Wilson	1
—		—	
24		23	

J.M. Marsh, Esq., Umpire and Scorer
After the match, the parties took dinner at Mr. McCarty's, Hoboken, as a wind up for the season. The Club were honored by the presence of representatives from the Union Star Cricket Club, the Knickerbocker Clubs, senior and junior, and other gentlemen of note.[35]

Several interesting things emerge from this notice of the game. Prominent Knickerbocker names are present—Wheaton, Tucker, Cone, Clair (Clare). So too are Gotham players of prominence—Lalor, Murphy, Johnson, Winslow, Case. The Davis who plays here and in the game of June 19, 1846, is not the Knickerbocker James Whyte Davis, who played opposite him in at least one contest after J. W. Davis's entrance on the scene in 1850. Venn is Harry Venn, celebrated Bowery icon and proprietor of the Gotham Cottage (a billiard and bowling saloon) at 298 Bowery, longtime clubhouse to the Gotham BBC. Gilmore may well be the Union Star cricketer who played baseball with the Brooklyns on October 21 and 24.

The game of November 10 was played nine to the side, clearly to 21 runs or more in equal innings, a rule that may have been invoked only for formalized contests. The two sides were unnamed. While the New Yorks were celebrating their second year as an organized club, on another field in Hoboken that very same day, the Knickerbockers were playing an intramural match all their own, eight to the side.

So who were these mysterious NYBBC players, so important to baseball's development yet nearly invisible in the shadow of the Knickerbocker Club? Let me supply a brief record with identifications for a few major figures. An addendum to this essay will portray, in a more perfunctory manner than it deserves, the reconstituted Gotham Club from 1852 until it drifted into inconsequence after the professionals formed their league in 1871. Someone ought to write a book.

* * *

According to Peverelly, the Gotham Base Ball Club of New York was organized early in 1852, with a mysterious Mr. Tuche as its first president. In his *Book of American Pastimes* he treated the Washington Base Ball Club as a separate entity, supplying slim details of their two matches with the Knickerbockers on June 3 and 17, 1851. For the first, which the Knicks won by a count of 21–11 in eight innings at the Red House Grounds, all that he had was a line score (both games went unreported in the press). For the second game, which the Knicks won 22–20 in ten innings, he listed the Washington players, several of whom we recognize as New York Base Ball Club players from the 1845

This Gotham Base Ball Club pin, the only example known, belonged to Henry Mortimer Platt, who had played a single match game with the club in 1854. The three men in a tub refers to an ancient Mother Goose rhyme: "Three wise men of Gotham went to sea in a bowl," it went; "if the bowl had been stronger, then my rhyme had been longer."

anniversary game and the purported match game of June 19, 1846: William. H. Van Cott, Trenchard, Barnes, William Burns, C[harles] Davis, Robert Winslow, Charles L. Case, Jackson, Thomas Van Cott. Peverelly also lists the officers of the Gotham Club since 1856 and describes the club uniform of ten years after as "a blue merino cap, with a white star in the centre; white flannel shirt, with red cord binding; blue flannel pants, red belt, and white buckskin shoes."

When the Gothams met the Knicks on July 1, 1853, a game interrupted by rain and resumed on the 5th, their players included: (William) Vail, W. H. Van Cott, Thomas Van Cott, (Robert) Winslow Sr., (Robert) Winslow Jr., Jonathan (John) Lalor, Reuben H. Cudlipp, and two highly skilled new players—Joseph C. Pinckney and Louis F. Wadsworth, both of whom would soon leave the club for greener pastures, perhaps lured by emoluments. Another Gotham with a vagabond temperament was second baseman Edward G. Saltzman, who in the spring of 1856 relocated his jewelry trade to Boston. With Brooklynites Augustus P. Margot and Richard Busteed, Saltzman organized the Tri-Mountain Club to play baseball by New York rules.

On November 7, 1857, correspondent "X" wrote of that year's edition of the club in Porter's *Spirit of the Times*:

Their best men are: Messrs. Vail, Van Cott, Cudlipp, [William] Johnson, [John] McCosker, Wadsworth, Sheriden [Phil Sheridan], Turner, and [Charles] Commerford. Mr. Vail, one of the oldest players in this city, and one of the original members, has had great experience; he has filled the position of catcher since Mr. Burns left (the club miss this player very much). He is a strong bat, and plays with good judgment. Mr. Van Cott stands very high as pitcher, combining speed with an even ball. Mr. Wadsworth formerly belonged to the Knickerbocker [which he joined in 1854, coming from the Gotham], and until the last year or so played in all their matches, but left them through some misunderstanding. It is claimed by his friends that he is the best first base man in any club, perfectly fearless—he will stop any ball that may come within reach—is a good player in any position, as his fielding last Friday will show. McCosker and Johnson are both fine catchers, and remarkably strong batsmen; and of the others it may be said, that if not powerful batters, they are what is termed sure ones, and good catchers…. The Gotham formerly played on the grounds of the Red House, and would probably have played there to this day, had there not some difficulty sprung up with the proprietor or lessee. They play at Hoboken, on grounds but slightly inferior to their old locality.[36]

The Gothams believed they were direct descendants from not only the Washington Club (which they averred to have organized in 1849, not 1850 as Peverelly had it), but also from the primal New York Club. The club limped along through the 1870s as the professionals took hold of the game. In 1871, following the formation of the National Association of Professional Base Ball Players, first professional organization, the Gothams joined with thirty-two other clubs, including the venerable Knickerbocker and Eagle clubs, hoping to keep top-level amateur play alive. In a last-gasp member-recruitment circular issued at the opening of the centennial year of 1876, the club's directors wrote, "The Gotham Base Ball Club dates its existence from the year 1849; it is, therefore, one of the oldest—if not the oldest—organization of its kind in the country."[37]

A few weeks later, *The New York Times* reported on the meeting of old Gotham players that resulted. It was noted that this club had "turned out more professional players than any other," which oddly may have been true. Buried in the notice was the still, to this day, not fully fathomed heritage of the club—like that of the game itself—in the rough and rowdy crowd that populated Washington Market long before.

The meeting on Monday evening was a large and very harmonious one. Old times were talked over, and a unanimous feeling prevailed in favor of reorganizing and keeping up the old club. Mr. James B. Mingay, a gentleman who has done business in Jefferson Market for over thirty years past, was elected president and Mr. Abraham H. Hummel, of the law firm of Howe & Hummel, at No. 89 Centre street, was made Vice President. [Hummel was the notorious underworld lawyer of his day.] The Secretary is Mr. Melchior B. Mason of No. 32 Chambers Street and the treasurer, Mr. Leonard Cohen, of Washington Market. There were about forty of the old members present; and among those who will take an active part in the new organization are Mr. Seaman Lichtenstein, of No. 83 Barclay street, who has been in business over thirty-five years…Mr. John Drohan, Mr. James Forsyth, and Mr. Richard H. Thorn, all merchants of Washington Market, of between twenty and thirty years' standing.[38]

PLAYER PROFILES

Cornelius V. Anderson — President of the Washington Club in the early 1850s after being the Chief Engineer of the Volunteer Firemen from 1837 to 1848. His portrait was prominently displayed at Harry Venn's Gotham Cottage at 298 Bowery, the ball club's headquarters after 1845. Born in New York City on April 1, 1809, Anderson was a mason by trade. In 1852 he became the first president of the Lorillard Fire Insurance Company. His health began to fail in 1856 and he died on November 22, 1858. He was revered among the city's firemen, who erected an elaborate tombstone in his honor at Brooklyn's Green-Wood Cemetery.

Charles H. Beadle — First baseman and officer of the Gotham Club during and after the Civil War, into the 1870s. Charles's brother, Edward Beadle, was also involved in the club and both brothers later moved to Cranford, New Jersey, where Edward served as mayor in 1885.

Edward Bonnell — Edward Bonnell was recalled by George Zettlein as "one of the players" on the Gothams. Born around 1825, Bonnell was a liquor dealer before becoming a member of the New York Board of Fire Commissioners in 1865. Zettlein reported that Bonnell was living in Philadelphia in 1887.[39]

William F. Burns — A Gotham catcher in 1855–56. According to the *Clipper* article quoted in the profile of Venn, Burns died in the 1857 sinking of the *SS Central America*. Contemporary coverage of that tragedy does indeed list among the missing: "William Burns of New York City. Had been in California about a year."[40]

C[larence] A. Burtis — The leading Gotham player of 1860, in which his runs per game ratio was the third best in the National Association, behind only Grum of the Eckfords and Leggett of the Excelsiors. In a game against the Mutuals on September 4, 1860, Burtis hit two home runs. After playing for the Gotham Club in 1859 and 1860, Burtis was absent from the lineup in 1861. He was back by the summer of 1862 and played through at least 1865. He also played in an 1888 old-timer's benefit game for John Zeller, crippled by a gruesome baseball injury. George Zettlein described Burtis [though recalling him as Bustis] as a "boss painter in the Ninth ward," so he can only be

Clarence A. Burtis, a painter who was born around 1835 and died in Manhattan on May 16, 1894. Burtis enlisted in the New York Infantry, Regiment 83, on May 26, 1861, and was a Sergeant-Major by the time of his discharge in June of 1862. Like many of his fellow club members, Burtis was also very active in the fire department.

Charles Ludlow Case — Born in Newburgh, New York, in 1818, he was a NYBBC player in the contest of November 10, 1845, when he resided at 7 Murray and was a merchant at 101 Front. He was at one time a butcher at Washington Market. He also played for the New York Club in the two games against the cricketers from the Union Star of Brooklyn on October 21 and 24, 1845. In the game of June 19, 1846, he played with the club designated as the New Yorks. Case arrived in San Francisco for the Gold Rush on February 27, 1849. At a meeting of January 6, 1851, he became a member of the Finance Committee of the newly formed Knickerbocker Association, composed of New York residents living in San Francisco. He was joined on that committee by Edward A. Ebbets and Frank Turk, who had been members of the Knickerbocker Base Ball Club of New York. It is reasonable to think that they were among the unnamed men reported to have played baseball in Portsmouth Square in 1851.[41] Case returned east and died in Newburgh on March 25, 1857.

Leonard G. Cohen — Officer of the Gotham Club during and after the Civil War; catcher for the ball club. As of 1869 he was a fruit dealer in Washington Market and living at 144 West Street. Cohen was born around 1839 in New York to a Polish-born father (though one census had Germany). He later moved to Westfield, New Jersey, where he served as the first postmaster and was still living as late as 1910.

Charles C. Commerford — Born in New York City, June 2, 1833; died in Waterbury, Connecticut, February 6, 1920. Played shortstop with Gothams and later the Eagles. Moved from New York to Waterbury, Connecticut, in 1864, where he continued to play ball. After some political successes, he was appointed postmaster there by President Grover Cleveland in 1886. His father, the chair-maker John Commerford of New York City, was an abolitionist prominently identified with labor interests, and was a candidate for Congress on the Republican ticket in 1860.

Three Gothams (L to R), all profiled herein: Charles C. Commerford, Harry Venn, and William R. Wheaton.

John Connell — George Zettlein described this man as a member of the Gothams and added that he "was on the *Herald* for some time, and is still [in 1887] a writer."

Reuben Henry Cudlipp — Reuben Cudlipp was a Nassau Street lawyer who served as vice president of the Gotham Club in 1856 and as one of the vice presidents of the NABBP in 1857. He also played for the first nine until 1858. One of the Gothams' better players, he was proposed for membership in the Knickerbockers on April 1, 1854, the same date as that of Louis F. Wadsworth's similar move.[42] Still active as a New York attorney in 1894, he resided at that time in Plainfield, New Jersey, as did Wadsworth (as shown in the NYC Directory for 1894, via ancestry.com). Cudlipp was seventy-eight when he died at his daughter's home in Yonkers on December 5, 1899.

C[harles?] Davis — A frequent entrant in the NYBBC box scores, he has been mistaken in print for the celebrated Knickerbocker James Whyte Davis, against whom he played.

William W. De Milt — Like Harry Venn and Seaman Lichtenstein, he was a member of the Columbian Engine Company, No 14. As a carpenter and machinist for the Union Square, Brougham's Lyceum (where fellow Gotham George W. Smith worked in 1850) and other New York theatres, he was responsible for producing a wide variety of stage apparatus and special effects. Born 1814, died 1875. Buried at Brooklyn's Green-Wood Cemetery.

Patsy Dockney — Born in Ireland ca. 1844, he was a catcher with Gotham in 1864–65. Paid under the table to move to Athletics of Philadelphia in 1866, according to the *Philadelphia Times*, Dockney "used to play ball every afternoon and fight and drink every night. He was a tough of the toughs."

Andrew J. Dupignac — Andrew Dupignac, Gotham Club secretary in 1860 and 1861, was born around 1828. He later became the president of the New York Skating Club and in 1903 was described as "the oldest living amateur skater."[43] Dupignac died in Brooklyn on November 27, 1908.

James Fisher — Identity not known for certain but after thorough review of the New York City directories and considering other factors, I tentatively conclude that this early player, according to Peverelly, was James H. Fisher. Roughly the same age as the two other prominent players who were named honorary Knickerbockers in June 1846—Col. James Lee and Abraham Tucker (the former born in 1796, the latter in 1793)—Fisher was born in 1798. Like Lee, he had made his fortune by 1850 and in the census lists his occupation as "gentleman." Previously he had listed his profession, with subtlety, as "agent." In 1847, the year of his death, his address was 134 Allen Street, the neighborhood from which Wheaton and his mates had begun their search for lively recreation.

Robert Forsyth — In 1855, the year after the death of the affluent patron of this independent military company, the *Herald* reported:

> The Forsyth Cadets, a well drilled company, composed chiefly of butchers belonging to Washington Market, will make their annual parade on the 18th inst.[44]

Shortly before his death, the *Clipper* observed:

> This organization is named in honor of Robert Forsyth, Esq., a gentleman whose name is a "Household Word" to all those who have occasion to visit Washington Market, being one of the most extensive dealers connected with that place. He must indeed feel honored at the compliment paid him by the "Cadets."[45]

Robert Forsyth's sons, Joseph and James, were both Gotham Club members. According to the 1887 *New York Sun* article, Joseph was already dead while James was an oyster dealer.

George H. Franklin — George H. Franklin was one of the club's representatives at the 1857 NABBP convention.

Andrew Gibney — Starting with Gotham Juniors in 1863, he graduated to senior club the following year and played second base with the Gothams in 1865, then center field with the Nationals of Washington in 1866. He played professionally with Olympics of Washington in 1870. Alfred W. "Count" Gedney played as Gibney with the Keystone club in Philadelphia in his early years, but these two are not the same individual.

John V(an) B(uskirk) Hatfield — Widely regarded as one of the best players of the 1860s, with the Eckford and Mutual clubs, he also played one year with the Gothams, in 1865.

Johnson — Played in the NYBBC anniversary contest of November 10, 1845. Harold Peterson, in his book *The Man Who Invented Baseball*, names him as a Knickerbocker and calls him F. C. Johnson. However, Francis Upton Johnston was a member of the Knickerbocker and the New-York Academy of Medicine., as were D. L. Adams and Franklin Ransom. One of his sons also practiced medicine for many years at Hyde Park, where he is buried. The NYBBC Johnson may, however, be neither man but instead William Johnson, named in a reminiscence of the Gotham Cottage by Colonel Thomas Picton in 1878, and a player for the club in the 1850s.

John Lalor — This sturdy New York and Gotham player is surely the Jonathan Lalor listed in the box score published in *Spirit in the Times* on July 9, 1853, detailing a match game between the Knicks and Gothams. He also played in the NYBBC second anniversary game of November 10, 1845. Harold Peterson, in his book *The Man Who Invented Baseball*, instead identifies the player as Michael Lalor, "Segar Seller." I think it is constable John Lalor, who umpired the Knickerbocker intramural game of June 26, 1846 and signed his name in full this way. This fellow was an up-and-comer in the Whig party in the Fifteenth Ward in 1845, and later its leader in the Seventh Ward. A lawyer by profession, he served in the Civil War, organizing the 15th Regiment, known as McLeod Murphy's Engineers. John Lalor was born in 1819 and died on February 21, 1884. His obituary in the *Herald* noted that he was "a member of the Gotham club." At his death he was chief clerk at Castle Garden.

Col. James Lee — According to Wheaton, he was one of the original Gotham Club members of 1837. Born December 3, 1796, he was a prominent businessman and sportsman. President of the New York Chamber of Commerce, he claimed to have played baseball in New York City ca. 1800. John Ward wrote, in *How to Become a Base-Ball Player* (1888),

> Colonel Jas. Lee, elected an honorary member of the Knickerbocker Club in 1846, said that he had often played the same game when a boy, and at that time he was a man of sixty or more years. [In fact he was fifty.] Mr. Wm. F. Ladd, my informant, one of the original members of the Knickerbockers, says that he never in any way doubted Colonel Lee's declaration, because he was a gentleman eminently worthy of belief.

In 1907 Ward added to his remarks about Lee a sentence that echoes editor Porter's reason for establishing the New York Cricket Club:

> Another interesting tale told me by Mr. Ladd was that the reason they chose the game of Base Ball instead of—and in fact in opposition to—cricket was because they regarded Base Ball as a purely American game; and it appears that there was at that time some considerable prejudice against adopting any game of foreign invention.[46]

Lee died June 16, 1874.

Seaman Lichtenstein — A candidate for the first Jewish player, Lichtenstein began to run with Columbian Engine No. 14 at the age of fifteen, becoming a member of the company in 1849, at age twenty-four. He began his business career salvaging scraps from the butchers at Washington Market, selling the meat to the Native Americans who lived in Hoboken and the bones to a manufacturer of glue (Peter Cooper). In the 1880s, he owned a trotter named for Gotham Cottage proprietor and archetypal Bowery B'hoy Harry Venn. He died at age seventy-seven on December 24, 1902.[47]

John McCosker — A third baseman, he began play with the Gothams in 1856 and played in Fashion Race Course Game 3 and in many games for the Gothams of the 1850s. Tom Shieber reported in the 1997 *National Pastime*:

> In a match game played between the Gotham and Empire clubs in September of 1857, McCosker hit a home run with the bases

full. While he was most probably not the first to accomplish the feat, the description in the *New York Clipper* is the earliest known recounting of what would later be termed a grand slam: "The Gothamites…scored 4 beautifully in their last innings, chiefly owing to a tremendous ground strike by Mr. McCosker, bringing each man home as well as himself."

George Zettlein described McCosker ("McClosky") as an engineer of the Fire Department, so there can be no question that the ballplayer was John A. McCosker, who was born around 1829 and was a fire department engineer prior to the war. When the war started, McCosker was one of the organizers of the 73rd Infantry—the Second Fire Zouaves—in which he served as a quartermaster until being discharged on August 4, 1862. His whereabouts become much harder to trace after that, but he may have died in 1881.

Dr. John Miller — According to Wheaton, he was one of the original Gotham BBC members of 1837. In 1842 John Miller, physician, is at 74 James Street. In 1845 he is at 186 East Broadway.

James B. Mingay — Mingay entered the poultry business in Jefferson Market in his youth and remained in it until age seventy-two. For 14 years he was a member of the Volunteer Fire Department with Hose Company 40, the Empire. He was a member of the Jefferson Market Guard and a judge of its target excursion on Christmas Day, 1857, an officer of the Gotham club 1861–64, and in 1876 a director of the North River Insurance Company. Born January 6, 1818, he died April 27, 1893, at his 19 Christopher Street residence.

John M. Murphy — According to Wheaton, he was a "hotel-keeper" and one of the original Gotham BBC members of 1837. He played in NYBBC anniversary contest of November 10, 1845, in Hoboken. Murphy's establishment is the Fulton Hotel at 164 East Broadway.

Joseph Conselyea Pinckney — In a celebrated early instance of revolving, or seeming professionalism, Pinckney played a game with the Gothams in 1856 while still nominally a member of the Union of Morrisania. Both the Unions and the Knickerbockers objected publicly. Along with Knickerbocker defector Louis F. Wadsworth, he played with the Gotham in 1857. The next year, back with the Unions, he was one of only three New York players selected for the Fashion Race Course match to play in all three games. Enlisting at the outbreak of the Civil War, he was Colonel of the Sixth New York Militia. In 1863 he was brevetted brigadier general of volunteers for war service. Afterward he served in New York City politics as an alderman. Born and died in New York City (November 5, 1821–March 11, 1881).

Henry Mortimer Platt — Born July 7, 1822, Platt died December 8, 1898. He played a match game in 1854 but otherwise served Gotham Club as scorekeeper. He merits mention because in 1939 his daughter donated the sole surviving badge of the Gotham Base Ball Club, featuring three men at sea in a tub, to the National Baseball Hall of Fame.

Dr. Franklin Ransom – In the game of June 19, 1846, Dr. Ransom played with the club designated as the New Yorks. In 1838 Dr. Ransom resided at 44 Wall. He was in a medical partnership with Dr. Lucius Comstock but also found time to invent a fire engine with a modified hydraulic system. Dr. Ransom exhibited his fire engine to the City Council in 1841 but came to believe that the city had stolen his design. In 1858 he took a patent infringement lawsuit against the Mayor of New York all the way to the United States Supreme Court, but did not prevail. Ransom was born near Buffalo in 1805 and earned his medical degree in 1832 from what was then known simply as the University of New York. He eventually returned to Buffalo, where he continued to file new patents but slipped into obscurity. He died there on March 25, 1873.

Edward G. Saltzman (Salzman, Salzmann, Saltzmann) – Born about 1830 in Jefferson County, New York, he was schooled in Hoboken, New Jersey. Saltzman played second base for the Gotham club of New York for five seasons, from 1852–56 and helped to bring the New York Game to Massachusetts via the Tri-Mountain Club. He brought baseball to Savannah, Georgia, in 1865, forming the Pioneer Club, then returned to Boston two years later and resided there until his final year. He died August 14, 1883, in Brooklyn.[48]

T. Seaman(s) – Playing in NYBBC anniversary match of November 10, 1845, he may be a billiard room proprietor of that name or, more likely, he is one and the same as the later Gotham player and treasurer Seaman Lichtenstein, discussed earlier.

James Shepard – After playing with Gotham, then Alpine BBC in 1860, he was a pioneer in establishing baseball in San Francisco, beginning in 1861.

William Shepard – Brother of James, he also played with Gotham, then Alpine BBC in 1860. Pioneer in establishing baseball in San Francisco, beginning in 1861.

Philip Sheridan – Sheridan Joined the Gothams in 1854 and frequently umpired. Said by Peter Nash in *Baseball Legends of Brooklyn's Green-Wood Cemetery* to have been buried in Green-Wood Cemetery in Brooklyn, but that interred Philip Sheridan is not the Gotham player.

George Washington Smith – A member of the Gotham Club after 1845, he was born and raised in Philadelphia. Smith was considered the only male American ballet star of the 19th century. He went on to become ballet master at Fox's American Theater. He also served in this capacity at the Hippodrome, where the costume of a dancer under his instruction caught aflame with fatal consequence. In his later years he opened a dancing school in Philadelphia. Born ca. 1820, he died February 18, 1899.

Oscar Teed – Oscar Teed, a celebrated ship's fastener and oarsman as well as a Gotham player, was born in 1828 and died November 4, 1866. A boat named in his honor ca. 1860 continued to race.

Austin D. Thompson – Born in 1820, Austin Thompson was described in his obituary as "a Connecticut Yankee, who came to New York when a youth and opened a coffee house in Pine street, near the old Custom House. … The coffee house, which was called the Phoenix, was frequented by the notabilities of the neighborhood, politicians as well as business men, particularly Democratic politicians, for Mr. Thompson was a Jeffersonian Democrat of the old school." As its proprietor, Thompson was the successor to the famed Edward Windust, 149 Water Street (Wall, corner Water). In 1851 his coffee rooms and restaurant relocated from 13 Pine to 25 Pine. It moved again in 1860, this time to 292 Broadway, where it remained until Thompson's death on June 7, 1892. By then Thompson was "probably the oldest eating-house keeper in the city," which made him "a man who knew nearly everybody and nearly everybody knew him."[49]

Richard H. ("Dick") Thorn – He played with Empire Base Ball Club in 1856, yet was a representative of the Enterprise Base Ball Club at the convention of January 22, 1857. With Gotham in 1858, he pitched for New York in Game 3 of Fashion Race Course Match that September. He returned to Empire 1859–61, then was with Gotham again in 1862, and the Mutual 1865–68. Since about 1850, a prominent member and revenue collector of the Washington Market Association, Thorn partnered with Lathrop and then Marcley in his produce business in the 1860s. In the 1870s he wholly owned Thorn & Co., 11–13 DeVoe Avenue, west of Washington St. On January 26, 1889 rode on horseback, with Seaman Lichtenstein, in a parade to mark the opening of the West Washington Market. In that year he lived at 233 West 13th Street, but does not appear in New York City directories thereafter, though he did testify at a hearing in 1890.

Tooker – He played outfield in Fashion Race Course Game 3, and later with the Henry Eckford Club. In 1871 he was a director of the Athletic Base Ball Club of Brooklyn. Possibly this is Theodore, son of William Tooker, ship's carpenter, who joined his brother-in-law George Steers in the shipyards that built the *America*.

Trenchard – This could be Samuel Trenchard, constable or marshal in various years from 1835 until 1861. In 1846 he resided at 86 Ludlow, and played with the club designated as the New Yorks on June 19, 1846. He also played with Washingtons against the Knickerbockers in match game of June 17, 1851. Born in 1791, he died February 15, 1865 in his seventy-fifth year. This would make him a bit of a graybeard for active play in the 1840s and 1850s, so perhaps he is billiard-hall proprietor Alexander H. Trenchard, at 139 Crosby Street in 1855.

Tuche – After the 1856 season, Porter's *Spirit of the Times* reported that the Gotham Club had been organized in the early summer of 1852 with "old ballplayer Mr. Tuche" at its head.[50] Other accounts also name Tuche as one of the principals, but his name soon disappeared from the club's annals and nothing more is known about him.

Abraham W. Tucker – Born in 1793, he was named an honorary member of the Knickerbocker Base Ball Club in June 1846, along with another New York Ball Club player, Col. James Lee. In 1822 he operated a "segarstore" at 205 Bowery. In 1837 he resided at 48 Delancey Street. Tucker is believed to have died in 1853–54.

William H. Tucker was a tobacconist in business with his father, Abraham, who was also a player with the New Yorks. They operated at 8 Peck Slip and lived at 56 E. Broadway. In 1849–50 he lived in San Francisco. In Alexander Cartwright's journal/address book he is listed as: "Wm. H. Tucker 271 Montgomery st. upstairs, San Francisco, Cal." Tucker appears to have died in Brooklyn, at the home of his son-in-law, on December 5, 1894, in his seventy-sixth year, which would conform to a birth year of 1819 recorded in the 1850 census.

Nicholas "Nick" Turner – He played left field in Fashion Race Course Game 2. A shoemaker, he resided in the Tenth Ward in 1860. He was born in Bavaria, 1831. His first name was supplied by Waller Wallace and Henry Chadwick in Sporting Life in 1889.[51]

William Vail – He was the tobacconist at 179 Prince Street in 1849. Born in 1817–18, his wife Mary was born in 1822–23, and their children as of 1850 were all sons: William, Francis, Martin, Daniel, George, in descending order of age. He was known affectionately as "Stay where you am, Wail," for his often disastrous derring-do on the base paths. In later years he played with Knickerbocker.[52]

Gabriel Van Cott – Gabriel acted as umpire for Gothams rather than player. There were a few Gabriels in the Van Cott family, but it appears most likely that this one was a cousin of Thomas and William. Another member of the family, Cornelius C. Van Cott (1838–1904), was the owner of the New York Giants of the National League from 1893 through 1895.

Theodore S. Van Cott – The son of Thomas, Teddy Van Cott later served in the Civil War and died in a home for old soldiers on August 23, 1905.

Thomas Van Cott – Thomas G. (1817–94), who married Harriet Murphy, was the Gothams' best player in the 1850s, and the great pitcher of all New York ball clubs. The *Elmira Gazette* obituary of December 19, 1894, called him "The Father of Baseball" and the first man to pitch a curved ball. He was a bookmaker in later years, at the Saratoga Track.

William H(athaway) Van Cott – This brother of Thomas was born September 26, 1821, in New York City, and died June 30, 1908 in Mt. Vernon, New York. He played in Fashion Race Course Games 1 and 2. Elected first president of the National Association of Base Ball Players when it formally organized in 1858, Van Cott was a lawyer and justice by profession. He continued his family's interest in trotters and began in the stabling business before entering the law. As Justice Van Cott he served sixteen years on the bench. His New York Times obituary reported that his efforts to rid New York of gangs led to two attempts to burn down his house.[53]

Harry B. Venn – Venn played in NYBBC anniversary match of November 10, 1845, and was a noted fireman with Columbian 14 and the proprietor of the venerable (1778) Gotham Saloon beginning in 1830, when he left his porterhouse at 13 Ann Street and took his first lease at the property. His successor in the lease, S.W. Bryham, transformed the cottage in 1836 to become the Bowery Steam Confectionary and Saloon. By 1842, under new ownership, it was renamed the "Bowery Cottage," and was the headquarters for firemen, sporting types, and Bowery B'Hoys. Venn resumed his proprietorship sometime before 1845. Behind the bar at the Gotham was a case with the gilded trophy balls from victorious Gotham Base Ball Club matches. (These survived, amazingly, and were sold to collectors in the 1980s; it would be pleasant to think that the Gotham rules survived too!) The back-bar also featured a big gilt "6" taken from the Americus engine (the inspiration for Christy Mathewson's nickname, "Big Six"). Boss Tweed was a regular patron at the bar. The Gotham Cottage was demolished in 1878, and Venn died a year later, on March 15, 1879. A contemporary wrote that his memorial might be inscribed: "Here lies one whose name was writ in whisky." Much more could be written about Venn and the Gotham Cottage, but suffice for now this snippet from a long paean to the demolished house by Col. Thomas Picton in the *Clipper* on June 1, 1878:

"The Gotham" became, moreover, extensively known in connection with our national pastime, as beneath its roof was held the first general convention of baseball players, one of the earliest clubs in existence deriving its significant title from this snuggery in the Bowery. "The Gotham" Club [as reformed in 1852] was a large association from the hour of its inception, organized through the election of Judge William H. Van Cott as president, and Gabriel Van Cott as secretary, with a roll of influential members, principally business men, embracing Harry B. Venn, Seaman Senchenstein [sic], James Forsyth, Joseph Foss, John Baum, George Montjoy, William Johnson, Edward Turner, E. Bonnell, Bates, Tooker, and a host of other notables. Its first playing members distinguishing themselves were Tom Van Cott, Sheridan, McCluskey [McClosky, "an engineer of the Fire Department," as George Zettlein recalled, in fact John McCosker, who played catcher with the Gothams in 1858], Cudliffe [Cudlipp], and William Burns, its pitcher [catcher?], afterwards lost at sea upon the *Central America*, wrecked in the Pacific [sic].

Louis F. Wadsworth – Born in Connecticut in 1825, he commenced to play baseball with the Washingtons/Gothams in 1852. After a few

The Old Gotham Inn and Bowling Saloon, at 298 Bowery, as depicted in 1862.

years with the Knickerbockers (1854–57) he returned to the Gothams, whom he represented in Fashion Race Course Games 1 and 3. One of the veteran Knicks, in recalling some of his old teammates for the *New York Sun* in 1887, said:

> I had almost forgotten the most important man on the team and that is Lew Wadsworth. He was the life of the club. Part of his club suit consisted of a white shirt on the back of which was stamped a black devil. It makes me laugh still when I recall how he used to go after a ball. His hands were very large and when he went for a ball they looked like the tongs of an oyster rake. He got there all the same and but few balls passed him.[54]

His time with the Knickerbockers, and his crucial role in affixing nine innings and nine men to the rules of baseball, are covered at length in *Baseball in the Garden of Eden*. Dissipating riches and fame, he died a pauper in the Plainfield Industrial Home in 1908.

William Rufus Wheaton – discussed amply above.

Robert F. Winslow – Robert F. Winslow, a lawyer, played in NYBBC anniversary game of November 10, 1845, Hoboken. In the game of June 19, 1846, Winslow played with the club designated as the New Yorks, and played center field for Gothams in mid-1850s. He and his son Robert Jr. played for the Gotham in the match against the Knickerbockers that commenced on July 1, 1853 and, after a rain interruption, concluded on July 5. In 1854, an Albert Winslow played with the Knickerbockers. Some evidence points to Robert Jr.'s earlier demise, but the Robert Winslows are the only father-son pairing of that surname in New York at the time.

George Wright – He joined the Gotham juniors when he was sixteen, in 1863. One year later he graduated to the senior team and was the club's regular catcher. He also caught for the club in 1866 under the name of "George" before transferring his allegiance to the Union of Morrisania, where he converted to left field and then shortstop. Born in 1847, George Wright was perhaps the greatest player of the nineteenth century and certainly its first national hero. He died in 1937, four months before his election to the nascent Baseball Hall of Fame.

Harry Wright – The Civil War so decimated the Knickerbockers' schedule that Wright (1835–95) decided to leave them and join the Gothams in 1863–64. But by the next year he had tired of baseball and resumed his 1850s career, as a cricketer, in Cincinnati, Ohio. He had to wait longer than brother George to enter the Baseball Hall of Fame (1953). Leaving his post as the Cincinnati Cricket Club professional in 1867, he was persuaded to take the helm of the Cincinnati Base Ball Club. The rest is history.

William P. Wright – With Gothams in 1865, played in five games. Not related to Harry and George. Appears to have gone to Cincinnati with Harry Wright at year's end. With that city's Buckeye club in 1868–69, Live Oak in 1870.

Other Club Members – John Drohan, Joseph E. Ebling, Hackett, J.A.P. Hopkins, N.W. Redmond, Charles S. Riblet, Peter Roe, Albert Squires, Cornelius Stokem, Andrew Whiteside. ■

Notes

1. For a full discussion of these three individuals, see the present writer's *Baseball in the Garden of Eden* (New York: Simon & Schuster, 2011).
2. His degree from Yale is reported in an untitled article in the Connecticut *Courant*, August 24, 1835, 3. His medical degree is reported in "Harvard University," *The Boston Medical and Surgical Journal*, September 26,

1838, 127. His work as an attending physician in New York is reported in "New York Dispensary," *The New-York Spectator*, February 27, 1840, 1.

3. "Dr. D. L. Adams; Memoirs of the Father of Base Ball; He Resides in New Haven and Retains an Interest in the Game," *The Sporting News*, February 29, 1896, 3.

4. "How Baseball Began: A Member of the Gotham Club of Fifty Years Ago Tells About It," anonymous journalist interviews William Rufus Wheaton, *San Francisco Examiner*, November 27, 1887, 14.

5. "City Intelligence," *New York Herald*, March 2, 1857, 8. *Eden*, 51–53.

6. *New-York Evening Post*, April 13, 1805, 3.

7. *National Advocate*, April 25, 1823, 2.

8. *Eden*, 80–81.

9. Peverelly, *Book of American Pastimes*, 340.

10. Col. Thomas Picton, "Among the Cricketers," in *Fun and Fancy in Old New York: Reminiscences of a Man About Town* (William L. Slout, editor; Borgo Press, 2007) 140.

11. *New-York Mirror*, July 15, 1837, 23.

12. Ibid.

13. *New-York Mirror*, July 15, 1837, 23.

14. *Commercial Advertiser* [from *New-York Gazette* of that morning], November 13, 1820, 2.

15. Cuyp Obituary, *New York Herald*, July 13, 1871. Also, Picton, "The New York Cricket Club," in *Fun and Fancy in Old New York*, 133–43.

16. Picton, "Among the Cricketers," in *Fun and Fancy in Old New York*, 140.

17. *Spirit of the Times*, March 16, 1844, 37.

18. *New-York Gazette*, March 3, 1803.

19. *New-York Morning Post*, September 19, 1788. Also, *New-York Daily Gazette*, April 20, 1789.

20. *American Citizen*, March 7, 1806.

21. Peverelly, *Pastimes*, 342–43.

22. Henry Chadwick, *Beadle's Dime Base-Ball Player: A Compendium of the Game, etc.* (New York: Irwin P. Beadle and Co., 1860), 6.

23. "The Military Spirit in New York…The Target Companies on Thanksgiving Day," *New York Weekly Herald*, December 14, 1850, 397; also, *The Subterranean*, October 25, 1845, 2

24. *New York Illustrated* (New York: D. Appleton & Co., 1870), 40–41.

25. Peverelly, *Pastimes*, 346..

26. Albert Spalding Baseball Collections, Knickerbocker Base Ball Club of New York, Club Books 1854–1868 at the New York Public Library.

27. *Spirit of the Times*, October 21, 1848, 414.

28. Randall Brown, "How Baseball Began," *The National Pastime* 24 [Cleveland: SABR, 2004], 51-54.

29. "The Old Atlantics of Fifty Years Ago," 1905 clipped article, perhaps from *Brooklyn Eagle*, otherwise undated. Albert Spalding Baseball Collections. Chadwick Scrapbooks, Volume 5. Chadwick quotes from a letter he received from Commerford. Also, *Auburn Citizen*, September 22, 1911, reprinted from *New York World*.

30. *Auburn Citizen*, September 22, 1911.

31. Albert Spalding Baseball Collections, Knickerbocker Base Ball Club of New York, Game Books 1845–1856 at the New York Public Library.

32. Tom Melville, *The Tented Field: A History of Cricket in America* (Bowling Green, OH: Bowling Green State University Popular Press, 1998), 168. Melville erroneously cited the game date as October 11.

33. *True Sun*, October 13, 1845, 2.

34. First names were located in Picton, *Fun and Fancy in Old New York*.

35. "Sporting Intelligence," *New York Herald*, November 11, 1845, 2.

36. Porter's *Spirit of the Times*, November 7, 1857, 148.

37. *New York Herald*, January 7, 1876, 8

38. *New York Times*, January 23, 1876, 7.

39. *New York Sun*, February 6, 1887, 6.

40. *New York Daily Tribune*, September 21, 1857, 7

41. Angus Macfarlane, "The Knickerbockers: San Francisco's First Baseball Team?" *Base Ball* 1:1 (Spring 2007), 7–21.

42. Albert Spalding Baseball Collections, Knickerbocker Base Ball Club of New York, Club Books 1854–1868, New York Public Library.

43. *New York Herald*, March 20, 1903, 12.

44. *New York Herald*, October 14, 1855, 1

45. *New York Clipper*, December 31, 1853.

46. Letter from John M. Ward to A.G. Spalding, stating his "opinion as to the origin of base ball," as Spalding submitted to the Mills Commission.

47. *The New York Times*, December 25, 1902.

48. *New York Clipper*, August 25, 1883, 365.

49. *New York Sun*, June 8, 1892, 4.

50. Porter's *Spirit of the Times*, January 3, 1857.

51. *Sporting Life*, January 16, 1889, 3.

52. *New York Herald*, December 14, 1881, 8.

53. *The New York Times* and *New York Tribune*, July 1, 1908.

54. "Ball Players of the Past," *New York Sun*, January 16, 1887, 10.

Captain John Wildey, Tammany Hall, and the Rise of Professional Baseball

Mark Souder

On Monday morning, before accepting of any civilities at the hands of the Nationals, the Mutuals [of New York] held a special meeting at Willard's Hotel, at which President [Andrew] Johnson was unanimously elected an honorary member of the club. After which such of them as felt like sight-seeing were taken in charge by the Reception-Committee of the National Club and escorted to the Capitol, Patent Office, Smithsonian Institute, Treasury, and the White House, where the entire party were received and presented to the President. The President of the Mutuals, Coroner Wildey, in a few appropriate remarks, informed the President of the action of the club in the morning and presented him with a badge of membership. The President, attaching the badge to his coat, made a few brief remarks, acknowledging and accepting the honor conferred upon him, paid high eulogy to the American game of baseball, and signified his intention of being present at the contest about to take place. The Mutuals and their friends then returned to the hotel.

— *New York Sunday Mercury*, September 1, 1867

This newspaper article gives us a glimpse of the nineteenth century. The *New York World* had carried a similar story a few days earlier which stated that "the Mutuals held a special meeting at their rooms at Willard's Hotel to-day, and elected President Johnson an honorary member of the club. They then visited the President's house, accompanied by the Committee of the Nationals, and held an interview with President Johnson." It also notes that Coroner Wildey presented the President with his badge signifying his honorary membership in their club.

What in the world was going on under the surface? How much of this actually was about *baseball*? Why is a New York City *coroner* the only name mentioned in all the stories except for the President of the United States?

Baseball existed before the Civil War but New York-style baseball, the game as we know it today, was focused almost exclusively in New York. The Civil War helped spread its popularity but most importantly, a new sense of nationalism boosted pride in the game. Politics accelerated the professionalization of it, and once it became publicly significant competition that people were willing to pay to see, baseball became part of public policy and politics from then to now. When President Andrew Johnson became the first President to refer to baseball as "our National Game" during the 1865 baseball matches in Washington, it boosted the idea, first put forth by the *New York Mercury* and other New York newspapers, that baseball was becoming America's national pastime.

Washington, Boston, Philadelphia and Cincinnati Base Ball Clubs began to hire better players post-War, even though the sport was still officially amateur. These "clubs" of young professionals included budding politicians and other emerging leaders often backed by key figures in the political, media, and economic establishment.

Upstate New York was then a powerful political counter-balance to the metro New York City area, and Brooklyn was still independent, but post-Civil War, Manhattan was increasingly dominant as the economic and media center of the country. A fire captain named William Tweed had re-vitalized the St. Tammany Society of New York into the most powerful local party political organization in American history.

The Mutuals were the first Tammany team and the dominant post-War Manhattan team, which was not unrelated. And the Tammany influence was carried forward from the Mutuals into the establishment of the major league Giants, Yankees, and Dodgers. Though the Mutuals were expelled from the National League after the 1876 season, baseball returned to Manhattan in 1883, when the New York Gothams joined the League. This would not have occurred without Tammany consent. The Gothams evolved into the New York Giants, which continued as Tammany's Team particularly during the ownership of Tammany powerhouse Andrew Freedman and influence of Manhattan Borough President James J. Coogan (Coogan's Bluff). It continued as such through the ownership of Tammany ally Charles Stoneham. Congressman Jacob Ruppert was but one of the prominent Tammany Yankees. State Assemblyman Charlie Ebbets and Walter O'Malley were the "Tammany Lite" Brooklyn Division.

This extraordinary linkage of professional baseball and Tammany Hall began with the rise of both baseball and Tammany prior to the Civil War. Fireman John Wildey was the point person for the Mutuals baseball team and aided Boss Tweed's rise to political power. Post-war, Wildey was the first and last President of the National Association of Base Ball Players (NABBP), the organization that represents the major turning point in the official professionalization of baseball.

It is an amazing story of firemen, war, politics, corruption, and baseball.

FIREMAN JOHN WILDEY: NY Fire Department Baseball and the Rise of Tammany Hall

John Wildey was born in New York City, March 28, 1823. He was a "plain but intelligent looking gentleman."[1] Wildey lived in the 8th Ward for over fifty years, moving late in life to Bayonne, New Jersey. He officially joined his first fire engine company in 1844, moving over to the Oceanus Engine Company No. 11 where he later served as foreman (i.e. chief).[2] Wildey took fifty of his firemen and "their splendid engine" by steamboat to Boston to participate in a celebration of the Battle of Bunker Hill, which built recognition for Oceanus.[3] Proving his popularity beyond his own engine house, in 1860 Wildey won a closely contested race for the New York area Board of Foremen and Engineers.[4]

He continued as a "prominent member of the Veteran Firemen's Association" after retirement.[5] When the Association visited Bayonne, they were "received by the Common Council and the Fire Department, John Wildey, an old New York fireman, acting as grand marshal."[6] In other words, while John Wildey was an enthusiast in numerous areas—baseball, politics, and the military—he was a fireman from his youth to his end. But the activities are not unrelated.

The Mutuals baseball team took its name from a firehouse. It wasn't just any firehouse but arguably the most historically significant firehouse in our nation. Founded in 1737, Mutual Hook & Ladder Company No. 1 of New York City was the first volunteer fire department in New York City. Among things credited to it were the first use of a horse as opposed to just manpower and creation of the fireman's hat design still used today.

Mutual Hook & Ladder Company No. 1 is yet another merging of politics and baseball. Fire and police departments were the backbone of the populist base of boss systems. The structures were hierarchical, with officer positions given through a combination of top down alliances, assessments, and the "bottom up" ability to deliver votes. Terry Golway wrote in *Machine Made:*

Tammany Hall and the Creation of Modern American Politics that the "firehouse was a finishing school in the fine art of local politics." While most would prefer the reputation of a firehouse as a finishing school in firefighting, in most cities it was the most disciplined early political force along with the police department.[7]

In 1846, at the invitation of Assemblyman John J. Reilly, 23-year-old William

Drawing of NAABP president John Wildey from the front page of *Frank Leslie's Illustrated Newspaper* (July 21, 1866).

Tweed organized Americus Fire Company No. 6, which took as its symbol a tiger. It later became one of the symbols of Tammany Hall.[8] Tweed lost his first race for alderman in 1850, then won in 1851, and was elected to Congress in 1852. The evolution of Tammany to a powerful organization built around graft began when Tweed was appointed to the County's Board of Supervisors in 1858.

An 1887 New York Fire Department history described the origins of the baseball team this way: "The famous Mutual Base Ball Club was named after this company and was organized in their house. John Carland was its first president, and John Wildey followed him. They had their grounds at the "Elysian Fields" in Hoboken, and their contests in 1859 and 1860 with the Atlantic, Eagle, Empire and Gotham Clubs will be remembered by all old-time lovers of the game."[9]

The *New York Sun* made the political linkage clear: "In 1857 a number of local politicians in the city conceived the idea of forming a base ball club, and at once set about it. Money was somewhat plentiful with them at the time and it did not take long to organize the Mutual Club. The Mutuals were controlled by a number of local politicians, who spent money freely on the results…Bill Tweed was the leading spirit of the Mutuals for several years, and could be found at many of the games played by that club. For several years the club ranked as the most popular and strongest in New York, and for a long period held the lead over all the other clubs."[10]

The New York Mutuals baseball team and the rise of modern Tammany Hall were simultaneous in part because they were the same people.

CAPTAIN JOHN WILDEY: The Fire Zouaves and the Battle of Bull Run

From 1861 to 1865 the United States of America had been rendered asunder. No community in the nation failed to avoid the tragic impact of the Civil War. Not only did families lose loved ones, but communities lost leaders. Men without limbs, the walking wounded, and those left in homes for the invalid were daily reminders. World War II left America scarred and wounded, but it was not the same as a war fought on our soil against fellow Americans. The Civil War defined American politics for decades afterward.

Heroes also come from war. The first major battle of the Civil War took place just west of Washington, near a creek called Bull Run just north of Manassas and west of Centreville, Virginia. One of the celebrated heroes to come from that first battle was Captain John Wildey, fireman, future Coroner, head of the Mutual Club of New York, and Tammany man. He was a senior officer of the famed 11th New York Fire Zouaves, who were a national phenomenon far greater than baseball.

The leader of the Fire Zouaves had fame nearly unfathomable today. Elmer Ellsworth was raised in the town of Halfmoon, New York, in a very poor family. He moved to Chicago where he met a former French officer in the Zouaves, famed for their distinctive uniforms. Colonel Ellsworth created the first American Zouaves. The Chicago Zouaves went on a tour of the East. When they paraded, they did acrobatic flips and landed with their rifles in firing position. Civil War historian Adam Goodheart referred to it as a nineteenth-century version of Cirque du Soleil. For example, 25,000 people lined the streets of Albany to watch them. They took a fascinated nation by storm. Charles Dickens wrote that the "Zouave drill, which is almost acrobatic, delights the Americans." President Buchanan hosted them at the White House. The fame of the Ellsworth Zouaves generated copycat units in all sections of the nation.[11]

Ellsworth's young men became part of the entourage of a candidate named Abraham Lincoln in Illinois. Ellsworth became so close to the Lincolns that he caught measles from the Lincoln boys. When Lincoln went to Washington, so did Ellsworth as part of his escort. In fact, President Lincoln was planning to name Ellsworth commandant of the militias of the United States. However, when the Civil War began, Ellsworth decided to go to New York City to form a volunteer division of firemen soldiers called the 11th New York Fire Zouaves.[12]

At the first call for Fire Zouave volunteers, firehouse foreman John Wildey raised a company of ninety men, all of whom belonged to a New York City firehouse. They were designated Company I of the Eleventh Regiment New York Volunteers. Wildey was elected captain.[13] He had demonstrated his interest in military organization as early as 1853 as captain of the Carlisle Light Guard, which was considered "one of the best-equipped and disciplined in the city."[14]

When Colonel Ellsworth's volunteers prepared to depart New York City, they were given the 1860's version of a ticker tape parade. From the time of their arrival in Washington, the Zouaves were treated uniquely.

Congress was not in session because Southern defections and disputed elections left Congress without a quorum for months. The Capitol Building was thus put to use in other ways. A Harper's Weekly etching from May 25, 1861, is titled: "The New York Fire Zouaves Quartered in the House of Representatives at Washington." The drawings feature the Zouaves lounging around on the House Floor and the officers at a table in one of the major committee rooms in the Capitol Building.

Their first battle, however, wasn't against southern soldiers. The City of Washington was filled with sympathizers to the Confederacy. Arsonists made an attempt to set the northern capital city on fire, beginning with buildings next to the Willard Hotel. As the fire spread unchecked, with the Washington fire department being a little slow to respond, the Fire Zouaves came to the rescue from their temporary home on the House floor. With smoke beginning to pour into the Willard, and fire right behind it, the New York firemen/soldiers saved the Willard. Harper's Weekly again featured an engraving of the Zouaves battling the Willard Hotel blaze entitled "The Ellsworth Fire Zouaves fighting their old New York enemy in their usual way." No wonder the Mutuals were welcomed at the Willard in 1867.

The Fire Zouaves moved out of the Capitol Building to a point across the Potomac River from what is now Ronald Reagan National Airport to help prevent southern sympathizers from launching attacks on Washington. The Zouave diarist noted that "in the absence of anything more exciting" that the Fire Zouaves began playing baseball with Wildey in "ball cap and ball shoes."[15]

On May 7, Colonel Ellsworth announced that the Fire Zouaves were to remove some threats in Alexandria. As Ellsworth turned on King Street, he stopped in front of the Marshall House Hotel on top of which was flying a huge rebel flag that could be seen from as far as the Capitol Building. He said to those with him, "That flag must come down." Ellsworth charged up to the roof, and as he re-entered the hotel lobby, the owner assassinated him. The celebrated Col. Ellsworth thus became the first recognized death of an officer in the American Civil War.[16]

In spite of all that I have just noted, it is still hard to fathom that upon his death, Col. Ellsworth's body was moved to the White House for viewing. The funeral was held in the East Room. This has been seldom done at any time in American history. Ellsworth's death was personal to the President and his family. For a long time, Lincoln was known to weep at the mention of his name.[17] Going into the Battle of the Bull Run, the Fire Zouaves of NYC had extraordinary national fame, critical to understanding Wildey's future fame in politics and baseball.

Wildey was the Zouave closest to Ellsworth. The more senior Lt. Colonel Noah L. Farnham, however, replaced Ellsworth as the Fire Zouaves commander. Farnham was "struck by a musket ball" during the Bull Run battle and soon died from complications from typhoid fever.[18] Farnham had been the head of the Mutual Fire Company unit. Post-Civil War the G.A.R. (Grand Army of the Republic), an organization of veterans of the Northern Army, became a powerful national political organization.[19] Not surprisingly, Wildey was a leader of the Noah Farnham G.A.R. Post No. 458 in NYC until his own death.[20]

The first Bull Run battle is enshrouded in more confusion and myth than most Civil War battles. Not only was soldier training minimal when the war began, but commanders were unfamiliar with one another and even uniforms were not coordinated. Some Southerners wore blue and some Northerners wore gray. This not only confused those trying to record what precisely happened, but was chaos on the battlefield during the fighting. Henry Hill became the pivotal ground during the Battle at Bull Run Creek. During the fight the N.Y. Zouaves and the rebels became confused as to whether oncoming soldiers were allies or enemies. Jeb Stuart spotted the Zouaves but then remembered there was a Southern unit dressed similarly so shouted out: "Are those our men or the enemy?"[21]

The Zouaves were in the heat of the battle and suffered serious casualties. They lost so many men that the unit did not survive. While most historians credit them with beginning the battle with bravery, they note that when counter-attacked the Zouaves panicked. Few reports, including those by soldiers present on the battlefield, agree on key facts. General Thomas Jackson received his nickname at Bull Run, though initially the reference to his standing there "like a stone wall" off the battlefield east of Henry Hill was not intended to be complimentary. When Stonewall Jackson did intervene, however, it was decisive.

The Union retreat at the First Battle of Bull Run stunned the North. Blame was flying everywhere. Today, with the advantage of hindsight, we know that the War would last four years and the other battles would have more significance. But in 1861, post Bull Run, the northern militia enlistment periods were about to expire. The Federal troops had been demoralizingly routed which put the survival of a united nation in doubt. Some heroes were immediately needed.

Captain John Wildey's exploits made him famous. The *New York Herald* reported that "in the midst of the battle-field the stalwart form of Jack Wildey could at all times be found at the head of his comrades." The *Herald* continued that when the regimental flag had been seized by Black Horse Cavalry Confederates of Jeb Stuart, "Wildey rushed forward at the head of his brave men, and after a bloody contest, in which he killed two men, recaptured the flag."[22] In the Civil War men died defending their regimental flags. In this case, it was the flag of Ellworth's famous Zouaves, firefighters from the largest city in America. Many sketches and lithographs appeared with the gallant Fire Zouaves fighting off the Black Horse Cavalry. More than 150 years later the image remains among the more prominent of the first Civil War battle.

Wildey's fame was spread throughout the nation. In New York City, Wildey had become a hero, a defender of the city's honor. Wildey was recalled home, ostensibly to recruit more soldiers. But Boss Tweed had other ideas. He needed Wildey to represent Tammany in the upcoming election.

CORONER WILDEY: The Mutual Interest of Politics and Baseball

Tammany Hall under Boss Tweed played an important role in backing the North in the Civil War's first years. It was a pivotal time for Tammany, which had begun as a national organization founded by Pennsylvania Revolutionary War leader John Dickinson as a more thoughtful alternative to Boston's Sons of Liberty. Aaron Burr in New York helped perpetuate New York City's branch long after others had faded away. Tweed's goal was to politically dominate the Democrat Party (sic), and New York through Tammany Hall.

In 1860 Confederate sympathizer Fernando Wood was the Mayor. He was tied to the South's cotton industry, which generated great revenue for the city and for his political base. Because of the Mayor's opposition, Lincoln's Secretary of War Edward Stanton desperately needed allies in New York City. Tweed made a deal: throw some support to Lincoln in return for, among other things, some shared power and, more importantly to Tammany's future, government contracts.[23]

Tweed's Tammany system required power, and maintaining power required some election victories. "It's hard not to admire the skill behind Tweed's system, though," Kenneth Ackerman writes in *Boss Tweed*. "The Tweed ring at its height was an engineering marvel, strong and solid, strategically deployed to control key power points: the courts, the legislature, the treasury and the ballot box. Its fraud had a grandeur of scale and an elegance of structure: money-laundering, profit sharing and organization."[24]

In the 1861 election Tweed had parts of the Tammany organization align with the Union tickets (there were multiple slates). "Tammany Democracy" ran a full slate, including for the Coroner positions and highlighted by Tweed himself for Sheriff. This slate was calculated for show, not victory. Boss Tweed also participated in putting together a "fusion ticket," with Tammany agreeing to support some non-Tammany candidates in return for enough Republican support for a few Tammany-selected choices. John Wildey for Coroner was one of the Tammany candidates selected to prevail (i.e. weak opposition slated against him). Included in the fusion ticket sweep of offices was Coroner John Wildey.

Coroner seems like an odd office for Tammany to focus upon. Even by Tammany standards, it is possible that Wildey's experience at the Fire Department, Civil War reputation, and as a baseball player did not give him enough plausibility for a position with more power regardless of his popularity. On the other hand, it was enough to make Wildey one of the top citywide candidates in the election in spite of lacking any qualifications for Coroner. Being a Tammany Coroner was not like serving as a coroner today. It was a political undertaking, not medicine. A PBS documentary pointed out that "even in an era of rampant corruption, New York coroners stood out."[25]

Obviously, the coroner does an autopsy to determine the cause of death. For each autopsy conducted the coroner received a fee plus all expenses covered. It would appear to have been a pretty scientific, straightforward post. As the city grew, in 1852 New York City went from two to four elected coroners to handle the increased load.

Because they were paid by the dead body, coroners had an incentive to process as many as possible and as quickly as possible. "Suspicious deaths" could be lucrative, which Tammany obviously recognized. "I don't want my husband to have committed suicide" was open invitation to assessing a fee to have that fixed. A study suggested that "skillful poisoning can be carried out almost with impunity." How many "errors" were due to incompetence (since no medical background was required for Wildey, nor years later Tammany Boss Richard Croker, would not have been

a coroner) and how much was the result of kickbacks to the coroners is impossible to determine.[26]

The funeral home business provided additional graft potential. After the negotiable death determination, if the coroner had a body a family wanted released, it was essential that one chose a Tammany-certified funeral home. This obviously provided more kickback opportunities.

Given that Wildey owed his political career to Tweed, it is likely that he was a willing participant in the corrupt coroner process. *The New York Times* 1889 obituary of Wildey states with a trace of irony: "He died in poverty. He had made plenty of money, but long ago lost the last of his fortune."[27] He didn't make a "fortune" as a fireman, Civil War vet, or in baseball.

A coroner named Henry Woltman, a ward politician prior to becoming coroner, was particularly excoriated by a New York State Senate inquiry in 1877. They concluded that "a more thoroughly expensive, wasteful and incompetent set of officials never existed." In addition to the opportunities for graft that I already raised, this inquiry cited many "gross abuses, among which were the following:

1. inquests were unnecessarily held.
2. juries were constantly called contrary to the intent of the statue.
3. in many cases jurors did not view the bodies of deceased persons, as required by law.
4. the inquest papers of the coroners were valueless as records, proving nothing.
5. there existed a ring of jurymen who served on hundreds of inquests, and were mere hangers-on, or creatures of the coroners.
6. the fees of the coroners were excessive, and their bills against the county, if legal, were far from being equitable or just."[28]

Baseball man John Wildey was part of an important Tammany Coroner tradition, which is rather different from being an honorable tradition. Wildey obviously had grassroots political skills demonstrated repeatedly in fire organizations, baseball organizing, and military organizations. He was elected to two three-year terms as coroner. He formed a "John Wildey Association" similar to the powerful ones later formed by Tammany powers such as Big Tim Sullivan, John Ahearn, and Maurice Featherson, which became the backbone structure of Tammany in the sprawling city. *The New York Times* noted John Wildey Association Annual Balls in 1864, 1865, and 1866.[29]

Tammany Hall headquarters, Manhattan, during the reign of Boss Tweed.

Wildey continued in politics post-Coroner. In 1869 and 1870 he ran for the position of election canvasser in the 8th Ward (Tweed was one of the two elected canvassers for the 7th Ward.)[30] In other words, should there be any doubt about Wildey being Tammany connected, his position as an official Tammany-style vote counter removes it. It was the last political position in New York City for Wildey. Not coincidentally, Tweed was chased away for corruption in 1871. Tweed fled to England and eventually went to jail. Wildey crossed the Hudson River to Bayonne, New Jersey. There is no record of Wildey being charged with any crime.

George Washington Plunkitt of Tammany Hall is among the most famous political books of all-time because it boldly proclaims how Tammany did business. Even for baseball.

"I hear a young feller that's proud of his voice…I ask him to join our Glee Club. He comes up and sings, and he's a follower of Plunkitt for life. Another young feller gains a reputation as a baseball player in a vacant lot. I bring him into our baseball club. That fixes him. You'll find him working for my ticket at the polls next election. I rope them all in by givin' them opportunities to show off themselves off. I don't trouble them with political arguments."

—George Washington Plunkitt[31]

Wildey's Coroner's office was one in which employment was found for Mutuals baseball players. But Tammany's assistance was more than just jobs. SABR historian Tony Morante noted: "By 1869, Tammany was contributing generously to the upkeep of the Mutuals, who were all on salary, making them a truly professional team. When the New York City Council voted the team $1,500 towards a trip to New Orleans in 1869, Tweed countered with $7,500 from his own pocket, another way to secure votes."[32]

Nothing in politics occurs in a vacuum. Once the context is understood—the Battle of Bull Run, Wildey's election as Coroner, the Tammany ties to the Mutuals—the opening story in Washington becomes clear today like it was to the readers at the time.

The visit of the Mutuals to Washington D.C. in the fall of 1867 came during one of the most politically contentious times in American history. Tennessee Democrat Andrew Johnson had been selected as the Republican Vice-Presidential candidate because the prolonged war made President Lincoln vulnerable in the 1864 election. Republicans had not expected Lincoln to be assassinated after his victory. President Johnson was opposed to the Radical Republican agenda for Reconstruction of the South.

When the Mutual baseball team arrived in New York, among the New York Congressmen were Fernando Wood, the former Mayor, and John Morrissey, former Dead Rabbits Gang leader, gambler, long-time Tammany boss, and purported owner of the Haymakers of Troy. New York Democrats were the core of the Party. The head of the Mutual Club of New York was military hero Wildey. New York Democrats had not been of one mind in support of the Union cause, but they were united in opposition to the Radical Republicans.

Vice-President Johnson was mostly scorned by his new party. In March of 1867, Congress passed the Tenure of Office Act. It prohibited Johnson from removing federal office holders who had been confirmed by the Senate as they battled each other over implementing Reconstruction. In early August— just weeks before the Mutuals visited to play baseball in Washington—Johnson tested the constitutionality of the Act. Republicans in Congress were furious.

President Johnson desperately needed some friends and the united help of Democrats to survive the Republican purge attempt. (His impeachment by the House occurred in February 1868; he—like later President Bill Clinton—survived the Senate trial.)

What could be more dramatic than the baseball team of the Mutual Fire Company of New York, led by former Fire Zouaves Bull Run battle hero Captain John Wildey, coming to Washington? And the Mutuals weren't just a baseball team. They were Tammany's team and their leader was an elected official, part of Tweed's political team.

When newspaper accounts recorded that the President hosted the team, was appreciative of being made an honorary member, and proudly put the Mutuals badge on his lapel, I'm sure they were completely accurate. In fact, Johnson was undoubtedly thrilled that the Mutuals had made sure that he was identified with the most prominent Democrat organization and a Civil War hero. Johnson might have liked baseball, but he loved important allies even more as he fought for his political life.

After the political tourism, they also played baseball. President Andrew Johnson attended, possibly still wearing his Tammany Mutuals badge. He was among political allies and friends. War and politics united them. Baseball was a respite from bitter politics.

NABBP President Wildey and the Rise of Professional Baseball

In 1865—the first post-Civil War convention of NABBP—baseball clubs gathered from ten states. The percentage of New York clubs had declined to 42% which reflected the increasing national popularity of the game (though clubs from New Jersey and Connecticut boosted the region to 56%). New York retained enough clout to elect Coroner John Wildey as the first truly national President (representatives from five states had been the previous high).[33]

The Mutuals were not known for honesty in baseball. The Mutuals cheated on a grander scale than most teams. John Thorn, the official historian of MLB, has written that gambling was the most important ingredient facilitating the growth of baseball (followed by statistics and publicity).[34] But Bill Ryczek notes that in the Mutuals case, it was much more serious. Whenever a big upset occurred involving the New York team, it was suspected that the losing Mutuals had thrown the game.[35]

For example, on September 28, 1865, the Mutuals faced the Eckford Club of Brooklyn in what is considered to be one of the most significant baseball games because it helped push baseball towards professionalism.

During the first four innings, the Mutuals played like the favorites they were. Gamblers moved through the crowds changing the odds around events during the game, as they generally did and especially in New York. But in the fifth inning, things on the field changed dramatically. In what became known as "the Wansley affair," the Eckfords scored eleven runs. It wasn't just that they scored that many in one inning. Games could be high scoring in the days when fielders, for example, had no baseball gloves and catchers were getting battered by trying to nearly bare-handedly catch pitched balls. It was the more than suspicious way that the eleven runs were suddenly accumulated. Experienced Mutuals catcher William Wansley had two missed catches, six passed balls and four wild throws in the pivotal fifth inning.[36]

The Fix Is In by Daniel E. Ginsburg, a history of gambling in baseball, describes how Wansley corralled two fellow Mutuals players to help ensure that the Eckfords won (it wasn't clear that his yeoman efforts to throw the game alone could have accomplished the mission). The gamblers' contact offered Wansley $100 to guarantee the success of their scheme. A few hours before the game, he drove the three players by wagon to the Hoboken Ferry where, once on board, Wansley kept $40 and gave the other two players each $30.[37] Obviously, the informed gamblers were able to maximize their betting odds going into that inning and cashed in.

Early baseball historian William Ryczek noted that "the Mutuals followers were avid bettors and generally sore losers."[38] So were the Mutuals' teammates of Wansley, Ed Duffy, and Tom Devyr. After the game, President of the Mutuals John Wildey charged Wansley with "willful and designed inattention" during the game.[39]

When a repentant Devyr confessed his role in throwing the contest, the Mutuals-Eckfords match officially became the first rigged game in baseball history. The significance reverberated in baseball far more than if it had been a more obscure match. Not only did the game involve the top teams in the largest metro area in the nation, but New York had been the cradle of baseball. The majority of the amateur teams were in the New York metro area. The game-rigging had occurred on the biggest baseball stage in the country.

But the time was nearing for John Wildey's last hurrah. In 1868 Wildey spear-headed the return of suspended Devyr, in 1869 Duffy was re-admitted, and at the 1870 meetings Wildey pushed to allow ringleader Wansley back into baseball. At the November 30, 1870, meeting in New York City, Wildey was again elected to head the National Association of Base Ball Players by a vote of 18 to 8. The NABBP also voted by a two to one margin to become professional. Wildey of the Mutuals was thus the last president before baseball officially went pro.[40]

Wildey was not one of those wringing his hands about the evils of the change. He stated in response to a proposal to remain amateurs: "We are perfectly willing to adopt such a rule," answered Wildey with a quaint smile, "but I fear, ladies and gentlemen, if we did, the players wouldn't observe it. It seems to me that the days are over when baseball is purely a game for amateurs."[41] Of course, in New York, they hadn't been purely amateur since the Civil War had ended. This just made professionalization official.

The National Association of Professional Base Ball Players (NA), the first professional baseball organization, began its first season in 1871. The Mutuals survived the Association but not without controversy. The National League was created in 1876, the official start of Major League Baseball, in order to provide more stability and integrity to professional baseball. The Mutuals were kicked out after the first season, officially for refusing to complete their schedule.

John Wildey had a very brief playing career for the Mutual Club prior to the Civil War but had been a leader of the powerful New York team for nearly two decades. He also served as an umpire, including an 1870 Mutual game against Brooklyn and at an 1871 game versus the Haymakers.[42]

Four years before Wildey's death, a history of the New York and Brooklyn fire departments concluded a brief biography of him by stating: "Everyone knows of Jack Wildey of 'Black Horse Guard' fame. He was always a great admirer of athletic sports of all kinds, and, although sixty-two years old, he would astonish some of the present generation should they try their strength against him."[43]

Capt. John Wildey, Tammany Hall, their baseball team the Mutuals, the Fire Zouaves at Bull Run, and the firehouses of New York City all played important roles, albeit stormy ones, in establishing professional baseball's role in our National Pastime. ∎

Notes

1. William J. Ryczek, *When Johnny Came Sliding Home: The Post-Civil War Baseball Boom, 1865–1870* (Jefferson N.C. and London: McFarland & Company, 1998); 20.
2. Frank Kernan, *Reminiscences of the Old Fire Laddies and Volunteer Fire Departments of New York and Brooklyn, Together with a Complete History of the Paid Departments of Both Cities* (New York: M. Crane: 1885); 474.
3. *New York Tribune*, June 16, 1857; 6.
4. *Brooklyn Evening Star*; October 19, 1860; 2.
5. Kernan; 474.
6. A. E. Costello, *Our Firemen: A History of the New York Fire Departments 1609–1887*; Chapter 45, Part V
7. Terry Golway, *Machine Made: Tammany and the Creation of Modern American Politics* (New York: Liveright Publishing, 2014); 60.
8. T. Jackson, Lisa Keller, and Nancy Flood; "Tweed, William M(agear) 'Boss'" *Encyclopedia of New York City: Second Edition* (New Haven and London: Yale University Press 2010).
9. Costello; 683.
10. "The Mutuals of New York," *New York Sun*, January 02, 1887; 11.
11. Adam Goodheart, *1861: The Civil War Awakening* (New York: Vintage Books, 2011); 194, 203.
12. Goodheart; 207, 211.
13. Kernan, 474.
14. *New York Tribune*; Feb 18, 1855; 7.
15. Brian C. Pohanka and Patrick A. Schroeder, *With the 11th New York Fire Zouaves in Camp, Battle, and Prison* (Lynchburg, Virginia: Schroeder Publications, 2011); 139.
16. Goodheart; 285.
17. Goodheart; 290, 291.
18. *White Cloud* (Kansas) *Chief*, June 20, 1861; 1.
19. "The Late Col Farnham," *The New York Times*; August 16, 1861.
20. Kernan, 474.
21. William C. Davis, *Battle of Bull Run* (Garden City, New York: Doubleday, 1977); 207, 208.
22. Kernan; 475–81 including a July 27, 1861, story in the *New York Herald*.
23. Kenneth D. Ackerman, *Boss Tweed* (New York: Carroll & Graf Publishers; 2005); 27.
24. Ibid, 357.
25. PBS Documentary series *American Experience*, "The Poisoner's Handbook," transcript at http://www.pbs.org/wgbh/americanexperience/ features/ transcript/poisoners-transcript.
26. Ibid.
27. "John Wildey Died in Poverty," *The New York Times*; June 1, 1889.
28. Jerome B. Parmeter, State Printer; *Documents of the Senate of the State of New York*; Ninety-Ninth Session—*1876*; Volume VII.—No 79; 1876.
29. *The New York Times*; Jan. 27, 1865; 4; *The New York Times*; Jan. 20; 1866; 3.
30. "Democratic Primaries," *The New York Times*, Sept 19, 1869; 5; "Official City Canvass" *The New York Times*; June 2, 1870; 3.
31. William L. Riordan, *Plunkitt of Tammany Hall: A Series of Very Plain Talks* (New York: E. P. Dutton & Co., 1963); 25, 26.
32. Steven A. Riess, *Touching Base: Professional Baseball and American Culture in the Progressive Era* (Westport, Connecticut: Greenwood Press; 1980), 66; Tony Morante, "Baseball and Tammany Hall;" *Baseball Research Journal*, Spring 2013, Volume 42, Issue 1.
33. Ryczek, 78–79.
34. John Thorn, *Baseball in the Garden of Eden: The Secret History of the Early Game* (New York: Simon & Schuster, 2011) 87.
35. Ryczek, 196.
36. Philip H. Dixon, "The First Fixed Game: Mutuals of New York vs. Eckfords of Brooklyn" *Inventing Baseball: The 100 Greatest Games of the 19th Century* (SABR, 2013); 46, 47.
37. Daniel E. Ginsburg, *The Fix Is In: A History of Baseball Gambling and Game Fixing Scandals* (Jefferson, NC: McFarland, 1995); 5, 6.
38. Ryczek; 75.
39. Dixon, 47.
40. Ryczek; 246–59.
41. Jimmy Wood, "Baseball of the Bygone Days, Part 3" from the blog of Major League Baseball historian John Thorn on MLB.com.
42. *Brooklyn Daily Eagle* August 8, 1870; 3 and *Brooklyn Daily Eagle*, October 6, 1871; 3.
43. Kernan; 474.

The Starring Tours of 1875

The "Amateurs" Tours, Tournaments and Regional Rivalries

Paul Browne

The Excelsior club of Brooklyn toured Upstate New York, Pennsylvania, and Maryland in 1860, only two years after the formation of the National Association of Base Ball Players. The Nationals of Washington carried the baseball gospel to the Midwest in 1867, shortly after the Civil War. And, of course, the Cincinnati club under Harry Wright accelerated the acceptance of professional clubs with their 1869 and 1870 tours.

Tours by ostensibly amateur clubs from the New York City area began to increase after the Excelsior's 1860 trip. These journeys, sometimes called starring tours—an example of the interaction between baseball clubs and theater troupes—were an outgrowth of playing on enclosed grounds where the owners of the fields charged admission to spectators, soon sharing part of those receipts with the clubs. Another movement in this trend was baseball clubs playing in trophy and prize games and tournaments. Creeping professionalism was an almost natural outgrowth of these developments.

By 1875, New York City teams were visiting those they identified as "country clubs" fairly routinely. Their more rural rivals were also on the rails visiting each other and their big city opponents. The Mutuals of Meadville in western Pennsylvania started out on a tour through Pennsylvania. Their journey eventually took them to Syracuse, Bridgeport, Connecticut, and New York City. Tours through Upstate New York became so common that the Comets of Norwich, New York, issued an invitation to all clubs touring Central New York to contact them about setting up games. This announcement was published in the *New York Clipper* on July 31, 1875. That paper's same issue carried a request from the Mutual Club of Washington, DC, for dates with clubs that had enclosed grounds during their tour of western New York in August 1875. This Mutual club was a black team and the notice was signed by their secretary, Charles R. Douglass, son of Frederick Douglass. Even the New Haven professional team, a member of the National Association of Professional Base Ball Players, played some of the same Northeast Pennsylvania teams that the amateurs

played. New Haven's 7–40 record against NA teams may explain why they were looking for competition at this level and why they only lasted one year in the NA.

The Arlington and Flyaway were two New York City teams that were representative of the class of teams that participated in the tours, tournaments, and regional rivalries which defined New York area baseball below the National Association level at this time. An exploration of the clubs' 1875 seasons will shine some light on the world of these lesser known "missing links" between the early amateurs and the major league, minor league, and semi-pro teams which were coming into existence at this stage in baseball's development.

When the professional clubs broke off in 1871 to form their own association, some of the remaining teams formed the National Association of Amateur Base Ball Players at the suggestion of Henry Chadwick, and led by the Knickerbocker and Excelsior clubs.[1] The group held no meeting in 1872 but was reorganized in 1873, meeting annually in convention for the next several years and maintaining active committees to deal with issues during the playing seasons. The Arlington and Flyaway were members of this organization, C.W. Blodget of the Arlington serving as Secretary going into the 1875 season.

The Amateur Convention on March 10, 1875, established the rules for the coming season and dealt with the two main issues troubling the amateur community at that time: payment of expenses and "revolving" (players switching teams). The convention determined that amateur clubs could split gate receipts to cover traveling expenses. Clubs that did that frequently played on enclosed grounds, while those that didn't—like the Knickerbockers—usually played on open grounds that charged no admission to spectators. In order to address revolving, the Association prohibited players who played on one club during a season from playing on another club during the same season.[2] In response to a May letter from the Chatham club complaining about Morris Moore's defection from their club to the Flyaway, the editor of the *New York Clipper* pointed out that since amateurs could not accept payment, and a contract could not be legally binding without compensation, the revolving rule could not be enforced.[3] The Sunday *Mercury* and the *Clipper* would complain about the leading amateur teams in the Association breaking the latter rule and bending the former during the season.

A review of the Arlington and Flyaway seasons published in the *Sunday Mercury* in December 1875 shows the Flyaway starting first with games against their second nines on April 22 and 26, with their first game in competition with other amateur clubs coming against the Cataract on May 1. The Arlington would jump into the fray with a game against the Star of New York on May 20. The Flyaway would play the Keystone, another premier amateur club in the New York City region, on May 24, beating them, 9–7. The Arlington would face the same opponent on June 10, "Chicagoing" the Keystone, 11–0. The Flyaway's first defeat would come on May 12, losing to the Rose Hill, a team from St. John's College, 11–7. The Arlington would not report a loss until they left the New York City area for their July Tour of Pennsylvania and Upstate New York. The Irving of Honesdale beat the New York City visitors, 8–6 on July 21. The *New York Clipper*, however, published two box scores on May 29, 1875. One showed the Rose Hill win over the Flyaway and the other showed the Arlington losing to the college club, 14–6.

The Flyaway were the much more active club, playing 45 games. They won 31 games, lost 11, and had three draws. In contrast, the Arlington played only 21 games, winning 16, losing four, and having one forfeit by the Olympic.

The two clubs met on June 24 on the Union Grounds in Brooklyn. Tied 4–4 after nine innings, the Arlington scored three runs in the top of the tenth and then shut the Flyaway out in their half of the inning. As was the custom of the time, Blodget(t) pitched all ten innings for the Arlington and Fallon for the Flyaway. All runs were recorded as unearned except for one by the Flyaway. No real details of which players did what were listed in the game accounts, including how the Arlington scored their three runs in the tenth.

Tournaments were a regular part of amateur clubs' seasons. The Flyaway participated in the Watertown, New York, Tournament that started on June 29. First-class clubs paid a $5 entry fee to compete for prizes of $450, $350, and $250. On their way to the tournament, the Flyaway would cross the border to face the St. Lawrence club of Kingston, Ontario, on July 1, beating the Canadian club, 9–2. The Flyaway would play their first game of the tournament on July 2 against the Syracuse Stars, who had lost the opening game of the

tournament the day before to the Lynn, Massachusetts, Live Oaks, 13–7. They dropped the July 2 game to the Flyaway, 14–12. The Flyaway's next game in the tournament would be a 7–1 loss to the Maple Leaf of Guelph, Ontario. Their last game would be a return match with the St. Lawrence on July 6, the Flyaway beating them, 12–2 and taking the $250 third prize. The Live Oaks took first and the Maple Leaf second.

The Flyaway provided the *Clipper* with a report of their opinion of the Watertown Tournament. While very complimentary towards the organizers, the City, and their host—Mr. Harris of the Kirby House—they could not resist the nearly traditional dig against one of their opponents, the Maple Leafs. They accused the team they lost to of playing a professional, a man named Kerl.[4] No player named Kerl is listed by Baseball-Reference.com, *Total Baseball*, or David Nemec's 19th Century Encyclopedia, so, if he was a professional, he was probably not of the highest caliber. In their adventures away from the Metropolis, it was not uncommon for these teams to find some excuse for a loss to any of the "country clubs."

The Arlington's western tour, consisting of games in Pennsylvania and Upstate New York, was announced in the *Mercury* on July 18. It started with the aforementioned loss to the Irving of Honesdale on July 21. The next day they lost to the Carbondale club, 4–3. It was reported that several thousand watched the game. Gillespie and Kennedy are credited among those making "beautiful plays" in the game for Carbondale.[5] Gillespie would go on to an eight-year National League career with Troy and the New York Giants. Kennedy would play four years in the American Association with the Metropolitans and Brooklyn.

The Arlington would recover their form once they hit Scranton, beating three teams in that city. The Scranton club fell, 7–5, in ten innings on July 22, the Hyde Park club being destroyed, 41–4, the day after, and Providence being wiped out, 28–7, the following. Wilkes-Barre would fare better on July 26 but succumb to the Arlington, 15–11. The New York City team returned to New York State on July 27, losing to Binghamton, 9–2. They would complete their tour with a 6–2 victory over the Star of Syracuse on July 28. Baseball in the hinterlands had improved by 1875. Three of the Arlington's four losses in 1875 occurred on this tour.

C.W. Blodget would provide the *Clipper* with a report of the tour, published on August 7. He expressed his club's thanks to the Honesdale, Scranton, and Syracuse people and congratulated Honesdale as the only team to win their game fairly. He criticized the Carbondale and Binghamton teams that had beaten them—as

CRAWFORD COUNTY HISTORICAL SOCIETY

The 1875 tour of the Mutuals of Meadville took them from Pennsylvania eventually through Syracuse, New York; Bridgeport, Connecticut; and New York City.

well as Wilkes-Barre whom they had beaten—for playing revolvers and picked nines. Wilkes-Barre's response was published in the *Clipper* of September 4. They denied they were a picked nine and stated that every player in the club was a member and resident of the city and that all but one player had been with the club the past two years. They also said that none of their players were paid.

Carbondale was a slightly more complicated matter. Early reports of the Arlington's planned tour indicate that they were to play a team called the Alerts in Carbondale. By the time they reached that city, however, the Alerts no longer existed. They had merged with another Carbondale team called the Lackawanna to form the Blue Stockings. This team existed before the Arlington tour and lasted into 1876. If this was a "picked nine," it is hard to imagine that a city of 6,393 in the 1870 census could have gained an unfair advantage against a New York City team drawing from an 1870 population of 942,292.

The Arlington's first baseman, Isherwood, seemed to have taken no offense to the Carbondales' behavior, joining them as their captain on the tour they launched on September 10. He also played first base for Carbondale, as he did with the Arlington, in at least four games. No games as a club are listed for the Arlington after August 17.

The Flyaway decided to skip the Lynn tournament and instead take a tour through New York State themselves. They began what turned out to be a very successful trip on August 23. They won all their games but for one loss and two draws. The loss was to the Syracuse Stars on August 30 by a score of 3–1. They had beaten the Stars in the Watertown tournament and

would win again on September 3, 7–4. The Flyaway's victories were over the Lone Star of Catskill, Murphy of Troy, Clipper of Ilion (twice), Uticas, Franklin of Auburn, Comet of Norwich and Active. They played to a draw twice, 2–2 with the Binghamton Cricket on September 1, the game being called after ten innings, and 7–7 with Sunnyvale on September 4. It was reported that the first game against Ilion was played in Johnstown, New York, with the Flyaway getting $300 for their 20–8 win.[6]

The $300 prize at Johnstown again raised the question of amateur status. This was a hotly debated subject during the 1875 season. The *Sunday Mercury*, in its preseason article for 1875, had raised the issue, stating in reference to amateur clubs, "It is questionable whether there are a hundred in the entire country."[7]

In its summary article at the end of the season, the *Brooklyn Eagle* stated, "It should be borne in mind, however, that in most cases of this kind the amateur nines were not exactly amateurs in the strict sense of the word, for two-thirds of the so-called amateur nines of 1875 included players who were compensated for their services, if not by regular salaries—as in the professional organizations—at least by a share of gate receipts, or some other form of remuneration. Hence such nines were able to devote the more time to that practice and training necessary to place them in a position to cope more successfully with the regular professional teams, than regular amateur nines could."[8]

While the article did not include the Arlington or Flyaway in their enumerated list of semi-professional teams, they ended that list with "and in fact every prominent amateur club of the country." The Flyaway were certainly among the prominent amateur clubs as the *Eagle* listed them as the leading such team in New York City for 1875. The Arlington placed several players on the New York City all-star team that played a series of games with the best Brooklyn players at the end of the 1875 season, so they would also most likely have been considered among the prominent clubs. It was stated later in the article, "Two tours of a genuine amateur character only are known in the history of the game, and they were the tour of the old Excelsior club in 1860 …; and the grand Western tour of the National Club of Washington in 1867."[9]

The division between professional and amateur clubs was not resolved with the 1871 formation of the National Association of Professional Base Ball Players. The status of those clubs which were not fully salaried stock clubs had varied before the divide and continued to evolve in the seasons leading up to 1875 and for years to come after. Before the launch of the 1876 season, the arrival of the National League would complicate matters for those clubs not included in the new organization even further. A review of the tours and tournaments of 1875 exemplifies the status of a confusing class of clubs on the verge of the next major change in the baseball world. ■

SOURCES
Articles

Brooklyn Eagle, 1875.
Carbondale Advance, 1875.
New York Clipper, 1874–76.
New York Sunday Mercury, 1874–76.
The New York Times, 1875.

Books

Nemec, David. *The Great Encyclopedia of 19th Century Major League Baseball*. New York, N.Y.: Donald I. Fine Books, 1997.

Seymour, Harold. *Baseball: The Early Years*. New York, NY: Oxford University Press, 1960

Thorn, John, Palmer, Peter & Greshman, Michael, Editors. *Total Baseball*, Seventh Edition. Kingston, New York: Total Sports Publishing, 2001.

Websites

www.baseball_reference.com

Notes

1. *New York Clipper*, March 18, 1876.
2. *Sunday Mercury*, March 14, 1875.
3. *New York Clipper*, May 29, 1875.
4. *New York Clipper*, July 17, 1875.
5. *New York Clipper*, July 31, 1875.
6. *New York Clipper*, September 4, 1875.
7. *Sunday Mercury*, March 28, 1875.
8. *Brooklyn Eagle*, November 23, 1875. (Thanks to Richard Hershberger for providing this reference.)
9. Ibid.

Women's Baseball in Nineteenth-Century New York and the Man Who Set Back Women's Professional Baseball for Decades

Debra A. Shattuck

New Yorkers love baseball. Their passion for the national game (and its bat-and-ball precursors) can be traced back into the earliest decades of the nineteenth century. Prior to the Civil War, scores of juvenile and adult teams in New York vied for bragging rights or trophy balls on emerald fields and dusty lots.[1] Boys and men weren't the only ones reveling in the excitement of smacking hard grounders past pitchers or putting runners out by catching a lofty fly ball (or on the first bounce by some early rules); girls and women were playing too—in cities large and small and in villages scattered across the rolling hills of upstate and western New York. In 1859 a twenty-seven-year-old dentist, Francis Guiwits of Steuben County, New York, informed *Harper's Weekly* that baseball had been a popular game "in nearly all the villages and among the rural districts of Western New York" for at least twenty years. He added that baseball was "*the* game at our district schools during intermission hours, and often engaged in by youths of both sexes."[2] Earlier that year, newspapers in Albany, Troy, and Genesee County had debated the propriety of women playing baseball. One individual argued that "there seems nothing violent in the presumption that ball playing would prove as agreeable and useful to ladies as to gentlemen," while another retorted, "Bosh! Just think of looking for the ball every minute or two under the circumference of crinolined players."[3] Criticizing the assumption that women had to wear cumbersome clothing while playing baseball, the *Troy Daily Times* responded: "Humbug! As if a woman must at all times and under every circumstance, be arrayed in the stiff and conservative propriety of drawing room attire."[4] When an unnamed advocate suggested that women could wear bloomers while playing, the *Troy* editor countered: "We are no advocates of the Bloomer costume, but we can imagine that there are occasions on which short dresses, minus the outlandish pantaloons—in brief, a rig permitting the free and natural exercise of the lower limbs—would be worth[y], healthful and proper."[5]

Fashion constraints weren't the only thing deterring women from playing baseball in the nineteenth century. They also had to decide whether playing baseball was worth risking their fertility and their lives. Girls and women were inundated with warnings from physicians that they would be irreparably harmed if they overexerted themselves physically or mentally—particularly during or after puberty. In October 1867 newspapers around the country reprinted an erroneous story that a twenty-one-year-old woman in Allen's Prairie, Michigan, had died after playing baseball.[6] (Amaret Howard actually succumbed to typhoid fever.)[7] That same year the Reverend John Todd warned about the dangers of encouraging women to ape men in their intellectual pursuits: "If it ministers to vanity to call a girl's school 'a college,' it is very harmless; but as for training young ladies through a long intellectual course, as we do young men, it can never be done—they will die in the process."[8]

Each girl and woman who threw herself into her academic studies or decided to pick up a baseball bat and dash around the basepaths in the mid-nineteenth century had to weigh the potential consequences of her actions. For the thirty-six young women at Vassar College in Poughkeepsie, New York, who organized three baseball clubs in 1866 and 1867, and for those who organized a junior and senior nine in Peterboro the following year, love of baseball outweighed warnings about infertility or death.[9] In 1875, scores of students at Vassar College organized seven or eight baseball teams with the frightening pronouncements of Harvard Medical School physician Dr. Edward H. Clarke ringing in their ears. In his bestselling book, *Sex in Education: Or, A Fair Chance for the Girls* (1873), Clarke explained that youth needed to carefully regulate both "muscular and brain labor" so that their bodies had sufficient "force" available to manufacture their "reproductive machinery."[10] He ominously warned that young women who ignored his counsel risked "neuralgia, uterine disease, hysteria, and other derangements of the nervous system."[11]

Fortunately for girls and women who loved to play baseball and to engage in other rigorous activities, there were also voices challenging Clarke's proscriptions.

Dr. Helen Webster was resident physician at Vassar College 1874–81. She encouraged students to keep playing baseball even after one of them injured her leg running the bases.[12] Webster, like a growing number of physical fitness experts, understood the positive correlation between robust health and vigorous exercise. By the 1880s and 1890s, colleges across the country were hiring physical fitness instructors like Dudley Sargent and Senda Berensen, as well as building gymnasiums, swimming pools, and sports fields to promote athleticism and robust health in male and female students.

The new emphasis on athletics for women inspired more girls and women than ever before to try their hand at baseball—especially in New York state. During the 1870s, girls and women in Rhinebeck, Poughkeepsie, Brooklyn, Erie, Kingston, Auburn, Rochester, Phoenix, Syracuse, and New York City played on baseball teams. In the 1880s and 1890s, dozens more female teams sprang up in at least two dozen New York communities.[13] Players came from all social strata. There were immigrants, like Maud Nelson, playing on New York-based barnstorming teams, black women, like Mary E. Thompson and Mary Jackson, playing on pick-up teams, and upper class girls and women, like those at Mrs. Hazen's School in Pelham Manor and "society buds" in Greenwich, playing on scholastic and civic teams.[14] There were so many women playing baseball by the mid-1880s that the *New York World* commented that sports like cricket and baseball were helping to "enlarge the sphere of the contemporaneous woman." The *World* described the transition of the female athlete it was observing: "When the [contemporaneous woman] first took to base ball she was a little limp on the pitch and scattered a little on the home base. She caught a ball with her head over her shoulder, and had an abnormal fear of being struck below the belt. But these absurd things have passed away with development."[15]

Girls and women played on the same types of teams as boys and men. In addition to school, college, civic, business, and pick-up teams, girls and women played on professional teams. The first women's professional team was organized by men in Springfield, Illinois, in 1875, but many nineteenth-century women's professional teams originated in New York City. They sported names like the Young Ladies Champions of the World Base Ball Club, the American Stars, the American Female Base Ball Club, the New York Giants, the Young Ladies Base Ball Club of New York, the New York Champion Young Ladies Base Ball Club, and even the deceptively named Cincinnati Reds.[16] The earliest of the New York City-based female ball clubs was Sylvester F. Wilson's short-lived American Brunettes and English Blondes, organized in late March of 1879.[17] (See the online supplement, "Female Baseball Teams in New York," at https://sabr.org/node/44959.) The team was short-lived because Wilson and his business partner, William Powell, were both arrested for "engaging girls under 16 for immoral purposes" and for having sexual relations with girls under sixteen.[18]

Wilson was the most notorious female baseball manager of the twentieth century. He was a narcissist, career criminal, and pedophile, and organized female baseball teams between 1879 and 1903 in places including New York City, Philadelphia, New Orleans, Chicago, and Cincinnati. James William Beul called New York City "the Great Maelstrom of Vice" in 1879 and Sylvester Wilson felt right at home in its seediest neighborhoods.[19] Because he was continually running afoul of the law, Wilson used multiple aliases like H.H. Freeman, Harry Richmond, W.S. Franklin, and Frank W. Hartright to hide his identity from the police and child protective agencies like the New York Society for the Prevention of Cruelty to Children (NYSPCC).[20]

Agents of the NYSPCC kept tabs on Wilson after his arrest for sexual impropriety in 1879 and were successful in bringing Wilson to justice on several occasions, including his arrest in August 1891 for allegedly abducting fifteen-year-old Libbie Agnes Sunderland from her home in Binghamton to join his barnstorming troupe. The Society not only brought the charges against

Sylvester Wilson (sporting his signature Dundreary whiskers) with his 1891 Black Stocking Nine baseball team.

PHOTO COURTESY OF JOANNE KLINE

Sylvester Wilson Promotional Publication, *The Young Ladies' Athletic Journal*, September 1890.

Wilson in the Sunderland case but also compiled testimonies from individuals around the country detailing how Wilson had duped, defrauded, or ruined them.[21] NYSPCC agents were delighted when Wilson received a five-year sentence to Sing Sing and $1,000 fine in 1892.

Two months after Wilson's release from prison in August 1898, Society agents began receiving reports that Wilson was making unwanted advances on a 17-year-old store clerk. The following May, Manager Fred Smithson of the St. George cricket grounds in Hoboken swore out an arrest warrant against Wilson (using the alias, William S. Franklin) and his partner H.A. Adams when they absconded with the gate receipts from a baseball game between their female baseball nine and the Hudson Athletic Club.[22]

Narrowly avoiding incarceration, Wilson headed for Philadelphia where he quickly attracted the attention of the Pennsylvania Society for the Protection of Children from Cruelty (PSPCC) on suspicion of being a "procurer" and enticing young girls from home. In its Twenty-Fifth Annual Report, the NYSPCC noted that it was "the pleasure of this Society to furnish from its records the complete criminal history of Wilson" to the PSPCC so it could prosecute Wilson.[23] Just over a year after walking out of jail in New York, Wilson was imprisoned in Pennsylvania's Moyamensing Prison for a year. His whereabouts between his release and December 1902 are unknown, but in January 1903 he was back in New York City advertising for a partner to put up $500 to help fund another female baseball team. He was using the alias Frank W. Hartright and using 23 Manhattan Avenue as his contact address. In April, agents of the NYSPCC spotted one of Wilson's ads

soliciting young ladies to join a basketball club. The girls were to report to the stage entrance of the Bon Ton Music Hall—a seedy theater located at 112 West 24th Street. Society agents sprang into action, immediately opening another investigation on Wilson that bore fruit in June when Max Bracklow—an employee of the Waldorf Astoria Hotel—claimed that Wilson had defrauded him out of $200 he invested in Wilson's "woman's base ball team and vaudeville show."[24] Bracklow reported that he had accompanied Wilson and a group of young women to Peekskill where they had played basketball for a week to get conditioned for the upcoming baseball season. He testified that Wilson's plan was to hold baseball games in the afternoon and vaudeville performances in the evening.[25]

Bracklow's charges of fraud against Wilson paled in comparison to the NYSPCC discovery that Wilson had not only lured underaged girls from their homes to join his entertainment troupe, but that he had also had sexual relations with some of them and shown them pornographic photographs.[26] NYSPCC detectives Pisarra and Fogerty gathered enough evidence against Wilson that he agreed to plead guilty to a first offense rather than go to trial. (Conviction on a second offense could have brought a 20-year sentence.) Wilson received a 9-year sentence to Sing Sing that ended up being a life sentence.[27] The 1910 federal census indicates that Wilson was a "patient" in Dannemora, New York—location of the State Mental Hospital where state prisoners were sent; he was still there in 1920 and died there on December 7, 1921. He was 69 years old.[28]

Had Wilson not been the crook he was, he might have made a positive contribution to the history of professional women's baseball instead of giving it a reputation for debauchery that took decades to overcome. Wilson was a masterful marketer whose hyperbolic flimflammery rivaled that of P.T. Barnum. He knew how to attract crowds—as evidenced by the dozens of hometown newspapers across the country that noted that attendance at Wilson's games were the largest to date in their locales. Approximately 65,000 individuals paid to watch Wilson's Young Ladies' Base Ball Club play its 37 games in 1883.[29] His biggest triumph as a baseball manager came in 1890 when 7,000 to 10,000 spectators turned out to see Wilson's Black Stocking Nine play the Allertons at Monitor Park in Weehawken, New Jersey. Wilson planned the grand event with future Tammany Hall leader Charles Murphy who was a big baseball fan and manager of Monitor Park at the time.[30]

Wilson's marketing brilliance was to recognize and leverage the shift in attitudes about women's physical fitness. Wilson launched his baseball enterprises just as the general public was acknowledging the connection between vigorous outdoor exercise and robust health. His oft-repeated pitch to reporters was that he was not organizing female baseball teams just to make money, but "to popularize open-air exercises among the Women of the land...as a Beautifying influence." He pointed out that the ancient Greeks had "understood the value of open-air Gymnastics, and produced those beautiful and graceful figures which, as shown in their marble representatives handed down to us, the world of today cannot rival."[31]

Wilson was drawn to female baseball teams because they provided easy access to young girls, but he also seemed genuinely interested in producing a financially viable entertainment commodity. He invested significant capital in his female baseball teams and military drill companies.[32] For his first foray into women's baseball in New York City, he obtained property at the corner of Madison Avenue and 59th Street and built "Wilson's Amphitheatre and Ladies' Athletic Grounds" complete with 400 feet of billboards for advertisers.[33] He announced in advertisements:

[M]y object is to start a new thing, to develop women of America. I am going to open here a field for their physical perfection. There is to be base ball, lacrosse, archery, polo, walking, running, velocipede riding and everything. Ponies are now in training. The doctors tell me it will knock seven-eighths of their business sky high.[34]

The idea of "developing" the women of America was a theme Wilson trumpeted with every new team

he established and many young women eagerly joined his baseball teams.

Over the course of his twenty-year involvement with female professional baseball, Wilson gave over 130 teenagers and young women the opportunity to travel the country and play baseball. Unfortunately, Wilson did not recruit highly skilled female baseball players; his focus was on physical beauty and most of his players were "well formed" actresses, former circus performers, and young runaways. He taught them only enough baseball to enable them to navigate on the diamond and make a show of pitching, hitting, and catching.[35] His rhetoric about promoting baseball as a "Beautifying influence" for women was bunk. Though a handful of Wilson's players, like Pearl Emerson and May Lawrence, were genuinely talented players, they were not Wilson's chief drawing card; he was selling sexual titillation and entertainment novelty.[36] The majority of his players saw through his false rhetoric and played only a single season or less, but a handful of them stayed for five seasons or more, sticking with Wilson through thick and thin and testifying on his behalf before numerous judges in courtrooms across the country.[37]

Sylvester Wilson undoubtedly harmed the reputation of professional women's baseball teams and of female players in general. During Wilson's 1891–92 trial for abducting Libbie Sunderland, New York State Assembly representative W. E. McCormick introduced a bill entitled "An Act to Prohibit Female Base-Ball Playing." Though nothing came of the bill, the fact that a New York politician thought to introduce it in the first place indicates the extent to which Wilson had besmirched the reputation of all female baseball players.[38]

Fortunately for the future of women's baseball, there were enough girls and women who continued to play baseball in New York and elsewhere that women were able to keep a foothold in the game. As Wilson headed off to Sing Sing for his first stint, the Young Ladies Base Ball Club of New York began operating. Two years later, its star, the highly talented pitcher, Lizzie Arlington, was wowing crowds and helping to rehabilitate the reputation of women's professional baseball.[39] As Wilson's sentence dragged on, girls and women engaged in games in Central Park, Rhinebeck, and on schoolyards and college campuses across the state and the nation.[40] These girls and women inspired others to play and passed their love of the game on to the generations who followed them. Over a dozen New Yorkers played in the World War II-era All American Girls Base Ball League and groups like the New York Women's Baseball Association and USA Baseball promote the game for countless New Yorkers today.[41] The future of women in baseball is bright. No thanks to Sylvester Wilson. ■

Notes

1. For details on baseball's evolution and New Yorkers' involvement with the emergence of the modern sport, see: John Thorn, *Baseball in the Garden of Eden* (New York: Simon & Schuster, 2011).

2. Correspondence, *Harper's Weekly* (November 5, 1859), 707. [Note: Guiwit's name is misspelled in the article; Census data provides the correct spelling along with his age and occupation.]

3. [No Title], *Albany Morning Times* (May 16, 1859), 2.

4. [No Title], *Troy Daily Times* (May 17, 1859), 2.

5. Ibid.

6. Examples: "The Daily Avalanche," *Memphis Daily Avalanche* (November 11, 1867), 1; "Local…Died of Baseball," *Coldwater Sentinel* (November 18, 1867), 3; [No Title], *Daily National Intelligencer* [D.C.], (November 22, 1867), 2; [No Title], *Indiana Herald* (November 27, 1867), 2.

7. "Local," *Coldwater Sentinel* (November 22, 1867), 3.

8. Rev. John Todd, *Woman's Rights* (Boston: Lee and Shepard, 1867), 25.

9. The Vassar teams were the Laurel and Abenakis, organized in Spring 1866 and the Precocious organized in Spring 1867. None of the players on the Precocious club had played the previous year on the Laurel and Abenakis. *The Vassariana*, Vol. 1, no. 1 (June 27, 1866), 2; Annie Glidden to John Glidden, April 20, 1866; *The Transcript*, No. 1 (June 1867). Vassar sources are available at the Vassar College Archives. Dozens of newspapers mentioned the girls' nines in Peterboro, New York. The first reference was contained in a letter written by Elizabeth Cady Stanton on August 1, 1868, and published in her women's rights newspaper, *The Revolution*, Vol. II, no. 5, (August 6, 1868), 66.

10. Dr. Edward H. Clarke, *Sex in Education: Or, A Fair Chance for the Girls* (Boston: James R. Osgood and Co., 1873), 42. Clarke's books went through seventeen editions between 1873 and 1886. See, Patricia A. Vertinsky, *The Eternally Wounded Woman: Women, Doctors, and Exercise in the Late Nineteenth Century* (Urbana and Chicago: University of Illinois Press, 1994), 51.

11. Ibid., 18.

12. Sophia Foster Richardson, "Tendencies in Athletics for Women in Colleges and Universities," *Appletons' Popular Science Monthly* (February 1897), 1–10. Richardson played on Vassar's baseball teams in the mid- to late-1870s.

13. See Appendix 1, Women's Teams of New York.

14. Maud Nelson, whose real name was Clementina Brida, was born circa 1873 in the Austrian Tyrol. She emigrated to the United States with her father and brothers in February 1887. Nelson played for numerous barnstorming teams, including some founded in New York City, beginning in 1892. She went on to a forty-year career in baseball as a player, manager, and team owner. The account of Thompson and Jackson is from: "Female Ball Players: How They Knocked Luke Kenney All Over the Diamond," *Brooklyn Daily Eagle* (July 23, 1889), 6. The article mentioning the "society buds" in Greenwich is from: "Atlantic Breezes: Echoes From Greenwich," *New York Herald* (July 9, 1893), 14. A photo of the Pelham Manor team is available from the town historian of Pelham, New York. See: http://historicpelham.blogspot.com/2010/02/photograph-of-only-known-19th-century.html.

15. "Girls Worth Having: What Muscular Evolution has Done for the Development of the American Young Woman . . ." *New York World*. Reprinted in: *St. Paul Daily Globe* (September 6, 1885), 13.

16. "Girl Base Ball Players: Have a Mighty Struggle With the Fort Hamiltons; and the Men Were Mean Enough to Beat by a Score of No One Knows How Many to One. Some Sliding Done, but Precious Little Catching," *Brooklyn Daily Eagle* (May 6, 1894), 7; "Carrollton," *Saginaw News* (June 28, 1892), 6; "A Female Base Ball Club in Danger: Attacked by a Cuban Mob and

One of the Players Hurt," *Brooklyn Daily Eagle* (March 6, 1893), 10; "Female Base Ballists," *Utica Sunday Tribune* (June 26, 1892); "Local News Gleanings," *The Denton* (Maryland) *Journal*, (May 20, 1893), 2; "How One of the Female Ball Nine Deserted Husband and Babes—Stuck on Being an Actress—She Tagged the Runner and He Hurt Her Arm," *Quincy* (Illinois) *Daily Herald* (June 8, 1894), 8; the Cincinnati Reds were organized in 1891 by Mark Lally. Numerous articles mention that the team was from New York. Examples: "Diamond Dust," *Wheeling Register* (July 28, 1891), 3; "Hard Lines for Female Baseball: The Girl Ball-Players Had to Stop Swing Bats," (New York) *World* (April 25, 1892), 1.

17. "Sporting Matters," *Lowell Daily Citizen* (March 27, 1879).

18. Wilson and Powell were arrested after players Kitty Byrnes (a.k.a. Gracie Clinton) and Mary Callahan went to their lodgings at Hamilton House and demanded their salaries. The men invited the girls to spend the night and seduced them. Wilson and Powell were arraigned in Police Court on the charges on May 24, 1879 and held on $1,000 bond. The charges were later dropped for lack of evidence and they were released. "Deluded Female Ball-Players," *Chicago Daily Tribune* (May 27, 1879), 5; "The Ladies' Athletic Association: Why the Manager and Treasurer Were Put in Jail Yesterday," *New York Herald* (May 25, 1879), 8.

19. See chapter 1 of James William Beul, *Mysteries and Miseries of America's Great Cities: Embracing New York, Washington City, San Francisco, Salt Lake City, and New Orleans* (St. Louis & Philadelphia: Historical Publishing Co., 1883).

20. References to each of the aliases: *New York Clipper* (November 10, 1883); *New Orleans Daily Picayune* (May 5, 1886); *Brooklyn Daily Eagle* (September 8, 1889); *Brooklyn Daily Eagle* (June 3, 1903). The NYSPCC was founded in 1875; within four years, its agents were targeting Wilson. Society reports contain several entries on Wilson. See, for example, *Twenty-Second Annual Report, New York Society for the Prevention of Cruelty to Children*, December 31, 1896 (New York: Office of the Society, 1897), 57; *Twenty-Ninth Annual Report, New York Society for the Prevention of Cruelty to Children*, December 31, 1903 (Albany: State Legislative Printer, 1904). Report contained in: *Documents of the Senate of the State of New York* 9.17 (1904): 32–33.

21. Wilson's 1891 arrest and trial were covered in scores of newspapers across the country and in the annual reports of the New York Society for the Prevention of Cruelty to Children. Examples from New York papers: "A Female Base Ball Manager Employed a Fifteen Year Old Girl as a Mascot," *Syracuse Courier* (August 15, 1891), 1; "A Wayward Lass: Abbie Sunderland, of this City, the Cause of a Base Ball Manager's Arrest…" *Binghamton Republican* (August 15, 1891), 1; "Christian Wilson, Abductor: Some Account of His Career—Near the End of His Rope," *The New York Times* (August 16, 1891), 14; *The New York Society for the Prevention of Cruelty to Children: Twenty-Fifth Annual Report*, December 31, 1899 (New York: Offices of the Society, 1900), 40–41.

22. "A Missing Partner: Lady Baseball Players' Manager Left With Cash; Levied on Bloomers; Manager Smithson of the Cricket Grounds Determined to Have his Share of the Receipts—Manager Franklin Arrested—His Partner Adams is Missing," *Jersey Journal* (May 31, 1899), 4.

23. *The New York Society for the Prevention of Cruelty to Children: Twenty-Fifth Annual Report*, December 31, 1899 (New York: Offices of the Society, 1900), 40–41.

22. "A Get-Rich-Quick Scheme? Max Bracklow Says He Dropped $200 in Promoting a Female Base Ball Team," *Brooklyn Daily Eagle* (June 3, 1903), 8. Another article claimed he invested $500. See: "Woman Ball Team Man Arrested: Sylvester F. Wilson, Man of Many Ventures, Is Charged with Abduction," *New York Evening Telegram* (June 7, 1903), 2.

25. Ibid.

26. "Gets Nine Years for Abduction: S.I. Wilson, Promoter of Women's Baseball Teams, Had Pleaded Guilty to Charge," *New-York Tribune*, (August 22, 1903), 11. Details on Wilson's numerous arrests and trials are available in an unpublished report written about Wilson by the New York Society for the Prevention of Cruelty to Children for prosecutors at

his 1903 trial. The unpublished "Brief for the People" is part of the files of the N.Y. Court of General Sessions for *People Against Sylvester F. Wilson*, New York City Municipal Archives.

27. NYSPCC Superintendent E. Fellows Jenkins and Agent Vincent Pisarra testified against Wilson at his final trial in June 1903. Pisarra later mentioned his role in apprehending Wilson in the *New York Evening Telegram* (May 13, 1919).

28. New York State Death Index, #67147.

29. I compiled these statistics from newspaper articles. The total is extrapolated by taking the average number of spectators for the 21 games with reported attendance (37,000 spectators/an average of 1,762 per game) and using that average for the remaining 16 games for which no figures are given.

30. Murphy had been a talented player in his youth and stayed involved with the sport as he worked his way up the ladder in New York City's political machine; he was unofficial "chief lieutenant" for the eighteenth district when he and Wilson staged the game in Weehawken. For background on Murphy's association with baseball see Nancy Joan Weiss, *Charles Francis Murphy, 1858–1924: Respectability & Responsibility in Tammany Politics* (Northampton, MA: Smith College, 1968), 22.

31. *Chicago Tribune* (March 30, 1879).

32. Several of Wilson's baseball troupes traveled with female military drill companies and/or music groups. See, for example, "Freeman in Bondage: The Manager of the Female Base Ball Club Punished as a Vagrant," *New Orleans Daily Picayune*, (5 May 1886); "Frolicking Freeman: The Man who was in Galveston with Female Base-ballers 'Detained' in New Orleans as a Dangerous Character," *Galveston Daily News*, (May 7, 1886), 15; *Shenandoah Herald* [Woodstock, VA] (October 25, 1889), 3.

33. An advertisement for the grand opening of the grounds appeared in: "Amusements," *New York Herald* (May 12, 1879). An ad in the *New York Herald* (May 14, 1879) announced that vendors could apply for "refreshment privileges" and "400 feet of Bill Boards." Thanks to John Thorn for bringing these to my attention.

34. "Red and Blue Legs: A High Old Game of Base Ball by Eighteen Women," *Washington Post* (May 12, 1879), 1.

35. For an example of a player advertisement see: *Pittsburg Dispatch* (September 21, 1889), 3. For details on what Wilson taught the players see: "Girls to Play Ball: A Team Composed of Pittsburg Young Ladies Being Organized; Good Material to Select From; Many of the Girls Enthusiastic Over the Open Air Pastime; Glad to Escape From Indoor Work," *Pittsburg Dispatch* (September 23, 1889), 5.

36. Pearl Emerson and May Lawrence (almost certainly stage names) played on Wilson's teams from 1883 to 1889. They usually played pitcher, catcher, and first base.

37. Information on player tenure was compiled by studying hundreds of available box scores on Wilson's teams. Newspaper articles about Wilson's numerous arrests abound and some mention his players testifying on his behalf. Example: "Winsome Witnesses: The Female Base Ball Club in Court—Sporr Discharged," *Kansas City Star* (2 Nov 1885), 5. Even Libbie Sunderland, the young woman Wilson routinely molested testified in court at his trial for abducting her that Wilson had treated her "as a father and furnished her a home." "Female Baseball Player: A Trial in New-York Discloses Interesting and Shameful Details," *Buffalo Express* (October 13, 1891), 2.

38. McCormick introduced his bill in March 1892. *Journal of the Assembly of the State of New York at Their One Hundred and Fifteenth Session* (Albany: James B. Lyon, State Printer, 1892): 785. Members of the Assembly seem to have considered the legislation a joke. See proposed amendments for March 25, 1892: *Journal of the Assembly of the State of New York at Their One Hundred and Fifteenth Session* (Albany: James B. Lyon, State Printer, 1892): 1326. "The Excise Bill: The Assembly Committee Reports A Compromise Bill…" *Auburn Bulletin* (March 4, 1892), 1.

39. Information on this team is culled from contemporary newspaper articles. It is quite difficult to distinguish between different teams as many had similar sounding names and newspapers sometimes confused them. It appears that the Young Ladies Base Ball Club of New York may have also been called the New York Stars and may have been renamed the New England Bloomer Girls at some point. Lizzie Arlington joined the team in either 1894 or 1895 and, after a brief stint playing for men's minor league teams, was still with them as late as 1901. "Lady Ball Players: Hit the Sphere and Run Bases Just Like Real Men; Some Incidents of the Cramer Hill Game," (Philadelphia) *Evening Item* (June 22, 1895); "Did You Ever?" *King's Weekly* [Greenville, NC] (July 26, 1894), 4.

40. "Throngs in Central Park…." *New York Herald Tribune* (June 11, 1894), 4. In July, the *Rhinebeck Gazette* (July 21, 1894) informed readers that the local all-female Ostrich Feathers would be playing a match game against the Pond Lillies on July 28. Schoolgirls in Lowville organized the Miss Allen and Mrs. Jones teams in June 1897. "Brief Mention," (Lowville) *Journal & Republican* (June 10, 1897), 5. Students at Vassar College played football, basketball and baseball. Annie E. P. Searing, "Vassar College," *Harper's Bazaar* (May 30, 1896): 469.

41. For information on New Yorkers in the All-American Girls Baseball League and on the New York Women's Baseball Association, see: http://nywomensbaseball.com. USA Baseball hosts a women's national team. See: http://web.usabaseball.com/womens_national_team.jsp.

The First and Last Games on the Polo Groundses

Stew Thornley

Examining the life span of a baseball stadium by profiling its first and last games is an interesting exercise—even more interesting when it becomes a number of different stadiums. This is the case with the Polo Groundses, four or five—depending on how one counts them—samely-named stadiums. Taking a look at ten different games over an 80-year span tells more than just the hits and errors in a particular game; it traces the history of baseball in America's largest city.

Varying definitions of stadiums also lead to differing numbering systems among stadium aficionados (some refer to the original Polo Grounds as two stadiums since it had two diamonds). Just to add to the provocativeness of it all, other issues of contention arise.

Contention isn't the goal of this article; it's to be a summary of the first and last games, with accompanying information perhaps at times illuminating the issues surrounding oddly-shaped stadiums with an equally odd name for most of them, since polo was played only in the original version.

While others may differ, the author here refers to the original site as Polo Grounds I—even though there were two diamonds. Because the grounds had one diamond in the southeast corner and another in the southwest corner, some have labeled the different diamonds as Polo Grounds I and Polo Grounds II; I consider the entire facility as one stadium, labeling it as such while noting that it had two diamonds.

POLO GROUNDS I

These were actual polo grounds, extending from Sixth to Fifth avenues and wedged between 110th and 112th streets just north of Central Park. Professional baseball first arrived in 1880, and major-league baseball (the focus here) came in 1883.

Since there were two diamonds, there were two first and two last games here. And the final game on the southwest diamond is, in this author's mind, not a certainty.

What is certain is the first major-league game on each of the diamonds.

First Game—Southeast Diamond

The New York National League team played its first game on the southeast diamond—the one with the elaborate grandstand—on Tuesday, May 1, 1883. This team eventually became known as the Giants. Many sources cite Gothams as the original nickname, although the author has yet to find that usage in any of the newspapers.[1]

The first game for the New-Yorks—as *The New York Times* referred to the team—was also the first major-league game on Manhattan Island.[2] A previous team representing the city in the National League played in Brooklyn, which still had nearly another 15 years as a separate city ahead of it.

The city was ready for baseball. "The residents of Harlem were awakened from their usual state of quiet and repose yesterday afternoon by seeing immense crowds of people coming up town on their way to the Polo Grounds," reported the *New York Tribune*.[3]

The crowd was reported at more than 15,000, one of the spectators being General (and former president) Ulysses Grant. New York batted first, built a 6–0 lead and held on for a 7–5 win over Boston. The New-Yorks had a lineup that featured four players now in the Hall of Fame—catcher Buck Ewing, first baseman Roger Connor, center fielder John Montgomery Ward, and pitcher Mickey Welch. (See Box Score 1.)

First Game—Southwest Diamond

New York had two new major league teams in 1883. In addition to the National League Club, a team called the Metropolitan played in the American Association.[5] Both the New-Yorks and the Metropolitan were owned by the Metropolitan Exhibition Company, of which John B. Day, a Tammany politician and wealthy baseball wannabe, was principal owner. Day planned to have his Association club play at the opposite end of the Polo Grounds from the New-Yorks and carved out a diamond in the southwest corner. The diamond wasn't ready for the Metropolitan's first home game, causing the team to use the southeast diamond.

On Decoration Day May 30, the southwest diamond was ready, and it was needed, because the New-Yorks were at home. Not only did the National League team have two games scheduled, the college national championship game was played in between.

On the southwest diamond, the Metropolitan also had two games scheduled—against two different teams, Cincinnati and then Columbus.[6] The game against Cincinnati, which started at 9:30A.M., was the first on the southwest diamond. Tim Keefe, another future Hall of Famer, shut out Cincinnati, 1–0, as the Metropolitan came up with a run in the top of the ninth for the win. (See Box Score 2.)

Mickey Welch at bat against Boston's Old Hoss Radbourn at the original Polo Grounds in 1886.

BOX SCORE 1 – Tuesday, May 1, 1883; New York 7, Boston 5 (Bolded name indicates Hall of Famer)

New York	r	1b	po	a
Buck Ewing c	0	1	7	4
Roger Connor 1b	1	2	13	0
John Ward cf	1	1	1	1
Patrick Gillespie lf	1	2	1	0
Mike Dorgan rf	1	2	0	0
Mickey Welch p	1	2	2	4
Ed Caskin 2b	1	2	0	1
Dasher Troy ss	0	0	1	3
Frank Hankinson 3b	1	1	2	1
	7	13	27	14

Boston	r	1b	po	a
Joe Hornung lf	2	1	1	0
John Morrill 1b	0	0	15	0
Jim Whitney p	0	0	0	3
Ezra Sutton 3b	1	1	0	1
Sam Wise ss	0	0	1	3
Jack Burdock 2b	0	1	4	2
Mike Hines c	2	2	4	9
Charlie Buffinton cf	0	1	2	0
Paul Radford rf	0	1	0	0
	5	7	27	18

Team	Line Score	R	H	E	Manager
New York	312/100/000-	7	13	6	John Clapp
Boston	002/111/000-	5	7	8	Jack Burdock

Runs earned[4]—New York 4, Boston 0. Errors—Caskin, Troy 5, Whitney, Wise, Burdock, Hines 3, Radford 2. First base by errors—New York 2, Boston 4. Struck out—By Whitney 2, by Welch 4. Total left on bases—New York 5, Boston 5. Three-base hit—Connor. Two-base hit—Hankinson. Total-base hits—New York 16, Boston 7. Passed balls—Hines 4. Umpire—S. M. Decker. Time of game—Two hours.

BOX SCORE 2 – Wednesday, May 30, 1883; Metropolitan 1, Cincinnati 0

Metropolitan	r	1b	po	a
Candy Nelson ss	0	1	0	2
Steve Brady 1b	0	0	6	0
Dude Esterbrook 3b	0	1	2	0
Chief Roseman rf	0	0	2	0
John O'Rourke cf	0	1	1	0
Bill Holbert c	1	2	13	2
Tim Keefe p	0	1	0	2
Ed Kennedy lf	0	1	0	0
Sam Crane 2b	0	0	3	0
	1	7	27	6

Cincinnati	r	1b	po	a
Joe Sommer lf	0	1	4	0
Hick Carpenter 3b	0	0	2	1
Charley Jones cf	0	0	3	0
Long John Reilly 1b	0	1	10	0
Phil Powers c	0	0	2	2
Pop Corkhill rf	0	0	2	0
Chick Fulmer ss	0	1	0	1
Bid McPhee 2b	0	0	4	2
Harry McCormick p	0	0	0	6
	0	3	27	12

Team	Line Score	R	H	E	Manager
Metropolitan	000/000/001-	1	7	1	Jim Mutrie
Cincinnati	000/000/000-	0	3	5	Pop Snyder

Runs earned—Metropolitan 0, Cincinnati 0. Errors—Holbert, Fulmer 3, McPhee, McCormick. First base by errors—Metropolitan 4, Cincinnati 0. Struck out—By McCormick 1, by Keefe 9. Total left on bases—Metropolitan 8, Cincinnati 2. Three-base hit—Keefe. Total-base hits—Metropolitan 8, Cincinnati 3. Passed balls—Holbert, Powers. Umpire—Mr. Magner. Time of game—One hour and forty-five minutes.

With games going on at both ends of the grounds, a flimsy, canvas-covered fence separated the playing areas. Balls rolling under the fence remained in play, causing the bizarre scene of an outfielder emerging into the opposing field in pursuit of a ball. Although outfielders proved agile and adept at getting under the fence and to the fugitive balls, occasionally a hit that rolled under the fence ended up as a home run.

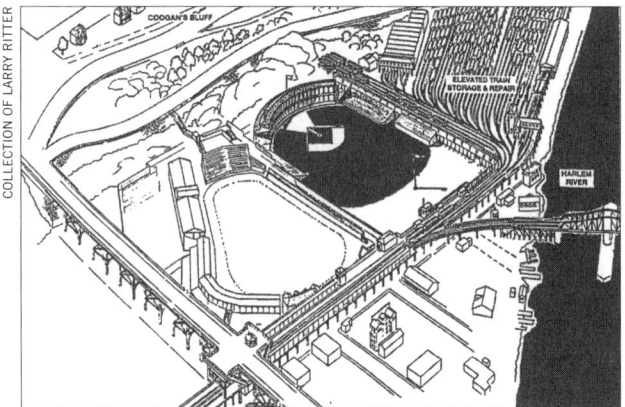

On the left is the Polo Grounds that opened in 1889. On the right is the new ballpark that opened to the north of the "New" Polo Grounds in 1890. Originally used by the New York team in the Player's League and known as Brotherhood Park, it was taken over by the National League Giants in 1891 and renamed the Polo Grounds. The stadium the Giants abandoned took the name Manhattan Field. Its grandstand remained for several years, and the playing area was used for a variety of activities.

Starting on Decoration Day, the League and Association teams were at home over the next couple of weeks, so the canvas fence remained up with the teams operating at opposite ends. The Metropolitan then took off on a long road trip and didn't return until July 23.

By then, the New-Yorks were away, leaving the entire Polo Grounds open. The question is, did the Metropolitan play on the southwest or southeast diamond? Many stadium scholars express certainty that the Association team played on the southeast diamond whenever it was available and played on the west end only when there was a conflict.

The author of this article—while acknowledging the likelihood of this—isn't as convinced as others, whom the author believes are being swayed by nebulous evidence.[7] Nevertheless, it seems more likely that the final game on the west diamond was September 4, two days before the Metropolitan's final home game, which was probably played on the southeast diamond.

Last Game—Southwest Diamond

The opponent September 4 was the Eclipse (Louisville), which took the lead with seven runs in the fifth inning. Down by five runs after six innings, the Metropolitan caught up and tied the score in the ninth. When the Eclipse couldn't counter in the bottom of the inning, the game was called by darkness and ended in an 8–8 tie. (See Box Score 3.)

BOX SCORE 3 – Tuesday, September 4, 1883; Metropolitan 8, Eclipse 8

Metropolitan	r	1b	po	a
Candy Nelson ss	1	3	1	5
John O'Rourke cf	1	3	1	0
Steve Brady 1b	1	1	12	0
Chief Roseman rf	1	1	0	1
Dude Esterbrook 3b	1	3	2	5
Charlie Reipschlager c	1	2	10	1
Ed Kennedy lf	0	1	0	0
Jack Lynch p	1	0	0	0
Sam Crane 2b	1	2	1	2
	8	16	27	14

Eclipse	r	1b	po	a
Pete Browning lf	1	1	4	2
Jack Gleason 3b	1	1	1	0
Guy Hecker p	1	1	1	4
Lew Brown 1b	0	0	12	0
Jumbo Latham 2b	1	1	4	3
Ed Whiting c	1	1	5	1
Leech Maskrey cf	2	1	0	1
Chicken Wolf rf	0	1	0	0
Tom McLaughlin ss	1	1	0	5
	8	8	27	16

Team	Line Score	R	H	E	Manager
Metropolitan	021/000/131–	8	16	7	Jim Mutrie
Eclipse	000/071/000–	8	8	9	Joe Gerhardt

Runs earned—Metropolitan 3, Eclipse 1. Errors—Esterbrook, Reipschlager, Kennedy, Lynch 4, Hecker 4, Latham, Whiting, Wolf, McLaughlin.
First base by errors—Metropolitan 5, Eclipse 5. Struck out—Metropolitan 2, Eclipse 6. Left on bases—Metropolitan 9, Eclipse 3.
Three-base hit—Esterbrook. Two-base hits—Reipschlager and O'Rourke. Total-base hits—Metropolitan 20, Eclipse 8.
Double play—Browning and Latham. Wild pitch—Hecker. Passed balls—Reipschlager, Whiting 4. Umpire—Mr. McNichol.
Time of game—Two hours and seventeen minutes. Called after nine innings because of darkness.

Last Game—Southeast Diamond

The southwest diamond disappeared from the Polo Grounds after the 1883 season; eventually, so did the Metropolitan. The National League team, soon known as the Giants, continued playing in the southeast corner and made it to the World's Series in 1888, playing the American Association champion St. Louis Browns in a series set at 10 games.

Four of the first five games were at the Polo Grounds, and the fifth game, on October 20, was the final game on the original Polo Grounds. The Giants trailed, 4–1, going into the last of the eighth but rallied for five runs. Buck Ewing brought in a run with a triple and then scored the tying run on an infield out. Roger Connor tripled and came home with the go-ahead run on a single by John Montgomery Ward, who added insurance via a stolen base, error, and passed ball. When the inning ended, umpire John Gaffney called the game because of darkness.

The Giants went on to win the series, six games to four. Until the Atlanta Braves closed Atlanta-Fulton County Stadium with a World Series game in 1996, the Polo Grounds on 110th Street was the only stadium to finish its history with a World's/World Series game. (See Box Score 4.)

POLO GROUNDS II

First Game

Early in 1889 New York City moved ahead with plans to re-open 111th Street, which had been interrupted by the Polo Grounds between Fifth and Sixth Avenues, the site occupied by the Giants.

The Giants opened 1889 as an itinerant bunch, playing first in New Jersey and then on Staten Island before Day found a site just off the Harlem River in the southern half of Coogan's Hollow in Manhattan, beneath the 155th Street viaduct and along Eighth Avenue. Day was concerned about confusion among fans as the team prepared for its third home of the season. He knew that New Yorkers associated the name Polo Grounds with his baseball team, so—to send an unambiguous message as to where the Giants would be headquartered—he christened the quarters the New Polo Grounds.[8]

Barely two weeks after work had begun to convert a field to a stadium, the Giants opened the New Polo Grounds with a game against Pittsburgh on Monday, July 8. Newspapers reported the crowd inside the stadium as more than 10,000, even though fewer than half that many seats were available. Many of those denied access retired to a beer garden across the street, an establishment that offered at least a partial view of the game through its windows. A larger group occupied the high ground to the west of the stadium. This area—officially Coogan's Bluff—was dubbed "Dead-Head Hill" by *The New York Times*, which observed that the onlookers from the hill "were bunched together as closely as chocks in a dude's trousers."[9]

Cannonball Crane outhurled Pittsburgh's Pud Galvin—a right-hander who had already amassed more

BOX SCORE 4 – Saturday, October 21, 1888; New York 6, St. Louis 4, 8 innings, called by darkness, Game 5, World's Series

Browns	r	1b	po	a
Arlie Latham 3b	2	1	1	1
Yank Robinson 2b	0	1	3	3
Tip O'Neill lf	0	0	1	0
Charles Comiskey 1b	0	0	9	2
Tommy McCarthy rf	0	0	2	0
Harry Lyons cf	0	0	1	0
Bill White ss	0	0	3	3
Jocko Milligan c	1	1	3	6
Silver King p	1	1	1	3
	4	4	24	18

Giants	r	1b	po	a
Mike Tiernan rf	2	2	0	0
Buck Ewing c	1	1	3	1
Danny Richardson 2b	0	1	2	1
Roger Connor 1b	1	2	12	0
John Ward ss	1	1	1	7
Mike Slattery cf	0	0	4	0
Jim O'Rourke lf	0	1	0	0
Art Whitney 3b	1	1	1	1
Tim Keefe p	0	0	1	8
	6	9	24	18

Team	Line Score	R	H	E	Manager
St. Louis	003/001/00-	4	4	5	**Charles Comiskey**
New York	100/000/05-	6	9	2	Jim Mutrie

Runs earned—St. Louis 2, New York 2. Errors—Comiskey, McCarthy, White 2, Milligan, Richardson, Keefe.
First base on errors—St. Louis 1, New York 2. First base on balls—Latham, Milligan, Ward. Struck out—Comiskey, King, Ewing, Slattery.
Stolen bases—Latham, Slattery, Ward 2. Double plays—Ward, Richardson, and Connor; Keefe, Ward, and Connor. Three-base hits—Ewing, Conner.
Wild pitches—King. Passed balls—Milligan 2, Ewing. Umpires—Messres. Gaffney and Kelly. Time of game—One hour and fifty minutes.

than 300 pitching wins in his career—and also started a four-run third-inning rally with a single. New York beat Pittsburgh, 7–5. (The Giants would go on to win the pennant in 1889 and beat the Brooklyn Bridegrooms of the American Association in the World's Series.) (See Box Score 5.)

Last Game

Brooklyn moved to the National League in 1890 and played the Giants more frequently. New York's final home game of the season—on Saturday, September 13—was against Brooklyn and also the final major-league game in this edition of the Polo Grounds.

A doubleheader had been scheduled, but the teams weren't even able to make it through all of the first game. The Giants trailed, 8–3, after six innings and scored a run in the top of the seventh before rain stopped play. The final score has been listed as 8–4 and 8–3, depending on if the Giants' final run is counted in the uncompleted inning. (Per the rules in the Spalding Guide, the run should not have counted.) (See Box Score 6.)

BOX SCORE 5 – Monday, July 8, 1889; New York 7, Pittsburgh 5

Giants	r	1b	po	a
George Gore cf	2	1	0	0
Mike Tiernan rf	2	2	4	0
Buck Ewing c	1	2	8	0
Roger Connor 1b	0	3	9	0
Danny Richardson 2b	0	2	2	4
Jim O'Rourke lf	1	1	3	0
John Ward ss	0	0	0	3
Art Whitney 3b	0	1	1	1
Cannonball Crane p	1	2	0	1
	7	14	27	9

Pittsburgh	r	1b	po	a
Ned Hanlon cf	0	0	1	1
Billy Sunday rf	1	1	2	1
Fred Carroll 1b	1	0	7	1
Deacon White 3b	0	1	1	3
Jack Rowe ss	1	2	5	1
Fred Dunlap 2b	1	1	1	5
Doggie Miller c	1	0	7	2
Bill Kuehne lf	0	2	1	0
Pud Galvin p	0	0	2	5
	5	7	27	19

Team	Line Score	R	H	E	Manager
New York	004/010/020-	7	14	1	Jim Mutrie
Pittsburgh	002/000/030-	5	7	9	Horace Phillips

Earned runs—Pittsburgh 2. Errors—Ward, Hanlon, Carroll, White 2, Rowe, Dunlap, Miller 2, Galvin. First base by errors—New York 7, Pittsburgh 1. Left on bases—New York 10, Pittsburgh 9. First base on balls—Off Crane 6. Struck out—By Crane 6, by Galvin 1. Three-base hits—Richardson. Two-base hits—Kuehne. Double plays—Ward, Richardson, and Connor; Whitney, Richardson, and Connor. Hit by pitcher—Sunday, White. Passed balls—Ewing. Umpire—Mr. Powers.

BOX SCORE 6 – Saturday, September 13, 1890; Brooklyn 8, New York 4, 6½ innings, rain

Giants	r	1b	po	a
Mike Tiernan cf	2	1	2	0
Dick Buckley c	0	0	4	1
Pebbly Jack Glasscock ss	0	1	1	1
Lew Whistler 1b	0	0	9	0
Jesse Burkett rf	0	0	0	0
Charley Bassett 2b	0	1	0	2
Joe Hornung lf-3b	1	0	0	0
Artie Clark 3b-c	0	0	1	1
Amos Rusie p	1	0	0	2
Pat Murphy c	0	0	0	0
Jack Sharrott lf	0	0	0	0
	4	3	17*	7

*Pinkney declared out.

Bridegrooms	r	1b	po	a
Dave Foutz 1b	0	0	10	0
Darby O'Brien cf	1	2	0	0
Hub Collins 2b	1	1	3	4
Oyster Burns rf	1	0	1	0
George Pinkney 3b	1	1	0	1
Adonis Terry p	1	1	0	3
Tom Daly c	1	1	5	0
Germany Smith ss	1	0	0	2
Bob Caruthers lf	1	2	2	0
	8	8	21	10

Team	Line Score	R	H	E	Manager
New York	102/000/1-	4	3	1	Jim Mutrie
Brooklyn	600/101/-	8	8	3	Bill McGunnigle

Earned runs—New York 1, Brooklyn 4. Errors—Glasscock, Foutz, Daly, Caruthers. First base by errors—New York 2, Brooklyn 1. Left on bases—New York 3, Brooklyn 4. Two-base hits—Tiernan. Stolen base—Caruthers. Sacrifice hits—Buckley, Glasscock, Clarke, Burkett, Foutz, Collins, Smith. Double play—Smith, Collins, and Foutz. Struck out—Burkett, Hornung, Bassett, O'Brien, Pinkney, Terry, Daly. First base on balls—Off Rusie 3, off Terry 2. Hit by pitcher—Buckley. Passed balls—Daly 2. Wild pitches—Rusie, Terry. Umpire—Mr. Lynch.

This box score, counting the run scored by New York in the top of the seventh, is from *The New York Times*. Retrosheet lists the score in this game as 8–3 for Brooklyn, indicating that the uncompleted seventh inning was erased with the score reverting to the sixth inning.

POLO GROUNDS III

In 1890 the National League had a neighbor in New York as a new league—the Players' National League of Professional Base Ball Clubs—formed. Backers of the New York team in what became known as the Players' League leased the northern section of Coogan's Hollow and built a stadium, Brotherhood Park, next to the Polo Grounds.

The Players' League lasted only one season, and the Giants moved into the northern space, carrying the name Polo Grounds with them again.

First Game

The first National League game in Polo Grounds III was played on Wednesday, April 22, 1891, and a huge crowd was on hand to see the Giants reunited. Before the game, Giants who had remained with the National League team lined up on one side of the field with those who had gone to the Players' League on the other. The two sides then came together to indicate that past differences were settled and that they were one team again.

Amos Rusie pitched for New York, John Clarkson for Boston, and the game was tied, 2–2, after eight. Rusie came home with the go-ahead run in the top of the inning on a single by George Gore, but Gore undid the good of his hit in the bottom of the inning. Boston had two on and one out when Herman Long sent a fly to center. "Gore started after it, and to the great discomfiture of the vast throng he lost his footing and fell," reported the *Times*.[10]

The *Boston Globe* provided a different perspective: "Long came up with his long bat and hit the ball hard, but it sailed high and George Gore started to get under it, having plenty of time. He misjudged, however, and then made a muff of it, high over his head, the ball rolling along the field as Gore lay in a heap on the ground, having tangled himself up in reaching for the ball."

The newspapers also differed on whether Gore was charged with an error or Long credited with a triple (as is indicated in the accompanying box score); in either case, two runs scored to give Boston a 4–3 win. (See Box Score 7.)

Last Game

The Giants remained in the Polo Grounds for nearly 20 years and expected to use the stadium longer. They lost to the Phillies, 6–1, in the second game of the 1911 season, a Philadelphia win preserved by a great catch

BOX SCORE 7 – Wednesday, April 22, 1891; Boston 4, New York 3

Giants	ab	r	1b	po	a
George Gore cf	5	1	2	1	0
Mike Tiernan rf	5	0	1	1	0
Pebbly Jack Glasscock ss	4	0	0	2	2
Jim O'Rourke lf	3	1	1	0	0
Roger Connor 1b	3	0	2	8	0
Danny Richardson 2b	4	0	2	3	5
Jerry Denny 3b	4	0	1	2	0
Dick Buckley c	4	0	0	7	5
Amos Rusie p	4	1	0	1	1
	36	3	9	*25	13

*One out in the ninth inning.

Boston	ab	r	h	po	a
Herman Long ss	5	1	3	5	4
Harry Stovey rf	2	0	0	2	0
Tommy Tucker 1b	4	0	1	10	1
Marty Sullivan lf	3	1	1	1	0
Joe Quinn 2b	3	0	2	2	2
Steve Brodie cf	4	0	1	2	0
Billy Nash 3b	3	1	0	1	2
Charlie Bennett c	4	1	1	4	1
John Clarkson p	3	0	1	0	3
	31	4	10	27	13

Team	Line Score	R	H	E	Manager
New York	101/000/001–	3	9	2	Jim Mutrie
Boston	100/100/002–	4	10	5	**Frank Selee**

Earned runs—New York 1, Boston 1. Errors—Tiernan, Rusie, Long 2, Tucker, Bennett 2. Two-base hit—O'Rourke. Three-base hit—Long 3. Stolen bases—Connor, Richardson, Stovey 2, Sullivan. First base on balls—Connor, Stovey 2, Sullivan, Nash, Clarkson. First base on errors—New York 3, Boston 1. Struck out—Connor, Denny, Long 2, Stovey 2, Bennett, Clarkson 2. Sacrifice hits—Glasscock, O'Rourke. Passed ball—Bennett. Wild pitch—Clarkson. Hit by pitched ball—Quinn. Time of game—2h ours and 3 minutes. Umpire—Lynch.

by center-fielder Dode Paskert.[11] Early the next morning a fire began in the grandstand, spreading quickly and destroying all but some bleachers in left field and the clubhouse/office building at the Eighth Avenue end.

A young sportswriter, Fred Lieb, was taken by the late-inning catch made by Paskert and years later reflected in his memoirs on the event and the fire that followed hours later. He wrote, "Reporters who were there liked to call the official account of the fire's origin nonsense: it was Paskert's electrifying and sizzling catch, they said, that sparked the Polo Grounds holocaust."[12] (See Box Score 8.)

POLO GROUNDS IV

The Giants accepted an offer from the nearby New York Highlanders/Yankees to move into American League Park as they figured out what to do about a new stadium. Owner John Brush decided to rebuild on the same spot but with more durable materials.

Coogan's Bluff is visible in the background as fans watch the 1905 World Series from center field.

BOX SCORE 8 – Thursday, April 13, 1911; Philadelphia 6, New York 1

Phillies	ab	r	h
John Titus rf	5	0	1
Otto Knabe 2b	4	2	2
Hans Lobert 3b	4	0	0
Sherry Magee lf	5	1	2
Dode Paskert cf	4	1	2
Fred Luderus 1b	4	0	3
Mickey Doolin ss	4	2	2
Red Dooin c	4	0	3
Jack Rowan p	3	0	0
	37	6	15

Giants	ab	r	h
Josh Devore lf	3	0	0
Larry Doyle 2b	4	0	1
Fred Snodgrass cf	1	1	0
Red Murray rf	4	0	1
Fred Merkle 1b	4	0	0
Al Bridwell ss	4	0	1
Art Devlin 3b	3	0	0
Chief Meyers c	3	0	0
Christy Mathewson p	2	0	0
*Beals Becker ph	1	0	0
Rube Marquard p	0	0	0
	29	1	3

*Batted for Mathewson in the eighth inning.

Team	Line Score	R	H	E	Manager
Philadelphia	110/100/210-	6	15	1	Red Dooin
New York	000/001/000-	1	3	0	**John McGraw**

Error—Knabe. Two-base hits—Luderus, Paskert, Murray. Sacrifice hits—Lobert. Sacrifice fly—Rowan. Stolen base—Doyle. Left on bases—Philadelphia 7, New York 5. Double play—Snodgrass and Bridwell. Struck out—By Mathewson 5, by Rowan 1. Bases on balls—Off Mathewson 1, off Rowan 4. Hit by pitcher—By Rowan (Snodgrass). Hits—Off Mathewson, 15 in eight innings; off Marquard, 0 in one inning. Umpires—Messres. Eason and Johnstone. Time of game—One hour and thirty-eight minutes.

In fewer than three months a burgeoning steel-and-concrete stadium with 16,000 seats was ready.

First Game

Christy Mathewson was on the mound against Boston—then at least informally known as the Rustlers—on Wednesday, June 28, 1911, for the first game of the final Polo Grounds.

Laughing Larry Doyle broke a scoreless tie in the bottom of the sixth with a home run into the right-field grandstand. It was all Matty needed, but his mates gave him two more runs as New York beat Boston, 3–0. (See Box Score 9.)

Through the decades the Polo Grounds expanded, keeping the familiar horseshoe shape of the predecessor, with the ridiculously short distances down the foul lines and even more absurd distance to center field. A gap between the bleachers was filled by the clubhouses and offices, set back to form a notch that contained monuments and stairways—all in play.

Last Game

The Polo Grounds had several last games—at least what were thought to be the finales for the stadium.

The end of the New York Giants came with a 9–1 loss September 29, 1957. The Giants were off for the West Coast, but the Polo Grounds survived—used for other events—to still be around when another New York team in the National League, the Mets, began in 1962. A new ballpark in Queens was being built and

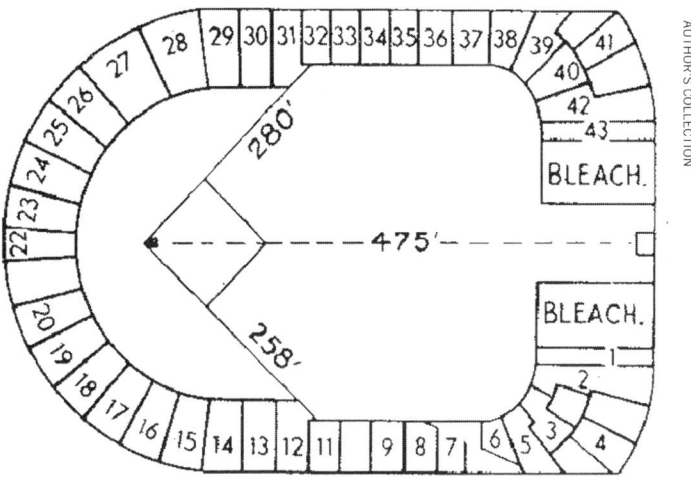

AUTHOR'S COLLECTION

For much of the history of Polo Grounds IV, a 483-foot marker was attached to the clubhouse wall in center field. When the Mets moved into the Polo Grounds, the distance was listed as 475 feet.

BOX SCORE 9 – Wednesday, June 28, 1911; New York 3, Boston 0

Rustlers	ab	r	h	po	a
Bill Sweeney 2b	3	0	1	4	4
Fred Tenney 1b	4	0	1	6	0
Buck Herzog ss	4	0	2	0	3
Doc Miller rf	4	0	1	3	0
Scotty Ingerton lf	4	0	2	3	0
Harry Steinfeldt 3b	3	0	1	0	2
Johnny Kling c	3	0	0	5	2
Al Kaiser cf	3	0	0	3	0
Al Mattern p	3	0	1	0	0
	31	0	9	24	11

Giants	ab	r	h	po	a
Josh Devore lf	3	0	1	0	0
*Fred Merkle	0	0	0	0	0
Beals Becker lf	0	0	0	1	0
Larry Doyle 2b	4	1	1	1	4
Fred Snodgrass cf	4	0	1	2	0
Red Murray rf	4	0	0	2	1
Hank Gowdy 1b	3	0	1	15	0
Al Bridwell ss	3	1	1	1	3
Art Devlin 3b	2	1	1	1	3
Chief Meyers c	2	0	1	3	2
Christy Mathewson p	2	0	0	0	2
	27	3	7	§26	15

*Batted for Devore in the seventh inning.
§Herzog out, hit by batted ball.

Team	Line Score	R	H	E	Manager
Boston	000/000/000-	0	9	2	Fred Tenney
New York	000/001/20x-	3	7	0	**John McGraw**

Errors—Tenney, Mattern. Two-base hits—Gowdy, Herzog. Home run—Doyle. Sacrifice hit—Sweeney. Sacrifice fly—Mathewson. First base on errors—New York 1. Left on bases—New York 4, Boston 4. Struck out—By Mathewson 2, by Mattern 2. Bases on balls—Off Mattern 3. Wild pitches—Mattern. Umpires—Messrs. O'Day and Frary. Time of game—One hour and thirty-five minutes.

was to be ready the following year as the Mets used the Polo Grounds in the interim.

On September 23, 1962, a crowd of 10,304 came out for another last game as the Mets beat the Cubs, 2–1.[13]

However, the new stadium still wasn't ready, so the Mets had one more year in the Polo Grounds. Fewer than 2,000 fans were on hand for what really was the final game, a 5–1 loss to the Phillies on Wednesday, September 18, 1963.

"Maybe the fact that there had been two previous 'last games' at the Polo Grounds took a bit from the occasion," wrote Gordon S. White, Jr. in *The New York Times*. "It is hoped that no more Mets games will be played at the Polo Grounds—if only to put an end to the string of finales."[14]

Jim Hickman gave the Mets their only run with the final home run ever hit in the Polo Grounds. (See Box Score 10.)

Baseball was still played there, one more time, in October in a Latin All-Star Game, the National League beating the American League, 5–2.[15] The New York Jets played out their football season, and the final event—a 19–10 loss to the Buffalo Bills—finished the Polo Grounds December 14, 1963.

History—from Merkle's Boner to Mays's Catch—all took place at some version of the Polo Grounds. ∎

Notes

1. Nicknames were nebulous in the nineteenth century and beyond. Although reliable reference sources list nicknames for teams, some are "blantantly bogus," according to SABR member and nineteenth-century expert Richard Hershberger.
2. The *Times* dropped the hyphen in New-York on December 1, 1896.
3. "Baseball News," *New-York Tribune*, Wednesday, May 2, 1883, page 2. The *Tribune* dropped the hyphen in New-York on April 16, 1914.
4. Note that here and elsewhere, "runs earned" are those earned by batting, not in the modern sense of "earned runs." Box scores replicate what appeared in the newspapers of the time.
5. The American Association had more of a focus on names than cities,

BOX SCORE 10 – Wednesday, September 18, 1963; Philadelphia 5, New York 1

Phillies	ab	r	h	rbi
8-Tony Taylor 3b	4	1	2	0
6-Johnny Callison rf	4	0	0	0
43-Wes Covington lf	4	1	1	1
24-Don Demeter lf	0	0	0	0
25-Tony Gonzalez cf	4	1	0	0
11-Clay Dalrymple c	4	1	2	0
5-Roy Sievers 1b	4	0	1	1
16-Cookie Rojas 2b	4	1	0	0
7-Bobby Wine ss	4	0	1	2
41-Chris Short p	4	0	1	0
	36	5	8	5

Pitching Summary	IP	H	R	ER	BB	SO
41-Chris Short (W 8-11)	9	9	1	1	2	6

Mets	ab	r	h	rbi
16-Dick Smith cf	4	0	1	0
18-Pumpsie Green 3b	3	0	1	0
33-Ron Hunt 2b	4	0	2	0
25-Frank Thomas lf	4	0	0	0
9-Jim Hickmn rf	4	1	2	1
3-Tim Harkness 1b	4	0	1	0
5-Norm Sherry c	3	0	0	0
(d) 10-Rod Kanehl ph	1	0	1	0
40-Al Moran ss	1	0	0	0
(b) 7-Chico Fernandez ph-ss	2	0	1	0
20-Craig Anderson p	1	0	0	0
13-Roger Craig p	0	0	0	0
(a) 23-Joe Christopher ph	1	0	0	0
19-Ed Bauta p	0	0	0	0
(c) 12-Jesse Gonder ph	1	0	0	0
31-Larry Bearnarth p	0	0	0	0
(e) 43-Ted Schreiber ph	1	0	0	0
	31	1	9	1

	IP	H	R	ER	BB	SO
20-Craig Anderson (L 0-1)	3.2	5	3	0	0	0
13-Roger Craig	1.1	3	2	2	0	0
19-Ed Bauta	2	0	0	0	0	0
31-Larry Bearnarth	2	0	0	0	0	0

(a) Popped out for Craig in 5th.
(b) Flied out for Moran in 7th.
(c) Grounded out for Bauta in 7th.
(d) Singled for Sherry in 9th.
(e) Hit into double play for Bearnarth in 9th.

Team	Line Score	R	H	E	Manager
Philadelphia	000/320/000-	5	8	0	Gene Mauch
Minnesota	000/100/000-	1	9	2	**Casey Stengel**

Errors—Hunt, Anderson. Two-base hits—Hickman, Hunt. Three-base hits—Wine, Green. Home runs—Hickman. Team Left on Base, New York—4. Team Left on Base, Philadelphia—8. Double plays—Philadelphia 1, New York 1. Caught Stealing—Green (2,2nd base by Short/Dalrymple). Wild pitch—Short (8). Umpires—HP—Doug Harvey, 1B—Lee Weyer, 2B—Al Barlick, 3B—Ed Vargo. Time of game—Two hours and nineteen minutes. Attendance—1,752.

differing from the National League. The Eclipse (representing Louisville), Alleghenys (representing Pittsburgh), and Athletics (representing Philadelphia) are among the examples of teams that shared the convention of the team representing New York, the Metropolitan.

6. Cincinnati and Columbus were also playing two games against different opponents, criss-crossing with one another by playing in Philadelphia as well as New York.

7. It's clear that the southwest diamond was not constructed to be used only when there was a conflict with the east diamond. However, it's possible that after seeing how inferior the playing and seating areas were in the southwest corner that John B. Day decided to have the Metropolitan play on the southeast diamond whenever possible. The nebulous evidence is that New York newspapers had ads for all home games, and the ads directed patrons to the Fifth Avenue or Sixth Avenue entrance, an indication of which diamond would be used. This is partially true; the specifics on the entrance, however, appeared only when both teams were at home. It's known which diamond was used by which team in these situations. The entrance information does not appear in the ads when only one team was at home—information that could confirm if the Metropolitan used the southeast diamond whenever it was available or if it used the southwest diamond, as was the plan before the season.

8. "A New Baseball Field: The Giants Will Play Games in This City Again: Grounds Secured on the West Side of Town in a Convenient Place," *The New York Times*, Saturday, June 22, 1889, 2; "The Giants New Grounds: A Home for Them on Manhattan Island at Last," *New-York Tribune*, June 22, 1889, 7.

9. "The Giants Are at Home: They Open Their New Grounds in Grand Style," *New-York Times*, Tuesday, July 9, 1889, p. 3; "A Royal Christening: Happy Giants Welcomed to Their New Grounds," *New-York Tribune*, July 9, 1889, 2.

10. "Boston Defeats New-York: Over 17,000 Persons Witness the Opening League Game: The Giants Looked Like Winners to the Ninth Inning, but Lost by an Accident," *New-York Times*, Thursday, April 23, 1891, page 2; "Grand Send Off: League Teams Begin the Battle for the Pennant: Over 17,000 People See the Game in Gotham: Boston Plays in Luck and Wins in the Ninth," *Boston Globe*, Thursday, April 23, 1891, 11.

11. Paskert's Catch: "Phillies Flay 'Big Six's' Pitching," *The New York Times*, Friday, April 14, 1911, p. 2.

12. Fred Lieb, Baseball As I Have Known It (New York: Coward, McCann & Geoghegan,Inc., 1977), p. 35; "Polo Grounds Swept by Fire," *The New York Times*, Friday, April 14, 1911, 1.

13. "Mets Beat Cubs, 2-1, in Farewell to Baseball at the Polo Grounds" by Robert M. Lipsyte, *The New York Times*, Monday, September 24, 1962, 24.

14. "Era of Mets Ends at Polo Grounds" by Gordon S. White Jr., *The New York Times*, Thursday, September 19, 1963, 32.

15. "National Leagues Triumph at Polo Grounds, 5-2: Latin All-Stars Paced by M'Bean" by William J. Briordy, *The New York Times*, Sunday, October 13, 1963.

The Asylum Base Ball Club

The Great Reunion Game September 29, 1905

Bob Mayer

The center of the baseball world had been New York City, but after the Civil War came a time of tremendous growth in the game. The National Association of Base Ball Players had been formed in 1858 and the number of member teams skyrocketed from 80 in 1860 to 202 in 1866, and more than 1000 by 1869. In New York State, teams were started all along the Hudson River during the 1850s and were evident in most inland towns by the 1860s. Orange County lies on the west side of the Hudson about 50 miles north of New York City. Along the river bank you will find West Point and Newburgh, and further west, Warwick, Goshen, and Middletown—where this story takes place.

Middletown's first reported baseball team was the Wallkills Base Ball Club. Founded in 1866 by many of the leading citizens, this amateur team played other towns and villages in the area as well as teams from northern New Jersey and New York City. Newspaper coverage of the Wallkills stops in the early 1870s, making it appear that the team had disbanded, but they resurfaced again with new personnel in 1880. In the interim, a team named the Lone Stars was formed and became the most prominent team in Middletown 1874–77. However, the resurgent Wallkills took back the local spotlight throughout the 1880s. During that decade the team won 79 games and lost 62, a fairly respectable showing. The team finally stopped playing shortly after a new Middletown powerhouse team came to life.

The rise of the Asylum Base Ball Club and its outstanding success is the story of an unlikely relationship between a hospital chartered to treat the mentally ill and a group of talented young men—some of whom would go on to careers in the major leagues, including Hall of Fame pitcher Jack Chesbro.

THE ASYLUM BBC

The Asylum Base Ball Club was formed in 1888 to represent the State Homeopathic Asylum for the Insane at Middletown, New York, and to provide amusement for the patients confined there. The State Homeopathic Asylum was the first of its kind in the United States, opening its doors in 1874. During its peak years in the late nineteenth and early twentieth century, it was the largest in the country. Baseball had been utilized in mental facilities as a recreational activity for patients for many years. However, Selden Talcott, the Superintendent of the Middletown SHA, believed that baseball could be therapeutic even for those patients unable to play the game, but who could be avid fans of a skilled team. He made it a priority to schedule games with the best teams in the region.

Between 1888 and 1894 the Asylum Base Ball Club was highly successful and posted an enviable record of 111 wins, 31 losses, and two ties against some of the top amateur, semi-pro, and professional teams in the New York area. In 1892 the team won 22 of 24 games played, and the only two losses were to the National League's New York Giants by scores of 2–1, and 6–5 in 10 innings.

Another indication of the team's strength was its record against two of the best professional Black Baseball clubs of the era, the Cuban

The Asylum Base Ball Club in 1891. Wilber Cook (manager) sitting in center.

Giants and the NY Gorhams. Between 1890 and 1894 the Asylum club won eleven of nineteen games against these fine teams.

THE CUBAN X GIANTS

In 1896, a rift between Cuban Giants owner John Bright and some of his players magnified. The players left the team and a new team, the Cuban X Giants, was formed under the management of E.B. Lamar. Bright sued Lamar over the use of the name but lost in court and renamed his own team the Genuine Cuban Giants. The Cuban X Giants took over the spotlight and became the Eastern Colored champions 1897–1903, and Colored champions in 1899. During 1896 and 1897, the Cuban X Giants opposed the Asylum Club four times, winning two (10–8 and 15–1), losing one (8–10), with one rainout.

In 2005, the National Baseball Hall of Fame in Cooperstown commissioned a group of baseball historians and other experts to investigate 36 ballplayers, managers, and executives who had been affiliated with the Negro Leagues or pre-Negro-Leagues teams. As a result, 16 men and 1 woman were enshrined in the Hall of Fame in 2006. Two black men who played periodically against the Asylum baseball teams were included in this group, Sol White and Frank Grant.

A PLAN UNFOLDS

Wilbur E. Cook had been the manager of the Asylum team since its inception in 1888. By 1905, he had spent 31 years at the State Hospital, mostly as Patient Supervisor. Weighing well over 200 pounds, Cook was an impressive figure with his walrus mustache. Cook had come to work for Dr. Seldon Talcott after Talcott successfully treated him for a severe injury he had received on the baseball field. Over the course of his employment, he served several superintendents, and his wife was also employed there for many years.

After many successful seasons, nine of the 1894 Asylum BBC starters left to join minor league clubs in 1895. The team was rebuilt, but over the ensuing years, baseball had slowly lost some of its local interest. Cook wanted to do something that would regenerate the previous level of interest in baseball at the hospital. He and former team captain John Degnan came up with what they thought was a great idea and as reported in the *Middletown Daily Argus* began corresponding with former Aslyum players by late summer

The Cuban X Giants circa 1902, E.B. Lamar standing in suit.

1905. They arranged for a "reunion" baseball game for the old Asylum players from the glory days to face the Cuban X Giants. Despite the years that had passed, Cook was still able to get many of the best players to commit to playing. Only one of the fan favorites—Pat McGreevy, the great Asylum catcher— had passed away in 1899 at age 32.

Wilber E. Cook, manager of the Asylum BBC

During the preceding decade, many of the former Asylum ballplayers had played with minor league clubs and a few had made it to the major leagues. When news of this reunion game broke, the old fans and rooters could hardly be contained. For weeks the game was anticipated with great interest by the baseball cranks (fans) of the city of Middletown and surrounding towns.

THE ASYLUM TEAM PLAYERS

"Happy Jack" Chesbro – Jack was a starting pitcher for the New York American League franchise—a team variously nicknamed by the press as Highlanders, Hilltoppers, and even Yankees. In 1904 Jack won 41 games and pitched 48 complete games, still top totals for seasons after 1893. The team would eventually officially adopt the Yankees moniker, and in 1946 Chesbro would be voted into the National Baseball Hall of Fame. Chesbro had come to the State Hospital in Middletown from North Adams, Massachusetts, in 1894 at age 19 to pitch for the Asylums and work as a hospital attendant.

Art Madison – Art was then a minor league shortstop for the Utica Pent-Ups of the New York State League. A boyhood friend of Jack Chesbro from Clarksburg, Massachusetts, as a youth he had played on local sandlot teams with Jack. In 1894 he also worked and played ball with him at the hospital, and was instrumental in getting Jack a tryout with the Pittsburgh Pirates in 1899. Art played with the Asylum team in 1894 and 1897, and went on to play briefly for the Pirates and the Philadelphia Phillies.

John J. "Jack" Lawlor – At the time of the reunion, he was player/manager of the Utica Pent-Ups. Lawlor had been playing minor league ball since 1891 primarily in the Eastern and the New York State Leagues. Jack was known as "The Gloveless Wonder" as he was one of the last professional players to field without a glove. He worked at the State Hospital from 1891 through 1909 during the offseasons, and would later be manager of Middletown's entry in the NY/NJ League in 1913 and the Atlantic League in 1914. John was also named manager of the Asylum team in 1922, but passed away early in the season at age 53.

Pete Lamer (aka Pierre Lamers) – Pete was with Dover in the Lackawanna League, and Pete's brother, E.B. Lamar Jr., was owner/manager of the Cuban X Giants. He had played with the Asylum club in 1896 and 1897. In 1898 he had gone to the Connecticut State League with New London. Per Mark Okkonen, Lamer spent several years in the minors and also played with Poughkeepsie (NY) in the Hudson River League in 1903. He had a cup of coffee in the major leagues with the Chicago Cubs in 1902 and later with Cincinnati in 1907.

George "Tuck" Turner – Tuck played on the Asylum team 1892–93. He went on to play in the majors with the Phillies 1893–96 and the St. Louis Cardinals 1896–98. Tuck had batted .418 for the 1894 Phils, and was playing minor league ball in New Bedford, Massachusetts, at the time of the reunion game. Tuck was inducted into the Staten Island Sports Hall of Fame in 2011.

Chris Genegal – Chris worked at the State Hospital from 1889 until 1901. He played minor league ball in the New York State League for Gloversville in 1895, in the Pennsylvania State League in 1896, and then Canandaigua, leading the NY State League in hits in 1897. He turned down several offers from the New York Giants to play in the National League. Chris continued to play locally for several teams and appeared in games as late as

1911 when he was 47 years old. He and Jack Lawlor were on the Middletown Athletic Club team that defeated both the Brooklyn Dodgers and NY Giants in 1908. Chris also played for the Middletown entry in the short-lived Eastern Association of 1909.

Charlie Tierney – Charlie was playing in Perth Amboy, New Jersey. He was from Goshen and worked as a clerk at Equitable Insurance, but always found time for baseball. He roamed the outfield when not pitching and he had played against Middletown teams since the mid-1880s, pitching effectively for strong Goshen and Walden teams. He also played with the Asylums on and off over a ten-year period, and played minor league ball with Albany/Johnstown in 1895 and Easton in 1896.

Tommy Murray – Tommy played with the Asylum team 1891–97 and had a brief stint in the minors for Albany/Johnstown of the NY State League in 1895. When Tommy left the semi-pro Allertons in 1891, Wee Willie Keeler took his place at second base on that team. Tommy previously worked for the railroad, but was now a liquor salesman in New York City.

Tom Morehead (Moorehead) – Tom was captain of the Dover team in the Lackawanna League. Tom had played with the Asylums 1891–93 and 1896–97. He was a cloth cutter for Hackett-Carhart and became his union's president.

Chris Rhinecker (Reinacker) – Chris was a member of the Asylum team 1896–97. He also played for many years in Hoboken, New Jersey. He was thought to be playing in Utica in 1905, and played for the New Rochelle (NY) Rough Riders, a semi-pro team in 1907.

Fisher Launt – Fish played for the Wallkills BBC of Middletown (1885–88) and became an initial member of the Asylum team in 1888. He played with the team through 1895, was a solid hitter to all fields, a great base runner, and the team's spark plug. Fish was most noted for his wild style of base coaching, which was a popular treat for the spectators and a terror for the opposition. He worked as a conductor for the Ontario & Western Railroad and lived in Sidney, New York.

John Degnan – Degnan, another original member, was the Asylum Captain 1889–96. He also captained Middletown's best amateur team, the Wallkills, 1883–90. On the three occasions when the Wallkills played the Asylum, Degnan and two other players, Launt and

McGreevy, would have to choose which team to play for. John was the owner of one of Middletown's plumbing companies, and quite active in local civic associations and politics. No longer actively playing, John was on hand to perform the umpiring duties.

THE BIG DAY ARRIVES
On the day of the game, the players were given a rousing reception upon arrival in Middletown via the Erie Railroad. The Giants emerged smiling from the train, and several of the Asylum team had accompanied them on the ride. Jack Chesbro and his wife, Tommy Murray, Tom Morehead, Tuck Turner, Charlie Tierney, Chris Rhinecker, and Pete Lamer had all taken the rails. From the station, a parade headed up to the State Hospital with the Cubans occupying a large side-seated wagon and the Asylum players seated in four automobiles driven by Charles Higham (Middletown's Chief Fire Engineer and former Wallkill BBC third baseman), and several other local businessmen.

Jack Chesbro had just come off his third year with the New York Americans winning 19 games and posting a 2.20 earned run average. It was a far cry from his 1904 season. In today's baseball world there are still exhibition games scheduled by team management, but these are rare, and there are contract restrictions that make it impossible for players to play on their own for another club. However, many of the early baseball teams allowed individual players to play for teams outside the major leagues if schedules permitted. This practice continued into the 1950s.

Everybody wanted to see Chesbro, who was now an $8000/year pitcher in the big city, and more than 3000 fans were on hand on the hospital grounds. Tommy Murray, who was originally expected to play,

acted as the second umpire. It was rumored that he had gotten too fat for any of the uniforms, and he did not deny this.

THE CUBAN X GIANTS PLAYERS
This was billed as the Cuban X Giants, but the players were essentially a black all-star team put together for this reunion game. These men played for a variety of black professional teams, and not all were on the Cuban X Giants 1905 regular season team.

THE LINEUP
Leading off and playing left field for the visitors was Pat Patterson. Since 1890, Pat had played with the NY Gorhams, Cuban Giants, Philadelphia Giants, Brooklyn Royal Giants, Page Fence Giants, and several other teams.

Danger Talbert at third base was batting second. Talbert started pro ball in 1900 and played mostly with Frank Leland's Chicago teams, but joined the Cuban X Giants in 1905. He would play pro ball until 1911.

Bobby Winston was batting third and playing center field. Bobby was just finishing his first professional year, having moved from the Norfolk Red Stockings in August. He would go on to become a superior base stealer and star outfielder with several black teams through 1923.

Batting clean-up and playing first base was Ray Wilson. In his prime, Ray was considered the best first baseman in black baseball. He played with the Cuban X Giants, then switched to their rivals, the Philadelphia Giants, where he played until 1910.

September 29, 1905 – Middletown State Homeopathic Hospital Base Ball Team vs. Cuban X Giants.

Standing (L to R):
Fisher Launt RF, Capt. Jack Degnan, John Lawlor CF, Chris Genegal 1B, Tuck Turner LF, Pete Lamer C, Tommy Murray Umpire, Art Madison SS, "Happy Jack" Chesbro P, Charlie Tierney RF.

Kneeling (L to R):
Tommy Morehead 2B, Chris Rhinecker 3B.

Frank Grant followed at second base. Grant is considered by many to be the greatest black player of the nineteenth century. He played in the minor leagues 1886–91 until black men were no longer allowed in the white leagues. He then played for the Cuban Giants, NY Gorhams, Page Fence Giants, Philadelphia Giants, and several other outgrowths from those teams including the Cuban X Giants. He was a consistent .300 hitter and a great fielder, and was elected to the Baseball Hall of Fame in 2006.

Harry Buckner was playing right field and batting sixth. Harry was a versatile player who pitched, caught, played outfield and infield for many teams in New York, Philadelphia, and Chicago between 1896 and 1918. Included in Harry's list were the Mohawk Giants of Schenectady and the Paterson Smart Set.

Clarence Williams was batting seventh and doing the catching. Clarence had been barnstorming through Middletown for 18 years, beginning with the original Cuban Giants with whom he played for 10 years, after joining in their first year 1885. Clarence played minor league ball in the Middle States League, the Connecticut State League and the Eastern Interstate League (with Frank Grant) until the color line was drawn, played briefly with the NY Gorhams and Philadelphia Giants, then several years with the Cuban X Giants. The *Negro Baseball Encyclopedia* indicates he played until 1912 as Player/Manager with the Paterson Smart Set, however he actually finished his career with them in 1913. Clarence should be seriously considered as a candidate for the Hall of Fame. SABR's Negro League Grave Marker project placed a stone at Clarence's unmarked grave in 2016.

Batting eighth was shortstop John Hill. Hill played 1900–07 primarily at third base, and was the backup for Hall of Famer John Henry "Pop" Lloyd on the Philadelphia Giants in 1907.

Pitching and batting ninth was John Nelson. John started his professional career with the NY Gorhams in 1887 and played for 17 years with several top clubs including the Cuban Giants, Page Fence Giants, and Philadelphia Giants. This included play in predominately white leagues (Trenton & York in the Middle States League, Ansonia in the Connecticut State League). John had often pitched against the Asylum teams.

Also present as substitute was Robert Jordan, who played with both the Cuban Giants and Cuban X Giants on a regular basis 1896–1906.

THE GAME BY INNINGS

First inning: Patterson grounded to Reinacker who threw to Genegal at first. Talbert struck out. Winston hit safely, but Wilson struck out, retiring the side. For the Asylums, Morehead struck out, Madison hit a grounder to third and was put out at first. Genegal grounded to Nelson who threw to first; three out. No runs on either side.

Second inning: Grant pounded a hot grounder to Chesbro who gathered it in nicely and threw to Genegal. Buckner made a base hit over in the right outfield. Williams knocked a grounder to Reinacker who threw to Morehead at second and Genegal at first, catching Buckner and making a nice double play; no runs. For the Asylums, Turner flied out to Winston in center field. Lawler made a two-base hit. Launt followed with a base hit and Lawler scored. Reinacker grounded to third and was put out at first. Lamar made a base hit but was caught in attempting to go on to second. While he was making his run for second, Launt scored. Score: Asylums 2, Giants 0.

Third inning: Both Hill and Nelson grounded to Morehead who gathered them in easily and threw them over in Genegal's bushel basket. Patterson hit a high

A game against the Cuban Giants on the Asylum Grounds in 1890.

AUTHOR'S COLLECTION

fly which was captured by Chesbro. In the Asylum's half, Chesbro grounded to Nelson who threw to first. Morehead was given his base on balls while Madison hit safely over second base. Genegal reached base while Madison was caught out at second. Turner made the third out leaving Morehead and Genegal on base.

Fourth inning: Talbot grounded out third to first. Winston flied out to Turner. Wilson fanned. For the Asylums, Lawler made a ground hit to Nelson and was thrown out at first. Launt, who followed, did likewise only he hit to second base. Reinecker was passed to first. Lamar hit to Nelson and was thrown out at first. Neither side scored.

Fifth inning: Grant flied out to Chesbro and Buckner rapped a ground hit to Morehead which the latter fielded. Williams made a nice two-bagger, but Hill hit an easy grounder to Chesbro and was put out at first. When the Asylum's half came, Chesbro threw the fans into an ecstasy of delight when he pounded out a three-bagger and ran like a deer around the bases. The team of Eagle Chemical Engine Company was standing in the road back of left field and the ball hit a horse named "Major," rolling under his feet. Morehead was thrown out at first and Chesbro attempted to sneak home on the play: Williams was watching, however, and Chesbro was caught between third base and the home plate, Williams starting after him ball in hand. It looked to be all over with "Ches" but he made several twists, eluded Williams, and was back safely on third. Madison had a ground hit, but Chesbro was unable to score on the play. Genegal made a long hit to center which was caught and Chesbro tagged and scored from third. Turner hade a nice base hit which scored Madison from second base. Lawlor was thrown out at first on a grounder to Nelson. Two runs for the Asylums. The score was now Asylums 4, Cuban Giants 0.

Sixth inning: Tierney took Launt's place in right field. Nelson was first at bat and made a base hit. Patterson flied out to Reinacker and Talbert did likewise to Morehead, who was also able to double Nelson who had strayed off first base. In the Asylum's half, Tierney knocked a grounder to second and reached first on a muff, going right on to second safely when the ball bounced into right field. Neither Reinacker nor Lamer were successful as both made outs. Chesbro was next to bat. He batted out a hot foul up the right field line and nearly upset the umpiring Tommy Murray. The effort to stop laughing at Tommy was evidently taking his attention from looking at the ball as Chesbro fanned on the next ball thrown. Score still 4 to 0.

Seventh inning: Winston banged a hot liner over Madison's head and reached first. His triumph was short lived as he was doubled up on a neat play by Chesbro, Morehead, and Genegal on a grounder of Wilson's. Grant expired at first in the effort to knock a grounder past Madison. The last half of this inning was even shorter then the first half, as Morehead grounded out to Nelson, Madison flied out and Genegal grounded out to Hill. No change in score.

Eighth inning: Jordan took Buckner's place and grounded out to Chesbro. Williams did the same, and Hill struck out. For the Asylums, Turner soaked out a hot one between first and second and reached second safely. He was put out a moment later on a double play made off Lawler's fly to first base. Tierney flied out to second. No change in score.

Ninth inning: Nelson grounded out to Genegal. Patterson made a safe hit between short and third and ran on to second. Talbert flew out to Tierney and Winston grounded out to Chesbro. Final score Asylums 4, Giants 0.

BOX SCORE

Cuban X Giants

Player	AB	R	H	2B	3B	RBI	BB
Patterson	4	0	1	1	0	0	0
Talbert	4	0	0	0	0	0	0
Winston	4	0	2	0	0	0	0
Wilson	3	0	0	0	0	0	0
Grant	3	0	0	0	0	0	0
Buckner	2	0	1	0	0	0	0
Jordan (8th)	1	0	0	0	0	0	0
Williams	3	0	1	1	0	0	0
Hill	3	0	0	0	0	0	0
Nelson	3	0	1	0	0	0	0
Totals	**30**	**0**	**6**	**2**	**0**	**0**	**0**

Asylum BBC

Player	AB	R	H	2B	3B	RBI	BB
Morehead	4	0	0	0	0	0	1
Madison	4	1	2	0	0	0	0
Genegal	3	0	0	0	0	1	0
Turner	4	0	2	1	0	1	0
Lawlor	4	1	1	1	0	0	0
Launt	2	1	1	0	0	1	0
Tierney (6th)	2	0	0	0	0	0	0
Reinacker	2	0	0	0	0	0	1
Lamer	3	0	1	0	0	1	0
Chesbro	3	1	1	0	1	0	0
Totals	**31**	**4**	**8**	**2**	**1**	**4**	**2**

EPILOGUE

As anticipated, Chesbro didn't disappoint the Asylum fans. His famous spit ball baffled the Giants throughout the game. The Cubans managed only five hits (the ninth inning hit may have been an error), four singles and a double, and Jack did not give any bases on balls. The Asylums didn't exactly knock Cuban pitcher John Nelson around, either. But with Madison and Turner each getting two singles, Lawlor's two-bagger, and Chesbro's three-bagger, the Asylums gained the victory with a shutout, 4–0. Launt, Lamer, Genegal, and Turner each had runs batted in for the winners.

Manager Cook was very pleased with the outcome and told the newspaper "…this…may be the starting of a new Asylum team for next year. We didn't think the people would take hold of it so strong and we're certainly pleasantly surprised."

At the conclusion of the game, there was another parade back to town where both teams took supper and headed back to New York City on the 7:35PM train.

One of the papers that covered the event, *The Daily Argus*, mentioned that photographs of the game were taken and would be printed on souvenir postal cards. The following represent two of those photos.

When I first saw this photo, I had been researching the Wallkill Base Ball Club and I was aware that there had been an Asylum BBC in 1892. In the photo below, I recognized Jack Chesbro immediately and had to find out more about this Asylum team. I originally thought that Chesbro was just brought in for this 1905 game, and wanted to find out what his connection to the State Hospital was. It was several weeks of investigation before I learned that he had worked at the hospital eleven years earlier, and had pitched 27 games (winning 21) for the Asylum BBC in 1894.

Researching the Asylum teams and individual players was most rewarding, and on one of my frequent trips to Thrall Library in Middletown, a staff member mentioned that a gentleman had come to Middletown to leave a book of thumbnail photos with the Historical Society. The original photos had been taken by his grandfather, Charles A. Ketcham, at the turn of the last century. Since the Historical Society was closed, he left the book with the library. As I looked through the

1905 Asylum BBC
Standing L to R: John Degnan, Fisher Launt, Chris Genegal, Tommy Murray, W. E. Cook Manager in suit, Charlie Tierney, Jack Chesbro, Art Madison, Tuck Turner. Kneeling L to R: Pete Lamer, Chris Rhinecker, Tommy Morehead, John Lawlor.
Photo by Charles A. Ketcham

1905 Cuban X Giants
Manager E.B. Lamar Jr. in center. Believe Ray Wilson 1B and Clarence Williams C are last two standing on right. Frank Grant 2B is kneeling on left with John Hill SS in the middle and John Nelson P kneeling 2nd from right. Other players: Pat Paterson LF, Danger Talbert 3B, Bobby Winston CF, Harry Buckner RF, Robert Jordan RF.
Photo by Charles A. Ketcham

book, I noticed that there was a copy of a photo that seemed familiar. It was of the Cuban X Giants in 1905, and I was certain that the background was similar to one of the Asylum team taken September 29 that year. At home that night, I looked through *A Collectors Guide to Post Cards of Middletown NY* and found a reference to Real Photo Post Cards of both the Asylums and Cubans. The photographer was anonymous, but was possibly an unsigned Charles Ketcham. As a result of additional interaction with the owner in Missouri, I was able to purchase the photo at the bottom of page 56.

The connection between Middletown and black barnstorming teams went beyond the field. The teams frequently shared banquets in town, and several of the players developed strong personal friendships. When Clarence Williams came back in 1913 with the Paterson Smart Set, it marked 26 years he had been barnstorming in Middletown. Over the years, he had become good friends with "Chick" Higham of the old Wallkill Base Ball Club who was now the Chief Fire Engineer and proprietor of the Commercial Hotel. Clarence expressed an interest in Chick's fancy white ceremonial fire helmet, and by the time Clarence made the trip back to New York City and Paterson, New Jersey, it was with the gift of Chick's helmet on his head.

With the exclusion of black players from white professional teams, barnstorming became the only stage for Americans to witness and appreciate the talented black players of the era. Middletown, New York, was extremely fortunate to have had this opportunity for so many years. ■

Acknowledgments
The bulk of my source data came from old newspapers. However, my research brought me in contact with so many wonderful people who were willing to either share information or point me in directions that led to many things that would have been overlooked. The staff at the Thrall Library, in particular the research and local history librarians were very helpful and supportive. The Historical Society of Middletown & Wallkill Precinct granted me access to their files and hard copy newspapers that were over a hundred years old. Curator Marvin Cohen and his team of volunteers were especially helpful, often finding articles and other tidbits for me.

The folks that worked at the Middletown Psychiatric Center made me feel like one of the family during the year I spent there. I had the privilege of working closely with Judy McGrath, the former librarian at MPC, and cannot say enough about the assistance she provided. Jim Bopp, Director of MPC, was also a big supporter, and attending the Center's formal closing dinner was an event I will never forget.

I also can't forget the minor league research, support and encouragement that were afforded to me by my friend and SABR mentor John Pardon. John was one of the original 16 men who founded SABR in 1971. Sadly we lost John in October 2008 and he is greatly missed.

Newspapers
Middletown Daily Argus
Middletown Daily Press
Middletown Daily Times
Orange County Press
The Conglomerate: Volumes 1 – 7 (published by the patients at the Middletown State Homeopathic Hospital) June 1890 – May 1897

Bibliography
Annual Reports of the Middletown State Homeopathic Hospital.
City Directories - City of Middletown, New York.
Gamwell, Lynn & Tomes, Nancy, *Madness in America: cultural and medical perceptions of mental illness before 1914*, Cornell University Press 1995.
Hopper, DeWolf with Wesley Stout, *Once A Clown, Always A Clown: Reminiscences of DeWolf Hopper*, Little, Brown, and Company 1927.
Kuntz, Jerry, *Lawson's Progress* (unpublished manuscript) [now *Baseball Fiends and Flying Machines – The Many Lives and Outrageous Times of George and Alfred Lawson*, McFarland 2009].
Laskaris, Peter, *Collectors Guide to Postcards of Middletown New York* 1995.
Peterson, Robert, *Only the Ball Was White*, Prentice Hall 1970.
Riley, James, *The Biographical Encyclopedia of the Negro Baseball Leagues*, Carroll & Graf Publishers, Inc. 1994.
White, Sol, *History of Colored Base Ball*, University of Nebraska Press 1995, incl. reprint of Sol White's Official Base Ball Guide 1907.
Wright, Marshall D., *The International League Year-by-Year Statistics, 1884–1953*, McFarland & Company Publishers 2005.

Internet Sites
Baseball-Reference.com
Baseball Almanac
Baseball Library
Deadball.com
Minor League Ball, John Sickels
www.hickocksports.com
The Baseball Index
www.anglefire.com
American Memory from the Library of Congress
National Baseball Hall of Fame
Ancestry.com

Other
Baseball Hall of Fame Research Library, Cooperstown
Conway, MA, Town Clerk
Middletown Historical Society
Middletown Psychiatric Center
New York State Archives, Albany
North Adams, MA, Library
North Adams Museum
North Adams Visitors Center
Norwich NY Museum
Ontario & Western Railway Archives
Sidney NY Historical Society
Thrall Library Middletown NY
United States Census Data
John Degnan, Director of Middletown's Business Improvement District (Asylum Photos)
Scott Fiesthumel (SABR Member) Utica Baseball
Vernon Hale Hawkins (Charles Ketcham RPPC)
Tony Kissell, Utica Baseball
Gerald Kleiner, Middletown City Council (Asylum Game Photo)
Joseph Lawlor (JJL Photo)
Peter Mancuso, SABR Member and Chair Nineteenth Century Committee
Marc Okkonen
John Pardon, SABR Founder

"A Foremost Part in the Work of Relieving Distress"

The Week New York, the Giants, and the Yankees Offered a Lifeline to the Titanic's *Survivors*

Dan VanDeMortel

Like 9/11, the sinking of the *Titanic* clings to American memory, slicing across sex, race, age, geographical, and class divides. Generations later, mental snapshots of the disaster develop at the briefest mention. An iceberg on a moonless night. The Law of the Sea: women and children first. The fortunate watching from insufficient lifeboats while others die in frigid Atlantic water.

What city was most traumatized by *Titanic*'s demise? Most would select its Belfast birthplace, perhaps European ports of call. Not so. New York was *the* catharsis epicenter, and the place baseball played an unexpected role in alleviating suffering.

The period from 1900 to World War I's commencement is sometimes labeled "The Quiet Years." World conflicts were few. Economic prosperity reigned. By 1912, post-diet, 270-pound President William Taft was facing a formidable election against Teddy Roosevelt and Woodrow Wilson. A Quiet Leader, he had left scant legislative impression but had tossed the first Presidential Opening Day pitch, chewed peanuts with common folks at others, and pronounced, "Any man who would choose a day's work over a day of baseball is a fool not worthy of friendship."[1]

Taft's bonhomie, however, contrasted with his nation, which was hardly quiet. Instead, America was beset with hectic change and unrelenting new technology. Henry Ford's mass-produced Model T was transforming isolated villages into a mobile, connected network. Cameras, movies, telephones, and telegraphs were accelerating communication. Farm life was giving way to urban employment at the mercy of industrial and financial corporations. The average person lived about 50 years, most of it spent working brutal hours, which was viewed as the key to success. Even children toiled at this rigorous schedule, and like their parents were provided scant economic protections. Women slogged along, too, at repetitive jobs and ritualized household chores.[2] Some fought the slowly successful battle for suffrage. Progressivism—political faith that science and rationality could salve America's condition —weighed in with incremental, mixed results.

No city embodied this hustle in 1912 more than New York. With its first skyscraper rising in 1889, Manhattan had commenced a construction boom previously unimaginable and unachievable, highlighted by the in-progress 792-foot Woolworth Building, slated to be the world's tallest building. With its boroughs recently consolidated, the city had trebled in size and exploded to 5.2 million people, second to London. Residents travelled via the new subway as well as horse, cable car, or trolley. Pennsylvania Station and the main library had just been built, and Ebbets Field had broken ground in March. With 80% of the city's inhabitants immigrants or their children, many viewed their fluctuating home as a foreign country. Immensity and innovation now characterized an "Imperial City," blessed by America's grandest mansions, shamed by its worst slums. Only Tammany Hall's corrupt governing machine, like a cockroach, remained stubbornly constant.

New York also hosted the world's biggest ships. Appropriately, the city anticipated the *Titanic*'s maiden voyage. The Sunday, April 14 *New York Times* heralded the April 17 arrival of "The New Giantess," marveling as we do at its 883-foot length and 94-foot width, the equivalent of an 11-story building laid end to end.[3] Coverage extolled the opulent spas, services, lodging, and meals available to the age's wealthy "1%." Unexpressed was how these socialites crested atop of the technologically-unsurpassed ship's "floating layer cake" while below, in a societal microcosm, one descended in class to the anonymous laborers fueling the ship deep in its boilers.[4]

Anticipation turned to dread when ominous reports surfaced regarding an iceberg encounter. Initial communication errors and journalistic speculation steered damage estimations into confusion and inaccuracy. One paper even proclaimed, "All Saved from *Titanic* after Collision."[5] The *Times* responded more cautiously, later revealing that developments, about 1,080 miles away, were far deadlier.[6]

As the grim news unfolded, New York entered post-9/11-like hellish days of waiting and wondering.

Highly imaginative conjectures, wavering fatality statistics, embellished tales of heroism and cowardice, and cold facts dominated public encounters. Some even questioned "The Law of the Sea," arguing Chinese hierarchy should have been followed by valuing women last.[7] Meanwhile, citywide half-mast flags and news coverage of ships searching for bodies confirmed undebatable fatalities. Crowds of up to 50,000 people huddled on streets at the ship's White Star Lines Broadway office or at newspaper buildings, waiting for publicly-displayed bulletins regarding survivors. Smaller groups clustered at hotels, stores, and other buildings. "Conversations, sometimes half hysterical, sometimes filled with sobbing, were heard on every side," the *Times* reported, even amongst those unconnected to anyone on board.[8]

President Taft cancelled his Opening Day appearance in Washington upon learning a close military aide had perished. But even the president was eclipsed by New York, which became the primary setting of suspense and resolution as the week dragged on. On a rainy Thursday evening, the rescue ship *Carpathia* passed 10,000 onlookers at the Statue of Liberty before docking at Manhattan's pier 54 with its cargo of 712 *Titanic* survivors. Amidst heavy security, 30,000 people, 50 ambulances, and numerous relief workers and customs officials waited for the saved. As they disembarked, "a low wailing sound started from the crowd. Its cadences, wild and weird, grew steadily louder and louder until they culminated in a mighty shriek," that swept the pier as if guided by "some master hand."[9] The following morning brought legal and political drama as a Senate inquiry into the sinking commenced at the Waldorf-Astoria.[10] Testimony pinpointed root causes already surmised by the *Washington Post*: "Speed, madness, and a reckless disregard for human life in the scramble for business."[11]

For many reasons, concern for the survivors abounded in New York more than anywhere in America. In a city that embraced size and technology, interest and suspense was already feverish. *Titanic*'s over 1,500 victims proved extremely personal, too: 11 city natives, 76 residents, and 146 people travelling to New York were on board; 129 died.[12] Among them were such notables as Waldorf-Astoria builder John Jacob Astor and Macy's co-owner Isidor Straus. New Yorkers could also easily relate to *Titanic* passengers seeking adventure or fresh opportunity. And most everyone recalled the 1904 *General Slocum* disaster, when a steamer filled with German-American families from the Lower East Side caught fire on the East River, killing 1,021 in the city's worst pre-9/11 tragedy.

At the exhibition game, two members of the Female Giants—a women's baseball team with connections to the New York Giants—roam the aisles to request donations to assist the *Titanic*'s survivors. A Polo Grounds employee, in hat and jacket, is in the background.

This empathy translated into action on many fronts. Mayor William Gaynor opened a relief fund that procured over $130,000 from socialites, companies, religious organizations, and average citizens. Prominent women organized another fund, raising almost $36,200. Newspapers, too, called for currency, including William Randolph Hearst's *New York American*, which collected $62,000. Hospitals contributed beds, medical professionals their time, and persons of modest means whatever they could.

Perhaps the most unexpected effort came from New York Giants owner John T. Brush, who Friday night offered his Polo Grounds to New York Yankees owner Frank Farrell for a Sunday fund-raising exhibition game between their teams. To do so, however, he challenged two traditions. First, the teams had a tense relationship. A decade previously, Brush had fought to prevent the new American League from moving a club into New York, then in 1904 had dismissively refused to play the junior circuit in the World Series when the Yankees looked primed to be its representative. A thaw began in 1910 and at season's-end, a best-of-seven series was won by the Giants four games to two. (The Giants' winning share of $1,110.62 and Yankee's losing share of $6358.60 helped explain the "thaw."[13]) A few more ice drops fell in April 1911 when Farrell, upon learning that a fire had destroyed the Polo Grounds, offered Brush shared usage of his home, American League Park, which the Giants quickly accepted to cover a three-month rebuilding process. But there had been no 1911 rematch.

Second were Sunday "blue laws." Governing protections for Sabbath rest had arrived from England in the seventeenth century, when behavior ordinances were printed on blue paper. The laws weren't always popular, yet they stuck. The National League ruled in

1876 against Sunday play, later retreating to allow games, as would the American League, upon local approval, which proved inconsistent and infrequent. By 1912, prohibitions against Sunday games were still in effect in New York and would remain so until the 1919 season.

Undeterred, Farrell quickly agreed to Brush's proposal, both owners scuttling animosity to express written gratitude that baseball would take "a foremost part in the work of relieving distress."[14] No words explained blue law workaround negotiations, but possibly Farrell offered Brush a slice of instructive personal history. In 1906, he had hosted a Sunday game versus the Philadelphia Athletics, with no objections, to raise San Francisco earthquake relief.[15] And in 1909, the Brooklyn Superbas had welcomed his team in a charity-driven Sunday match. With these likely precedents, both owners agreed to play Sunday, a first for the Polo Grounds, and the first in-season interleague game since the American League's formation.[16] Program sales would substitute for admission, all proceeds directed toward survivors.

From a public relations standpoint, Farrell was in no position to decline Brush, nor was his team. Despite wearing their April 11-debuted pinstripes, the Yankees bore little resemblance to their modern, dominant counterparts. The team known in the press by numerous nicknames—including Americans, Invaders, Hilltoppers, Highlanders, and Yankees until officially adopting the last the following year—played second fiddle to the Giants.[17] Farrell's club was consistently outdrawn by a heavy ratio, and habitual second-division finishes gave fans good reason to stay away.

Broadway icon George M. Cohan, a Polo Grounds habitue and friend of Giants manager John McGraw, in the process of selling copies of the *New York American* to benefit the *Titanic*'s survivors. Assisting right behind him is Jack Sullivan, founder of the Newsboys' Home, an organization with connections to assorted nefarious, nocturnal activities.

A 1911 .500 mark conveyed slight optimism, but spring training rains in Georgia had limited practice to a mere three days, paving a 0–6 start.[18]

The Giants were everything the Yankees were not. Brush's public frailty due to debilitating locomotor ataxia was the club's only infirmity.[19] Regular first-division finishes, league-leading attendance, a 1905 World Series, and appearances in 1911 and 1912 testified to vitality. The Giants reflected the smarts and will of manager John McGraw, a man of amazing contradictions. Off the field, he frequented race tracks, pool halls, fancy restaurants, and vaudeville, and was regarded for his soft-touch generosity. On the field, he was known as "Little Napoleon" and his "great heart contract[ed] to the dimensions of a bean."[20] Supported by pitching legends Christy Mathewson and Rube Marquard, he personified the Deadball Era and hurled invective that "would have to be written on asbestos paper."[21] His team had swiped a post-nineteenth century high 347 bases the previous year, would pilfer 319 in 1912, and had a champion's swagger.

The Giants would bring another advantage: mascot Charles "Victory" Faust. Mascots in 1912 mirrored industrial overlords' relationship to its workers: top-down and exploitive. "Colored boys," dwarves, hunchbacks, and "retarded" adults filled these roles, providing amusing good luck charms in a sport rife with superstition. The slow-witted, gap-toothed, eccentric 31-year-old Faust, from rural Kansas, fit right in. He had materialized the previous year, claiming a fortune teller had predicted a Giants championship if he were allowed to pitch. A windmill motion and soft tosses revealed little skill, but he became an all-star butt of practical jokes and purveyor of pre-game comedy—some intentional, some not. Newspapers devoured this burlesque, and the team was 36–2 when he was in uniform, showcasing his act.[22] He was even allowed to participate in two meaningless season-ending games, sporting a 4.50 ERA while being hit by a pitch and permitted to steal twice in a plate appearance. A World Series loss, however, burst the bubble. By 1912, McGraw had tired of Faust, refusing to let him "sign" with the team or don a uniform. But for the charity game, announcements signaled his resurrection.

Sunday afternoon delivered welcoming sunshine and moderate southern winds over Coogan's Bluff, then a virtual countryside from which residents could view part of the playing field below. As the gates opened, a "wild clatter of howls" erupted as fans purchased programs entitling them to unreserved seating.[23] Brush arrived by limousine and sat in left center. Farrell attended, as did other Giants and Yankees employees, who assisted with the crowd: rich, poor, Tammany Hall cogs, Wall Streeters, and Broadway aficionados.

And what a horseshoe-shaped park to be in! Concrete-and-steel with detailed, captivating architectural flourishes had replaced the wooden firetrap. A clover-shaped infield even featured ornamental circles built into the dirt. As *Baseball Magazine* marveled, the 34,000-seat "beauty" now rivaled the "silent grandeur" of the Pyramids.[24]

To ensure victory—and laughs—Faust took center stage in a discarded 1911 World Series uniform, pitching left-handed and running bases to the crowd's delight. Also on hand was McGraw pal and park habitue vaudeville icon George M. Cohan, "the man who owned Broadway," the entertainment capital of America. Covering the city on an aid-seeking mission, he roamed the stands in sweater and slanted cap, soliciting relief and selling *New York American* newspapers on the survivors' behalf. Assisting him was a far murkier character: Jack Sullivan, founder of the Newsboys' Home. Outwardly, this "Home" was an athletic/meeting place for boys who hawked newspapers on street corners. On a primal level, the hard-scrabble club was linked to prostitution, the Mafia, and other nefarious, nocturnal activities.[25] Months later Sullivan would be indicted in the murder of bookmaker Herman Rosenthal (whom he possibly collected for), a crime memorialized in *The Great Gatsby*.[26]

With flags at half-mast, World Series-like rituals were enacted. As the teams entered—Yankees outfitted in road grey, Giants in home white with pinstripes—they were greeted by loud cheers. Both managers received a warm reception as they shook hands at home plate. Soon thereafter, veteran chief umpire Cy Rigler and second-year base umpire Bill Finneran appeared. Each had been vilified for controversial calls in the preceding two days, but bygones were bygones now, and they were given a big hand as they volunteered their time. Movie men and photographers moved about, capturing the scene. Rigler neared home plate at three o'clock, barked out the starting batteries via megaphone, and the game was on.

Leaving their box seats, some Female Giants began working the crowd, requesting *New York American*-relief fund donations and storing their gatherings in caps borrowed from Giants players. Patronized as "featherweights" in one news account, they were anything but. Rather, these Giants—led by Broadway celebrity, Hollywood actress, and "the best all-around athlete of America," pitcher Ida Schnall—consisted of 32 young women athletes who played each other

throughout the city, sometimes joined by the Giants.[27] Clad in restrictive, layered clothing and ornately-plumaged "tray hats," they accepted contributions from similarly-garbed female fans and men in dark suits, ties, and derby hats.

Due to injuries and illness—and Harry Wolverton's decision to sit many starters—the Yankees led off against seldom-used youngster Bert Maxwell with a lineup of scrubs. Smooth-fielding but notoriously corrupt first baseman Hal Chase, the lone infield regular, singled in a run for a promising start for the visitors.

Then the Giants batted. Pre-game reportage that Brooklyn would contribute players proved inaccurate, which was unfortunate: The Yankees needed help. McGraw fielded several front-line players, who came out electrically charged. Five runs were tallied off starter George McConnell's spitball before an out was recorded. Two walks, four hits, sloppy fielding, and a blown "safe" call by Finneran authored quickly daunting math. And "McGraw ball" ran amok: Tillie Shafer and Fred Snodgrass swiped the first of two Giants double steals that afternoon, while Fred Merkle and Red Murray scampered for solo bags. Five-foot-10, 175-pound catcher Gus Fisher suffered a nightmarish inning, unsure where to throw next, once even wisely declining an attempt to nail a runner.

In the second, the Yankees scratched out another run and held the Giants scoreless for two frames. Then, in the fourth, slaughter returned. Whacks of Giants hits rang out while the Yankees assisted with a walk, a hit batter, three errors, and overall infield ineptitude. Five runners scored. After that, everything else was garbage time. McGraw inserted subs wholesale. His roster's depths delivered the tongue-twisting Phifer Fullenwider, who allowed no runs in the highest-profile game of his career: He would never pitch in a regular season major league game.[28]

During the sixth, another exhibition briefly flared. Two men in front of the lower grandstand commenced fighting, "maul[ing] away regardless of Queensberry [rules]" until stopped by police.[29] (Yankees fans surely welcomed the distraction.) In the stands, fans smoked cigars and cigarettes, and purchased pie slices and hot dogs—a recent Polo Grounds innovation—from coat-clad waiters. Sunday laws banished alcohol, outfield fence ads promoting it notwithstanding.

The contest concluded in two hours: an 11–2 Giants "bragging rights" pasting. Available box scores differ slightly but enumerate a grim Yankees afternoon: Eight innings of 12–13 hits, three-four walks, and a hit batter surrendered by McConnell; six-seven stolen bases allowed; and four-five errors recorded along with other unclassifiable folly.[30] In perspective, though, only these numbers mattered: 14,083 patrons, $9,425.25 raised at the game, nearly $20,000 gathered by Cohan's newsboy efforts and evening theatrical performance.[31] And no number could quantify the value of a pleasant afternoon diversion during a tumultuous week in which the national pastime helped humanity when it was most needed. ∎

Acknowlegments

My appreciation goes out to MLB historian John Thorn, Hall of Fame librarian Matt Rothenberg, and the New York Giants Preservation Society for their research assistance. Blessings to Ken Manyin's proofreading eyes, to SABR stalwarts Stew Thornley and Greg Erion for reviewing parts of this article, and to Leslie Cassidy for tracking down information at the New York Public Library.

Notes

1. Mike Vacarro, *The First Fall Classic* (New York: Doubleday, 2009), 158.
2. Ibid., 208. A typical schedule of the times: Monday—Wash Day, Tuesday—Ironing Day, Wednesday—Sewing Day, Thursday—Market Day, Friday—Cleaning Day, Saturday—Baking Day, Sunday—Rest Day.
3. "The New Giantess Titanic," *The New York Times*, April 14, 1912; Robert D. Ballard, *The Discovery of the Titanic* (New York: Warner/Madison Press, 1998), 18.
4. Ballard, op. cit., 15.
5. James Barron, "After Ship Sank, Fierce Fight to Get Story," *The New York Times*, April 9, 2012, https://cityroom.blogs.nytimes.com/2012/04/09/after-the-ship-went-down-scrambling-to-get-the-story/?_r=0.
6. Ibid.; George Behe (*Titanic* Historical Society), email message to author, May 8, 2017.
7. "Topics of the Times—Displayed Mild Enthusiasm," *The New York Times*, April 19, 1912.
8. "Women Sob as News Bulletins Appear," *The New York Times*, April 16, 1912.
9. "Rescue Ship Arrives, Thousands Gather at the Pier," *The New York Times*, April 19, 1912.
10. The Senate inquiry was transferred to and continued in Washington, D.C. the following week.
11. "American Press Comment on *Titanic* Disaster," *New York Herald* (European Edition), April 18, 1912.
12. New York City, Encyclopedia Titanica, https://www.encyclopedia-titanica.org/titanic-places/new-york-city.html.
13. "Giants Divide Winnings," *New York Tribune*, Oct. 24, 1910; "Mathewson Beats Yanks Fourth Time," *The New York Times*, Oct. 22, 1922. Each Giant and Yankee received an additional $190.29 and $120.79, respectively, for a played game that ended in a tie due to darkness. Each Giants player's total share was also reduced slightly to apportion funds to the team's trainer, masseur, and three players who were either no longer with the Giants or who joined the team late in the year.
14. John T. Brush and Frank Farrell, "The Human Side of Baseball," *Baseball Magazine*, June 2012; Frank Farrell, "A Word on the Recent Benefit Game for the Survivors of the *Titanic* Disaster," *Baseball Magazine*, June 1912.
15. Prior to the *Titanic* exhibition, this was the first and only Sunday game played by two major league teams in Manhattan. Walter LeConte, In-Season Exhibition Games (or ISEGs), http://www.retrosheet.org/Research/ LeConteW/ISEG.pdf.
16. Ibid.; "Play for Newsboys," *New York Tribune*, July 5, 1909. Brooklyn hosted the Yankees for a Sunday, July 4, 1909 exhibition game to benefit newsboys. Although technically the first in-season, inter-league exhibition game since the American League's 1901 formation, the teams exchanged batteries to circumvent a National Commission (baseball's then three-man governing body) rule forbidding inter-league exhibition games. It is unclear whether this edict was still in effect on April 21, 1912. If so, it was circumvented.
17. Donald Dewey and Nicholas Acocella, *Total Ballclubs*, (Toronto: Sport Media Publishing, Inc., 2005), 392; Keith Olbermann, "End of Story: The 1912 New York Yankees," MLB Pro Blog, http://keitholbermann.mlblogs.com/2012/04/21/end-of-story-the-1912-new-york-yankees.
18. A last-place 50–102 finish loomed, stained by a league-leading, deplorable 384 errors. Manager Harry Wolverton intrigued with his sombreros and long cigars, but Farrell's saloon and casino operations, Tammany Hall servitude, and racetrack and bookmaking activities dominated headlines.
19. Later that year, Brush was seriously injured in a Manhattan car crash. He died on November 26.
20. G.H. Fleming, ed., *The Unforgettable Season* (New York: Penguin Sports Library, 1982), 201.
21. Christy Mathewson, *Pitching in a Pinch* (New York: Stein and Day, 1977), 111.
22. Gabriel Schechter, Charlie Faust. Society for American Baseball Research, http://sabr.org/bioproj/person/d1ee8535.
23. Damon Runyon, "American Sports Pay Tribute to American Manhood," *New York American*, April 22, 1912.
24. Stew Thornley, *Land of the Giants* (Philadelphia: Temple University Press, 2000), 66.
25. "Who Was 'Jack' Sullivan," Newsies Historical Research, http://newsieshistory.tumblr.com/post/98207741743/whowas-jack-sullivan.
26. Ibid. Sullivan, aka Jacob Reich, real name John Abraham Rich, testified at the murder trial, was released from jail in 1913, and cleared his name in 1936.
27. "14,083 See Game for Charity," *The New York Times*, April 22, 1912; "Girl Wonders in Athletics," *San Francisco Chronicle*, Oct. 30, 1921. Sources claim 1913 as the women's first game. But, the Female Giants were likely already playing unreported games in 1912. Exhibition game coverage describes them as "a noted female baseball club." Runyon, op. cit. Their box seat-presence demonstrates an obvious yet unclear connection to the Giants. One source, repeated by others, indicates they were probably created by McGraw. No available evidence confirms this probability, rendering it speculative. However, the Female Giants would be unable to fund-raise or use "Giants" without the approval of Brush and/or McGraw. McGraw's affinity for and excursions to Broadway, and his friendship with Cohan, likely facilitated his introduction to Schnall. And a photo shows a Giants catcher participating with the women. "And Now the New York Female Giants: (Briefly) A League of Their Own," Bowery Boys: New York City History, http://www.boweryboyshistory.com/2015/06/and-now-the-new-york-female-giants-briefly-a-league-of-their-own.html.
28. Fullenwider, who pitched the previous season for the delightfully-named Columbia Commies, was released on a one-way ticket to the minors two months later.
29. "Giants Too Rapid for Players from Hilltop," *New York Sun*, April 22, 1912.
30. Ibid.; "14,083 See Game for Charity," op. cit.; "For Titanic's Victims," *Baltimore Sun*, April 22, 1912; "Giants Toy with Yankees," *New York Tribune*, April 22, 1912.
31. Attendance was 63% higher than the 8,621 Giants home attendance average.

The 1920 Brooklyn Robins

Uncle Robbie Leads Brooklyn to Third National League Championship

Gordon J. Gattie

The Brooklyn Robins reached the World Series for the third time as a National League franchise, under manager Wilbert "Uncle Robbie" Robinson during the 1920 season. Brooklyn's first National League championship occurred in 1890, when they finished first in the NL with an 85–44 record; they tied the American Association champion Louisville Colonels in the 1890 World Series 3–3–1. The team celebrated its second NL championship in 1916, but lost the World Series to the Boston Red Sox in five games.

The 1920 Robins were led by future Hall-of-Fame pitcher Burleigh Grimes, Hall-of-Fame outfielder Zach Wheat, star pitcher Leon Cadore, and solid third baseman Jimmy Johnston. The Robins started strong by winning eight of their first 11 games and never dropping more than four games from the National League lead throughout the season. On September 9, Brooklyn defeated St. Louis to secure sole possession of first place, and clinched their fifth National League pennant on September 27 after their crosstown rival New York Giants lost to the Boston Braves.[1] Brooklyn completed the regular season with a 93–61 record, finishing seven games ahead of the Giants. The Robins ultimately lost to the Cleveland Indians, 5–2, in a best-of-nine series that featured two notable firsts in World Series history—both accomplished by Cleveland players during the momentum-shifting Game 5: a grand slam and an unassisted triple play.[2]

As such, the 1920 Robins may be remembered more by the Indians' achievements and events on the national stage rather than their own successes and failures. The 1920 season marked the introduction of the liveball era and the only fatality occurring during game play, and the Black Sox scandal cast a shadow during the World Series.[3,4] In Brooklyn, Uncle Robbie's ballclub overcame an unsettled infield, a stretch of 58 innings covering three games in early May when the club went 0–2–1, the loss of outfielder Tommy Griffith, and a late June swoon, by playing .800 baseball during September to earn the pennant. The team overcame preseason prognosticators and challenges throughout the year; following the regular season, Uncle Robbie

quipped, "No special system of playing won the 1920 pennant for the Brooklyn Superbas."[5]

Like all major league clubs, the Robins were severely impacted by World War I. Although they made their third World Series appearance in 1916, four years later the only regulars playing in the same positions included shortstop Ivy Olson and left fielder Zach Wheat. During that span, Johnston moved from the outfield to infield and the other players no longer played for Brooklyn. The pitching staff had changed too, with Grimes and Cadore complementing Jeff Pfeffer and Rube Marquard. Staff ace Burleigh Grimes topped 20 wins and 300 innings for the first time in his career, Zach Wheat finished fourth in the NL with a .328 batting average, and outfielder Hi Myers paced the National League in triples for the second straight season.

Twenty-one Robins appeared in at least 20 games during the 1920 season; nine were purchased outright from other ballclubs, four joined via the Rule 5 Draft,

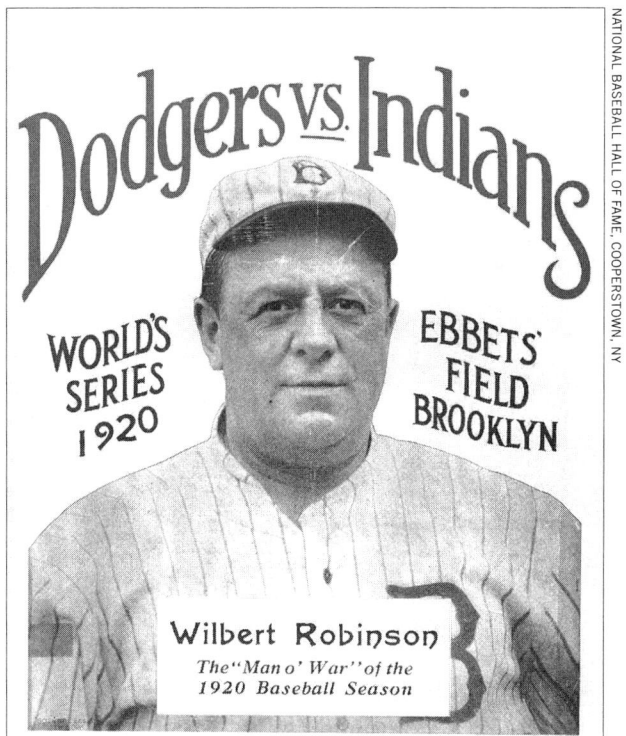

NATIONAL BASEBALL HALL OF FAME, COOPERSTOWN, NY

1920 World Series program cover.

four were acquired via trade, and four were selected off waivers. The top four players appearing in the most games that season—Johnston, Myers, Wheat, and Olson—had also played in the 1916 World Series against the Boston Red Sox. Catcher Otto Miller was the only other non-pitcher acquired before 1916. Table 1 describes how the Robins' roster was compiled for all players who appeared in more than 20 games for the team during the 1920 season. Brooklyn owner Charles Ebbets wanted his team set entering the 1920 season; a month before training camp started, Ebbets had signed 27 of 28 ballplayers by mid-February. The lone holdout was Tommy Griffith, who was debating retirement from professional baseball.[6]

Table 1. 1920 Robins' team assemblage.

Player	Position	1920 GP	Year Acquired	How Acquired
Jimmy Johnston	3b	155	1915	Purchase
Hi Myers	of	154	1909	Purchase
Zach Wheat	of	148	1909	Purchase
Ivy Olson	ss	143	1915	Waivers
Pete Kilduff	2b	141	1919	Trade
Ed Konetchy	1b	131	1919	Purchase
Bernie Neis	of	95	1919	Purchase
Tommy Griffith	of	93	1919	Trade
Otto Miller	c	90	1909	Rule 5 Draft
Clarence Mitchell	p	55	1917	Waivers
Ernie Krueger	c	52	1917	Waivers
Burleigh Grimes	p	43	1918	Trade
Rowdy Elliott	c	41	1919	Purchase
Bill McCabe	util	41	1920	Purchase
Al Mamaux	p	41	1918	Trade
Leon Cadore	p	35	1914	Rule 5 Draft
Sherry Smith	p	33	1914	Rule 5 Draft
Jeff Pfeffer	p	30	1913	Purchase
Ray Schmandt	1b	28	1917	Rule 5 Draft
Rube Marquard	p	28	1915	Waivers
Bill Lamar	of	24	1920	Purchase

The 1920 Brooklyn Robins opened their season with a 9–2 victory over the Philadelphia Phillies on April 14 at Ebbets Field during unseasonably cold weather. Both pitchers went the distance, with Cadore allowing two runs on eight hits while striking out two hitters and walking none, and Philadelphia starter Eppa Rixey allowing nine runs (five earned) on nine hits with four walks and no strikeouts. According to *The New York Times*, the game was more lost by the Phillies than won by the Robins: "Weak pitching in the pinches, uncertainty in fielding and a generally poor performance made the Phillies appear even worse than the preliminary dope on the team had promised."[7] Konetchy was the offensive star, registering two singles and three RBIs. Hitting third in the Phillies lineup that afternoon was right fielder Casey Stengel, who famously guided the Dodgers 1934–36 during the first stop in his 25-year major league managerial career.

The Robins continued to play solid ball throughout April, although the infield struggled during the season's first month. The initial team report printed in *The Sporting News* concluded, "The new Brooklyn infield is showing rather more brains than skill as yet. It was responsible for the seven mechanical errors in the two games with the Phillies, but it made no mental mistakes."[8] Brooklyn finished the month with an 8–4 record, a half-game behind Cincinnati. The Robins were second in runs scored, and allowed the third fewest runs in the league, only six fewer than the Boston Braves, who had played only nine games through April 30. The team was pointed in the right direction.

The first weekend in May proved to be an extremely long one for the Robins, first playing the Boston Braves in Boston, then back to Brooklyn for a game against the Phillies, followed by a return to Boston before taking on their crosstown rival Giants in a three-game series at the Polo Grounds. The estimated 4,500 fans who attended the Saturday, May 1 game between Brooklyn and Boston were treated to a marathon pitching duel that lasted for 3 hours and 50 minutes—26 innings.

Leon Cadore, the Robins' starting pitcher, had started the season strong. After his complete game win against Philadelphia, he fired an 11-inning, 7-hit shutout against the Braves, then allowed two earned runs over six innings in a loss against New York, bringing a 2–1, 1.38 ERA into the contest. His mound opponent, Joe Oeschger, also pitched three games in April: a 6-hit shutout against the Giants, a tough-luck 1–0 loss against Brooklyn where the lone run was scored in the bottom of the 11th inning, and a third consecutive complete game win against the Phillies when he allowed a lone earned run and two unearned runs, to increase his ERA to 0.63. These two hurlers pitched the entire 26-inning game, with Brooklyn scoring in the fifth inning when Olson singled home Krueger. Boston responded with their only run during the following frame when Tony Boeckel singled home Walton Cruise after Cruise tripled to left-center field. Cadore allowed 15 hits and five walks while striking out seven hitters and Oeschger allowed nine hits—all singles—and struck out seven with four walks before the game was called because of darkness.[9] Interestingly, as the game progressed through the extra innings, the two sportswriters covering the game—Eddie Murphy from *The New York Sun* and Thomas Rice of *The Brooklyn Eagle*—were receiving story requests from other area newspapers; they were also exhausted by night's end.[10] The previous record for longest game occurred when the Boston Americans lost to the Philadelphia Athletics, 4–1, in 24 innings on September 1, 1906.

The Robins returned to Ebbets Field the following day, hosting the Phillies, with Philadelphia starter George Smith facing Brooklyn ace Grimes. The Phillies struck first in the third inning as Bevo LeBourveau crossed the plate on a Dave Bancroft double. Philadelphia padded their lead on a two-run LeBourveau homer. The Robins responded with two runs later that inning: Neis scored when Myers doubled and reached third on a dropped ball; subsequently, Konetchy plated Myers. In the bottom of the ninth, Wheat tied the game when he blasted a 3–1 pitch over the right field wall. The teams remained scoreless until the 13th inning when Bancroft scored on a sacrifice fly after Stengel was walked to load the bases, giving the Phillies a 4–3 win. Once again, both pitchers went the distance, and now Brooklyn established a record of playing 39 innings in two games on successive days.[11]

The next day, Brooklyn appeared in Boston with Sherry Smith taking on Braves' starter Dana Fillingim, who brought an 0–2 record and 0.00 ERA into the Monday afternoon contest. Fillingim pitched 17 innings over two starts but all his runs allowed were unearned. The Robins scored first when Johnston reached on a fielder's choice but Smith came home on an error during the fifth inning; Olson also attempted to score on the play but was thrown out at home. The Braves tied the game in the sixth inning as Walter Holke's sacrifice fly brought in Charlie Pick. The game remained tied for the next 11 innings when manager Robinson asked the game to be called on account of darkness; his request was denied. Two innings later, John Sullivan scored the winning run on a Boeckel single and Boston won, 2–1. Both starting pitchers threw complete games; Fillingim earned his first victory and now carried a 0.00 ERA over 36 innings into his next start. After playing 58 innings in three consecutive days—or six full nine-inning games with four additional innings—during which they went 0–2–1, the Robins fell into third place. *The New York Times* opened the game report, "Rumors were circulating around Braves Field late tonight the members of the Braves and Dodgers baseball clubs were about to assemble in mass

meeting in Faneuil Hall and declare themselves on this business of working overtime."[12]

In addition to their marathon extra-inning games to begin the month, Brooklyn proceeded to play five more extra-inning games during May, including three of the six subsequent games. The Robins still finished the month with a 13–10 record; with an overall 21–14 record, they were a half-game behind the Chicago Cubs and percentage points ahead of Cincinnati. Although their offense sputtered during the month, their strong pitching and fielding kept them competitive. During the month, the Robins strengthened their bench by purchasing utility player Bill McCabe from Chicago and selecting outfielder Wally Hood off waivers from Pittsburgh. In addition, Tommy Griffith returned to the diamond after threatening retirement from baseball. During the preceding offseason, Griffith profited from working as a stock salesman, and was still upset over his trade from the Cincinnati ballclub the year before. Once Griffith was assured his salesman career would not suffer from playing ball, he returned to the Robins.[13]

During the first week in June, the Robins reeled off a four-game winning streak, which included a 7-hit shutout by Pfeffer and a 6-hitter by Grimes, to take over first place. However, their success was short-lived; after the streak, Brooklyn lost nine of their next 11 ballgames. After a late-inning rally fell short, resulting in a 9–7 loss to Pittsburgh on June 22, the Robins extended their losing streak to four games and dropped into third place.[14] The papers called out their poor play: "Such baseball as was produced would have shamed a respectable sand-lots team."[15] Brooklyn was now only a half-game in front of surging St. Louis. The Cardinals were in the midst of their own five-game skid, but had won 13 of 14 starting June 1 to jump from sixth to third place. The Robins rebounded with a three-game winning streak

1920 World Series Opening Day crowd at Ebbets Field, October 5, 1920.

following their loss to Pittsburgh, but their inconsistency resulted in a following six-game losing streak, which included losing five games to the struggling Braves. Although the Brooklyn offense was showing signs of life, they couldn't capitalize on opportunities and the pitching was ineffective.[16]

Brooklyn's fortunes improved over the summer, as their 23–12 July record and 14–13 August record moved them back into contention with Cincinnati and New York. Although the Robins suffered a four-game losing streak in the final week of August, they captured back those games with an equivalent four-game winning streak that included back-to-back shutouts by Grimes and Cadore. The Robins were swept by Philadelphia in a Labor Day doubleheader, and promptly returned the favor the following day, initiating a 10-game winning streak which culminated with a doubleheader sweep of the Cubs on September 13.[17] Their sweep resulted in a five-game lead over both Cincinnati and New York and commanding control in the pennant race. Cadore delivered back-to-back shutouts during the streak, and the team's overall offensive production was increasing. John McGraw's Giants were coming on strong with a 20–11 August record, but it wasn't enough to catch the cruising Robins, while Pat Moran's Cincinnati Reds played .511 ball from July 1 onwards. Finally, on September 27, Brooklyn won the pennant after the Braves dramatically ended the Giants' World Series hopes on a Boeckel ninth-inning clout during the second game of a doubleheader.[18]

Hall-of-Famer Zach Wheat enjoyed another great season at the plate. He led the Robins with personal career highs in runs (89), hits (191), and slugging percentage (.463), and also led in batting average (.328), OPS (.848), and home runs (9); he finished second in doubles (26), triples (13), and RBIs (73). He still remains the Dodgers' all-time franchise leader in hits, doubles, triples, and total bases.[19]

Although the Robins lost their fourth attempt at securing a world championship, two lesser known events occurred that October: a curse created by a slighted mascot, and brothers who faced each other for the first time in World Series history.

The 1920 Robins were arguably victimized by one of the earliest curses in the twentieth century, when Brooklyn's mascot Eddie Bennett was prevented from joining the Robins for the four games scheduled in Cleveland following Game 4. Although Bennett had served as a good-luck charm for the Robins during the season and during the previous year with the American League pennant-winning Chicago White Sox, his disappointment over not traveling with the team led

to his supposedly "placing a curse" on his hometown Robins.[20] Bennett joined the Yankees the following season, and for twelve years served as a batboy/mascot for four World Series winners.[21] The curse tale gained notoriety during the next decade; while the Yankees enjoyed success, the Robins wouldn't return to the World Series for another 21 years.

Secondly, brothers faced each other for the first time during the 1920 World Series. Doc and Jimmy Johnston were born just over two years apart in Cleveland, Tennessee. Doc, whose given name was Wheeler Roger Johnston, tended first base for the Indians while his younger brother Jimmy, or James Harle Johnston, covered third base for the Robins. The brothers enjoyed similar careers; Doc played 1056 games, compiling a .263 career batting average with 14 home runs and 381 RBIs and Jimmy played 1377 games, compiling a .294 career batting average with 22 homers and 410 RBIs. In 1920 their batting averages were extremely close—Doc hit .292 over 535 at-bats while Jimmy delivered a .291 average over 635 at-bats: "Wheeler has it on Jimmy in the Frequency (sic) and weight of his hits, but Jimmy has it on Brother Wheeler in stealing and sacrificing."[22]

Doc debuted in 1909 with the Cincinnati Reds, playing three games while going hitless in ten at-bats. According to his younger brother, Doc received his nickname from his father, "who used to say that he would grow up some time to be a Doctor."[23] The following three years he played in the minors, with the Chattanooga Lookouts (1910), Buffalo Bisons (1910), and New Orleans Pelicans (1911–12), before returning to the majors with Cleveland for 43 games toward the end of the 1912 season. Three years later he was purchased by the Pirates; during the following season, Pittsburgh sent Doc to the Birmingham Barons—as one of the players to be named later for a young spitball pitcher named Burleigh Grimes, whom he also faced during the 1920 series. Grimes reached the majors during the 1916 season with Pittsburgh before the Pirates traded him, pitcher Al Mamaux, and infielder Chuck Ward to the Robins for second baseman George Cutshaw and outfielder Casey Stengel in January 1918.[24]

Jimmy played a single game with the Chicago White Sox in 1911; he was selected by the Chicago Cubs in the 1913 Rule 5 draft, appearing in 50 games with the Cubs the following year. He joined Brooklyn in 1916, and played with the Robins until the 1926 season. Jimmy played all the infield and outfield positions during his early years before Brooklyn manager Wilbert Robinson settled on him playing third base, a position with a revolving door in the preceding years: "Here Johnston has played a resolute, active game, which has given abundant satisfaction to the public accustomed as it was to seeing a new performer at third base about three times a week."[25] In 1920 and 1921 Johnston played 146 and 150 games at third base, respectively, the steadiest assignment he held throughout his 13-year career.

Both brothers attained career highs in games played that season (Doc 147, Jimmy 155), with Jimmy tying for the National League lead with New York's Highpockets Kelly and St. Louis's Milt Stock. Doc also reached career highs for his 11-year career in hits (156), doubles (24), and RBIs (71). Jimmy posted solid numbers, leading the Robins in plate appearances (707), stolen bases (19), and finishing second to teammate Zach Wheat in runs (87) and hits (185). Jimmy posted career highs in batting average, doubles, triples, home runs, and stolen bases the following season. Although Jimmy had the lower regular season batting average, Doc held a slight edge during the 1920 Series—going 3-for-11 and scoring once in five games compared with Jimmy's 3-for-14, two-run performance covering four games. Doc's lone run scored came on Cleveland pitcher Jim Bagby's home run during the notable game five. Both brothers retired to farms following their playing careers, and both passed away in Chattanooga, Tennessee.

The 1920 Brooklyn Robins were more than just the Indians' opponent during the Series; Uncle Robbie led the team through a challenging season of peaks and valleys, a three-way season-long pennant chase with the New York Giants and Cincinnati Reds, and unique performances from key players. ■

Additional References

Baseball Reference: http://www.baseball-reference.com

Blanpied, Ralph B. (2005). Brooklyn v. Boston in 26 Innings. In Andrew Paul Mele (Ed.) A Brooklyn Dodgers Reader. Jefferson, North Carolina: McFarland & Company, Inc., Publishers.

Golenbeck, Peter. (2000). Bums: An Oral History of the Brooklyn Dodgers. Chicago, IL: Contemporary Books.

James, Bill. (1997). The Bill James Guide to Baseball Managers from 1870 to Today. New York: Scribner.

Retrosheet: http://www.retrosheet.org/

Simon, Tom. (2004). Deadball Stars of the National League. Cleveland, OH: Society for American Baseball Research.

Thorn, John; Palmer, Pete; Gershman, Michael; and Pietrusza (2004). Total Baseball: The Official Encyclopedia of Major League Baseball. New York: Viking Press.

Notes

1. Daniel, "Fifth National League Pennant for Brooklyn," *The Sun* and *New York Herald*, September 28, 1920: 14.

2. Joseph Wancho, "October 10, 1920: A game of World Series firsts: unassisted triple play and grand slam," SABR Baseball Games Project. Accessed 04 December 2016 at http://sabr.org/gamesproj/game/october-10-1920-world-series-game-firsts-unassisted-triple-play-and-grand-slam.

3. Associated Press, "Ray Chapman Dies of Blow by Ball; Mays Exonerated," *Brooklyn Daily Eagle*, August 17, 1920: 1.

4. Associated Press, "Indict Two Gamblers in Baseball Plot; Men Named by Williams in Confession; Inquiry Here to Guard the 1920 Series," *The New York Times*, September 30, 1920: 1–2.

5. Thomas S. Rice, "Nerve and Spirit Won Pennant, Says Robinson," *Brooklyn Daily Eagle*, September 30, 1920: 1.

6. Thomas S. Rice, "All Dodgers Signed Early in February," *The Sporting News*, March 4, 1920: 2.

7. "Giants and Yankees Lose But Robins Win in Opening Game of Major League Season: Dodgers Open With Easy Victory," *The New York Times*, April 15, 1920: 15.

8. Thomas S. Rice, "Dodgers Please By Display of a Punch," *The Sporting News*, April 22, 1920: 3.

9. "Brooklyn Ties in Record Game of 26 Innings," *The Sun* and *New York Herald*, May 2, 1920: 1.

10. Frank Graham Jr., *Brooklyn Dodgers: An Informal History* (Carbondale, IL: Southern Illinois University Press, 2002): 78.

11. "Ruth's Home Run Liner Enables Yankees to Defeat the Red Sox, 7 to 1—Dodgers Succumb to Phillies by 4 to 3: Dodgers Go 13 Innings to Defeat," *The Sun* and *New York Herald*, May 3, 1920: 9.

12. "Yankees and Giants Lose in Nine Innings, Brooklyn in Nineteen," *The New York Times*, May 4, 1920: 12.

13. Nelson "Chip" Greene, "Tommy Griffith", SABR Biography Project, https://sabr.org/bioproj/person/00873ae1.

14. "Dodgers Continue to Slip: Brooklynites Drop Fourth Straight Game, Losing to Pirates," *Democrat and Chronicle* (Rochester, NY), June 23, 1920: 26.

15. "Late Rally Fails to Save Dodgers," *The New York Times*, June 23, 1920: 12.

16. "Yankees Score 3 Runs in Ninth, Beating Red Sox by 6 to 5—Giants Win From Phillies by 7 to 1—Dodgers Lose: Cadore Ineffective Against the Braves," *The Sun* and *New York Herald*, June 30, 1920: 13.

17. "Giants Win and Dodgers Take Two Games While Reds Lose—Ruth's 49th Homer Enables Yankees to Beat Tigers: Dodgers Twice Rout Cubs, Increasing Lead in Race," *The Sun* and *New York Herald*, September 14, 1920: 10.

18. Thomas S. Rice, "Brooklyn Wins Pennant—World Series Opens in West," *Brooklyn Daily Eagle*, September 28, 1920: 20.

19. Eric Enders, "Zack Wheat," SABR Biography Project, https://sabr.org/bioproj/person/c914f820.

20. Jack Kavanagh and Norman Macht, *Uncle Robbie* (Phoenix, AZ: Society for American Baseball Research, 1999): 126.

21. Peter Morris, "Eddie Bennett" In Jacob Pomrenke (Ed.) *Scandal on the South Side: The 1919 Chicago White Sox* (Phoenix, AZ: Society for American Baseball Research, Inc., 2015): 265–68.

22. Thomas S. Rice, "Others Have Beaten Indians Sluggers—Why Not Superbas?," *Brooklyn Daily Eagle*, October 4, 1920: 2.

23. F.C. Lane, "When Brothers Meet in a World's Series: How the Two Johnston's (sic) of Cleveland and Brooklyn Hope to Clash for a World's Championship," *Baseball Magazine*, November 1920: Volume 25, Issue 6, 578.

24. Charles F. Faber, "Burleigh Grimes," SABR Biography Project, http://sabr.org/bioproj/person/0957655a.

25. F.C. Lane, "When Brothers Meet in a World's Series: How the Two Johnston's of Cleveland and Brooklyn Hope to Clash for a World's Championship," *Baseball Magazine*, November 1920: Volume 25, Issue 6, 578.

Graham McNamee

Broadcast Pioneer

Cort Vitty

The excitement was electric, as crowds filled Yankee Stadium to capacity on October 10, 1923. For the third consecutive year, the Fall Classic was an all-New York affair, pitting the dominant National League Giants against the upstart Yankees, representing the American League. The latter fittingly christened their magnificent new ballyard in the Bronx by going on to win their first World Series title.

1923 also marked the third Fall Classic broadcast over the new phenomenon called radio. Broadcast licenses were rapidly being granted to stations all over the country; airtime was difficult to fill, prompting the coverage of unsponsored sporting events (like the World Series) as a public service. An early radio experiment had involved broadcasting the first game (only) of the 1921 Series. The methodology used involved *Newark Call* reporter Sandy Hunt phoning the action from the Polo Grounds to colleague Tom Cane broadcasting from the WJZ studio.

Commissioner Landis assigned broadcast duties for the 1922 series to prominent sports writer Grantland Rice. Seated in the upper deck of the Polo Grounds, the respected scribe spoke into a microphone crudely perched atop a wooden plank, wired directly to station WEAF in New York. A man of few words, Rice spoke in a slow monotone, devoid of any excitement or enthusiasm. His habit of taking frequent breaks—to allegedly rest his voice—produced extended periods of dead-air silence.

New York Herald-Tribune writer William McGeehan took on the announcing duties for the 1923 Fall Classic, and Graham McNamee was hired to assist him. McGeehan walked off the job in the fourth inning of game three, leaving the broadcast in McNamee's hands.[1] Taking a deep breath, Mac confidently spoke into the microphone with a line that became his standard opening: "How do you do, ladies and gentlemen of the radio audience? Graham McNamee speaking."[2]

Red Barber described the circumstances suddenly thrust upon McNamee: "There was no lamp of experience for the pioneer broadcasters. They had no past by which to judge the future. This is what made McNamee and the others so great. Nobody had ever been called upon before to do such work. They had to go out and do it from scratch. If ever a man did pure, original work, it was Graham McNamee."[3]

Five months earlier, McNamee was an unemployed opera singer, in receipt of a notice to serve jury duty. Fulfilling his civic obligation on a beautiful spring day in May 1923, McNamee decided on a long exhilarating walk during his lunch break. Selecting a route by-passing his usual diner, he chose instead to lunch at a pricey upscale establishment near the AT&T building, at 195 Broadway; the decision cost him an additional fifty cents.

McNamee paused upon noticing a mesmerized crowd listening to a radio broadcast emanating from station WEAF in the AT&T building. Reacting on impulse, he ventured in and upstairs to the WEAF studios. Fortuitously catching the attention of station manager Sam Ross, he boldly inquired about a position as a singer.

Ross indicated no such opening existed, prompting McNamee to mention a window sign he spotted for a staff announcer. Ross liked the appealing tone of McNamee's voice and definitely needed help in that department. Mac was hired on the spot at a starting salary of $3 a day. His job description was to "fill in between appearances of important people."[4]

Early radio announcers worked gruelingly long hours, performing a laundry list of duties around the station. Jobs included general maintenance, answering phones, chauffeuring celebrities, and improvising to fill airtime. As described by author Gerald Nachman, McNamee's "magnetic voice and dramatic flare were tempered with an easygoing personality that set him apart from the mellifluous voices that dominated the microphones of the 1920s."[5]

The newest hire at station WEAF New York was the son of John and Anne McNamee, both of Irish ancestry and Ohio residents when they married in 1885. The couple moved to Washington, DC, after John accepted a position as a legal assistant to the Interior Secretary

NATIONAL BASEBALL HALL OF FAME, COOPERSTOWN, NY

Graham McNamee at the second game of the 1924 World Series, broadcasting from Griffith Stadium in Washington, DC.

during the Cleveland administration. Thomas Graham McNamee, their only child, was born in DC on July 10, 1888.

The family relocated to St. Paul, Minnesota, when Graham was two years old, after his dad accepted a position as a railroad attorney. A trained musician in her own right, Anne McNamee taught her son to sing by age four and play piano at age seven. Attending high school in St. Paul, Graham did well academically in languages and music, while excelling at football, baseball, and wrestling.

After graduation, John McNamee arranged for his son's first job as a freight clerk with the Great Northern Railroad. Graham was next employed as a deliveryman (by horse and buggy) for the Chicago-based Armour & Company. After wrecking eleven buggies in twelve months of employment, he was terminated.

Graham's ambitious mother was convinced an opera career awaited their son; his dad leaned heavily toward law as a profession. Family upheaval due to John McNamee's work-related travel ultimately led to a divorce. After the split, Graham accompanied his mother to New York, where she assumed her son would receive superior vocal training. The 1920 census lists Anne as the owner of a rooming house on West 57th St.; Graham resided on the premises.

McNamee joined an opera company, there meeting aspiring singer Josephine Garrett from nearby Bronxville. The couple sang in the Dutch Reformed Church choir as their relationship blossomed. When they married on May 3, 1921, Josephine's classically trained voice

made her the more likely spouse to potentially have a singing career. Opportunities existed for Graham too; in 1922 he received an invitation to perform at New York's prestigious Aeolian Hall, a legitimate stepping stone for aspiring opera singers. His new job at WEAF meant placing operatic aspirations on hold.

McNamee cut his teeth as a sports broadcaster on August 31, 1923, when assigned to announce the Harry Greb-Johnny Wilson championship fight. His next foray was at the Polo Grounds on September 14, where a crowd exceeding 60,000 fight patrons gathered for the Jack Dempsey- Luis Firpo bout. Thousands more heard Major Andrew White (assisted by McNamee) describe the action on radio. This important live broadcast of a championship fight was a significant radio milestone, greatly increasing the popularity of the fledgling medium. Dempsey retained his heavyweight championship despite being knocked through the ropes (and landing on McNamee) in the second round.

A deluge of positive fan mail followed, attesting to McNamee's style; "The few detractors generally commented about his slight exaggeration, but the listening audience loved the hype and couldn't get enough of the announcer with the baritone voice. McNamee freely admitted to being an entertainer first and a broadcaster second."[6] His approach to radio was simple: "You make each of your listeners, though miles away from the spot, feel that he (or she) too is there with you in the press-stand, watching the pop bottle thrown in the air, Gloria Swanson arriving in her new ermine coat; McGraw in his dugout, apparently motionless, but giving signals all the time."[7]

Miscues were common (and even expected) during a McNamee broadcast. Realizing nothing could be done to correct a mistake, the broadcaster thought it best to simply admit regret and go on to the next factoid. "Once at a baseball game, he confused the players and plays to such an extent, sportswriter Ring Lardner was prompted to observe that there had been a doubleheader yesterday–the game that was played and the one that McNamee observed."[8] Quick with a pun, Mac observed a fight in the stands resulting in a pop bottle being hurled at an umpire. McNamee called it: "a ball…and a strike."[9]

McNamee's broadcast of the 1926 Rose Bowl included extensive details regarding the changeable California weather, accompanied by overly thorough descriptions of attendees' attire; game details were occasionally mentioned. Humorist Will Rogers later publicly scorned McNamee for his insignificant tangents, unrelated to sports, but the listening audience couldn't get enough of the announcer with the baritone voice.

Stations WEAF and WJZ merged to become the National Broadcasting Company, forming a cross-country network, connected by 3,600 miles of phone lines. The official kick-off ceremony took place on November 15, 1926, with a celebratory broadcast from the grand ballroom of the Waldorf-Astoria. An estimated 10 million listeners heard Graham McNamee open the festivities by officially greeting the vast NBC audience. This milestone broadcast marked the start of what would become radio's Golden Age. "When asked to name radio's greatest asset, NBC president Merlin Hall Aylesworth replied—Graham McNamee."[10]

McNamee's voice became synonymous with fall and the World Series. His broadcast of the Yankees-Pirates 1927 Fall Classic marked the first year a nationwide audience enjoyed the play-by-play over network radio. Mac's immense popularity warranted assignments to cover prominent newsmakers such as Charles Lindbergh, Admiral Byrd, Neville Chamberlain, and Amelia Earhart. The Lindbergh coverage at the Washington Navy Yard resulted in an unruly crowd crashing through a Marine guard, trampling the press area. In the commotion, McNamee was knocked to the ground; miraculously unhurt, he continued broadcasting from a prone position on the pavement.

McNamee pursued assignments with dogged determination, often driving poorly lit back-roads, in the dark of night, to arrive for an early morning interview. If time was of the essence, Mac wouldn't think twice about hitching a ride aboard a rickety crop-duster and landing on a corn-field to conduct an interview. He once covered a college regatta while hovering above the race in a chartered plane.

The broadcaster graced the cover of *Time* magazine when the October 3, 1927, edition hit the newsstands. The announcer's fame segued into his personal syndicated newspaper column, appropriately titled "Graham McNamee Speaking." Under his byline, the announcer waxed poetic regarding news events, while providing insightful anecdotes to accompany celebrity interviews. His commentary included analysis of current events while responding to reader inquiries, often of a personal nature.

No slouch on the lecture circuit, McNamee was scheduled to conduct a 1927 speaking engagement in New Castle, Pennsylvania. The well-publicized event was sold out at curtain time, as a filled-to-capacity audience sat in anticipation of his arrival—but he never showed. Mac personally kept his own schedule and apparently jotted down the wrong date. *The New Castle News* published an unflattering editorial, blasting the announcer's blatant snub of the event.

Learning of his error, McNamee took full-responsibility, contacted organizers and insisted all attendees be invited back the next evening, to enjoy the lecture at no charge. "The next day's news took back its raspberry-laced criticism and praised the great man to high heaven."[11] Remarkably, McNamee, "never prepares his program in advance but depends on his extraordinary extemporaneous speaking ability to entertain his audience."[12]

At the close of the 1920s, McNamee's style placed him at the top echelon of all radio announcers. His annual income was estimated to be in the $50,000 range, a remarkable sum at the time. The salary allowed the former out-of-work juror to comfortably reside in a vine-clad cottage atop a swanky New York penthouse.

In 1930, close pal Babe Ruth opened a haberdashery shop in New York for men and boys. Serving as master-of-ceremonies, McNamee: "cheerfully addressed the crowd through a loudspeaker; the ever-confident salesman casually covered the lines of apparel stocked in Babe's new retail shop."[13] Other celebrities accompanying Babe to the grand opening included Knute Rockne of Notre Dame, Yankees manager Bob Shawkey, and teammate Lou Gehrig.

McNamee's crowded workload increased further when assigned to narrate *Universal Newsreels* in 1930. Josephine began referring to herself as "the original microphone widow."[14] Tabloid publications didn't help solidify the couple's relationship, alluding to rumors of an ongoing affair, apparently discovered by Josephine. The couple divorced in 1931.

McNamee re-married on January 21, 1934, tying the knot with Ann Lee Sims, a Louisiana native and aspiring New York actress. The *Washington Post* reported the ceremony as taking place in Elkton, Maryland, "where the couple hurriedly motored into the little town, secured a license and were married by one of the town's marrying parsons."[15] The bride was over twenty years younger than her new husband.

McNamee's favorite radio gig was his stint as the announcer on the *Texaco Fire Chief*, a highly rated NBC radio program, starring veteran comic Ed Wynn. The energetic comedian essentially performed variations of his old vaudeville routines before a live, in-studio audience. In addition to handling the announcing chores, Mac also dutifully performed as a stooge to Wynn's madcap brand of comedy.

Author Elizabeth McLeod noted:

Wynn apparently was a very insecure man. It was McNamee who calmed him down each week, McNamee who gave him the courage he needed to face that forbidding black enamel box. The two men became close friends—and McNamee's regular-guy enthusiasm acted on the air as the perfect complement to Wynn's manic comedy.[16]

While broadcasting the National Soap Box Derby from Akron, Ohio, McNamee was behind the mike on August 12, 1935, when a young participant accidently crashed into the judge's stand. McNamee sustained a serious head injury after being struck by the youngster's two-hundred-pound racer. Recuperation and ultimate recovery required a two-week hospital stay; lingering effects of the head injury would remain with the announcer for the rest of his life.

A new generation of sportscaster began arriving on the scene, loosely following McNamee's style, but more analytical and thorough in broadcast preparation. By 1935, Red Barber became the heir apparent to announce the World Series. Ironically, McNamee attended, solely as a spectator, seated silently next to Red during the broadcast. Barber poignantly noted in his book: "The parade had passed the pioneer that rapidly, that harshly, that remorsefully, in only a dozen years."[17]

McNamee's distinctive voice and proven ability to sell advertisers' products made his work on network radio-programs more valuable than sports reporting. In addition to being on the Wynn program, his regularly scheduled announcer slots included: *Major Bowes Original Amateur Hour*, *Ripley's Believe It Or Not*, *Treasury Hour*, *Millions for Defense*, and *The Rudy Vallee Program*. Periodically Vallee gave McNamee the opportunity of stepping away from his announcer's duties to perform as a featured singer.

The December 7, 1941, Pearl Harbor attack thrust the country into war. Among the high-profile stories making headlines in the aftermath was the conversion of luxury liner *Normandie* into the troopship *Lafayette*. On February 9, 1942, in New York harbor, a blaze of unknown origin consumed the entire ship. Reporters converged on the dock area as sabotage was initially suspected. The fire was ultimately determined to be accidental, caused when welding equipment ignited a spark. Broadcasting from the cold, rainy dock area, McNamee came-down with a sore throat.

Continuing to work his grueling schedule, the throat ailment developed into strep, and the announcer's health progressively deteriorated. He entered St. Luke's Hospital in April, where a new series of tests revealed evidence of a serious heart ailment. The golden baritone voice was permanently silenced on May 9, 1942, with the official cause of death listed as a brain embolism. Services were held at the Frank E. Campbell funeral church in New York.

Shortly before his passing, a broadcast colleague asked McNamee to identify the greatest sports moment he'd ever witnessed during his extensive career. Without hesitation McNamee responded: "Babe Ruth and the 'called-shot' in the 1932 World Series."[18]

At the time of his passing, *The New York Times* estimated "the late broadcaster uttered ten times the number of words in an unabridged dictionary during his radio career."[19] McNamee was just shy of 53 years old, however, as Red Barber remarked: "He'd lived a thousand years."[20] The broadcaster was buried in Akron, near the location of his father's interment.

Broadcast partner and fellow WEAF announcer Phil Carlson commented: "His voice was the most trusted and vibrant in radio, for nearly 20 years it thrilled the people who heard it. There was never such a voice of excitement heard in this land, as that of Graham McNamee."[21]

McNamee was inducted into The American Sportscasters Association Hall of Fame in 1984. The National Baseball Hall of Fame and Museum presented the Ford C. Frick Award to McNamee in 2016, commemorating his significant contribution to the origin of baseball broadcasting. ∎

Notes

1. Stu Shea, *Calling the Game* (Phoenix; SABR, Inc., 2015). 363.
2. Robert Weintraub, *The House That Ruth Built* (New York: Little, Brown and Company, 2011). 23.
3. Red Barber, *The Broadcasters* (New York: DaCapo Press, 1970). 23.
4. T.R. Kennedy, "A Voice to Remember," *Baltimore Sun*, April 17, 1942.
5. Gerald Nachman, *Raised on Radio* (New York: Pantheon Books, 1998). 264.
6. Robert Weintraub, *The House That Ruth Built* (New York: Little, Brown and Company, 2011). 301.
7. Robert Weintraub, *The House That Ruth Built* (New York: Little, Brown and Company, 2011). 300.
8. "Graham McNamee," *Terre Haute Saturday Spectator*, August 16, 1930.
9. Ibid.
10. Robert Weintraub, *The House That Ruth Built* (New York: Little, Brown and Company, 2011). 301.
11. "The Way We Were 1927," *New Castle News*, May 8, 1992.
12. "Graham McNamee to be in City Next Friday," *Canton Daily News*, January 20, 1929.
13. "Babe Ruth Opens Broadway Shop with Ceremonies," *Moorhead Daily News*, September, 29, 1930.
14. Helen Hulett, *McCalls*, May, 1930.
15. "McNamee Marries," *Washington Post*, January 24, 1934.
16. Elizabeth McCloud, *The Life and Times of Ed Wynn, The Fire Chief*. Web article, 1999.
17. Red Barber, *The Broadcasters* (New York: DaCapo Press, 1970). 27.
18. Robert Weintraub, *The House That Ruth Built* (New York: Little, Brown and Company, 2011). 394.
19. "Graham McNamee is Dead Here at 53," *The New York Times*, May 10, 1942.
20. Ibid.
21. Ibid.

The Day Babe Ruth Came to Sing Sing

Gary Sarnoff

On September 5, 1929, Babe Ruth and the New York Yankees played an exhibition game against the top team of the Mutual Welfare League inside the walls of Sing Sing Correctional Facility in Ossining, New York.

"I hear we're going to Sing Sing next Thursday," Yankees catcher Ben Bengough announced in the Yankee Stadium dugout.

"Yeh,"said Babe Ruth, "It's a good thing we ain't going to play in a bughouse. They may keep some of you birds there."[1]

The Yankees are coming! The news spread through the penitentiary like wildfire, and the inmates began counting down the days until the Bambino and his teammates would appear. The exhibition game would be against the penitentiary's top team, the Ossining Orioles of the Mutual Welfare League. The Yankees wouldn't be the first major league team to play on the sunbaked skin surface of Sing Sing Stadium. The New York Giants had made six appearances during the 1920s, with their most recent visit occurring nine days before the Yankees were scheduled.

The idea to bring big league teams to Sing Sing evolved from Warden Lewis E. Lawes's theory of rehabilitating prisoners through building morale rather than hammering discipline. When appointed as warden of Sing Sing by New York governor Alfred Smith in 1919, Lawes arrived with a goal to focus on building the inmates' morale through recreation, athletics, work, books, and medical treatment. Under his tenure, sports and recreation became a big deal at Sing Sing, with not only inmate baseball but an annual field day consisting of track and field events. Handball, bocce, and other recreational gamesere played throughout the warmer months of the year.

On September 5, 1929, Babe Ruth, Lou Gehrig, and most of the players on the Yankees roster journeyed to the prison. Tall stone walls impounded the buildings located on the bank of the Hudson River in the town of Ossining, 28 miles north of Yankee Stadium. Not attending the day's event were Tony Lazzeri, Bob Meusel, Leo Durocher, some of the pitchers, and manager Miller Huggins, who was said to be very ill and in need of a day off. (Little did anyone realize how sick the New York skipper really was, and that he was within a month of living the final day of his life.)

When the big iron-plated front door was opened, a security guard carefully counted each player passing through the gate. The team was escorted through several barred gates—some plain, some fancy—toward the jail's cells to begin their tour. While heading to the cellblocks, the players got a glimpse of the officers' mess. Ruth decided to step inside and snatch a slice of gingerbread resting on a plate.

Inmates were star-struck by the sight of the Bambino, who was well-dressed for the occasion in spotless golf togs: white shirt, black tie, white knickers pleated in black, with black stockings and black and white shoes. When the prisoners said hello, Ruth responded with a smile, a salute, or by answering with his familiar "Hello, kid."[2] One of the temporary residents, too ill to attend the game that day, asked Ruth to sign his cell wall, which Ruth gladly did.

The Yankees noted that the prisoners were uniformed in dark gray pants, white shirts or sleeveless white undershirts and black shoes, the fashion for jailbirds since striped suits and pillbox hats went out of vogue. The defending American League champs were amazed over how young looking and pleasant-faced the inmates appeared. They seemed happy, content, healthy, and were tan from their daily outdoors jobs and recreational activities, which was also noted by the Giants during their recent tour. "These guys look like they'd just come back from a month on the beach," one of the Giants had said. "Where is that parlor I've read about?" another player kidded.[3]

The next phase of the tour took the players to the new cells built into the hill on the grounds, described as "ritzy,"[4] with each new cell furnished with radio headphones. The Yankees also saw the correctional facility's new auditorium in the process of being equipped with machinery to show motion pictures with sound. At this juncture of the tour, prison life looked as if it may not be so bad. However, the next part of the journey would be "a somewhat gruesome reminder of prison life."[5]

Although Warden Lawes had always bitterly opposed the death penalty, the law existed in New York, and in order to comply, Sing Sing had a Death Row. The tour guide conducted the Yankees to the death chamber, furnished with a big wooden electric chair mounted to the floor. Ruth sat in the big chair, which seemed "to sober him for the next half hour," according to *New York Evening Journal* sportswriter Ford Frick.[6]

While on their way through the prison yard following their exit from the death house, the Yankees came across an elderly blind inmate on his way to a workshop. The tour paused while Ruth assisted the elderly prisoner through the yard and to a workshop entrance. "There's a nice chap," Ruth said when he rejoined his teammates. "I wonder what he did? Stole something, I suppose. He's too gentle to do any rough stuff."

"Up to a short time ago that old fellow was in the death house awaiting execution," the tour guide informed Ruth. "He murdered his wife and was sentenced to die. Now that he lost his sight, his sentence has been commuted to life imprisonment." Surprised to hear this, Ruth looked down as he shook his head. "Gosh," he said. "Gosh."[7]

The Yankees then met the man in charge, Lewis E. Lawes, the distinguished forty-five year-old head official of Sing Sing who had started his career as a prison guard and had earned the utmost respect while working

Autographing was as prevalent an activity for Ruth at Sing Sing as pitching, fielding, and batting.

his way to the top. The warden hosted a luncheon for the players, and then it was finally time to play ball.

The Yankees were guided to the dressing room where once again they were carefully counted. After putting on their famous pinstriped uniforms with numbers on the jersey backs, they were again counted before being directed to the playing field. The minute the players appeared on the field they were confronted by the inmates for autographs. As one would expect, Ruth received the majority of autograph requests, and as usual, the Bambino obliged by signing and signing. "I didn't know that there were so many of you here," Ruth said with a laugh after he had signed the first fifty or sixty baseballs.[8] After twenty minutes of autograph-seeking, the guards cleared the field in order to give the Yankees time to warm up before the game.

The high walls that encompassed the entire facility also served as the outfield wall. "Those gray walls are twice as insurmountable when you're on the inside," wrote Frick.[9] Though the distance from home plate to the outfield walls is unknown, it was said that it didn't take a wallop to clear the left-field wall. Only once in Sing Sing Stadium history had a ball topped the right field wall, hit by Bill Terry during a Giants' visit in 1924. Never had a home run traveled beyond the center-field wall, although a drive of Ruthian proportions was thought possible to manage it.

Above the towering walls were six watchmen with machine guns, stationed in three towers, unresponsive and uninterested in the score yet closely monitoring the ballgames. Among the armed watchmen was a former major leaguer, William Leith, who had played for the 1899 Washington Senators and had spent time with the New York Giants after Dan Brouthers had highly recommended him. Now in his tenth year as a guard at Sing Sing and wearing a cap bearing the letters "N.Y.S.P." Leith insisted that the Giants and Yankees were lucky that they did not have to play the best at Sing Sing. According to Leith the most talented team was the all-colored team of the institution's Shop League. "The really classy team of the institution, better than the official nine representing the Mutual Welfare League," insisted Leith.[10]

Down the left-field foul line were covered bleachers that the inmates occupied. For the Yankees game, all spots on the benches were taken. Inmates unable to fit in the seating area sat atop the bleachers cover, in front of the stands, and on the field along the left-field wall.

The right-field bleachers were reserved for outside spectators. Because this was no average ballpark, there were rules for these fans, one requiring that they arrive prior to game time. When it was time to enter, a gate was opened, the only way to or from these bleachers. These stands were backed by a wall and fronted by a wire screen. All spectators were admitted at the same time and only at that time. Late arrivals were not admitted and nobody was permitted to leave until the game was finished. There were no vendors, no concession or souvenir stands. There were also no tickets and no charge for admission. However, during the game an optional donation was taken up among the crowd for funds to buy equipment, mitts, and baseballs for the Mutual Welfare League.

Behind home plate a cozy suite was elevated above the field, used by Warden Lawes and the press. Inside the box were cushioned seats, photos of Abraham Lincoln, Charles Lindbergh, and movie stars, plus a window with a view of the Hudson.

The Mutual Welfare League team entered this game with a season record of 32–6, but it didn't count for much. They were not in a league, were not battling for a pennant, nor were they motivated to win one for dear old Sing Sing. The team never left the prison. They had no road games. All games were at home, usually played on Saturdays or Sundays against visiting amateur ball teams. There were few privileges in playing for the Mutual Welfare League, other than getting to play the great game of baseball and receiving an extra meal on game day. The players were also entitled to an early leave from their daily jobs at workshops in order to practice from 4:00 to 7:00. They did not get paid for playing. They earned the same 1½ cents per day that the other inmates earned for laboring in the workshops.

The best team in the Mutual Welfare League, decked out in castoff New York Giants gray road uniforms, took the field for the top of the first. Pitching for the inmates was Charlie McCann, who had earned a reputation as a hitter the week before by clouting one out of the yard off of Giants pitcher Joe Genewich. The team's best pitcher, William Conklin, would appear later in the game. Known by his nickname, "Red," Conklin had once played semi-pro baseball for $75–85 per week.[11] He was paroled in 1922, but by the end of that season he was returned to Sing Sing in handcuffs when charged with disorderly conduct.[12] Because Conklin had violated Baumes Law by committing more than three felonies, he was automatically sentenced for life. His only hope for release was a pardon by the state.

The manager of the Mutual Welfare League team was the team's third baseman, Mike Lawlor, in for ten to twenty and hoping to be pardoned while he still was young enough to play professionally. At first base was

another inmate named Mike, a resident for so long that it was said he was almost happy to be there. He had arrived fifteen years ago as a kid and still had ten years to go on his sentence.[13] Old and grizzled, he was still counting on a career in professional baseball. "By the time I'm out of here I'll be able to play first base like nobody's business."[14] Another Mike was the megaphone announcer, said to be a handsome fellow with a pleasant smile who kept announcing that he would be a free man in twenty-two days, "And when I get out the big gate I won't ever come back here again. Not even to manage this club."[15]

A former dentist now living in Sing Sing called the balls and strikes from behind the plate. "It's better to have a dentist for an umpire rather than an umpire for a dentist," quipped a sportswriter. The sportswriter noted that a dentist became an umpire because there were no umpires in Sing Sing, "Although one would think, after listening to the remarks made by baseball fans, the jails would be full of umpires."[16]

Ruth smiled as he stepped in for his first at bat in the top of the first. There was a feeling that he would hit a home run—maybe two or more—on this day. He had already energized the prison populace by clearing the right field barrier during batting practice.

After hitting a hard grounder that rolled into the far distance of the outfield for a double in his first at bat, Ruth got hold of one in the top of the second and sent it for a long ride to center. The ball seemed to travel for miles and miles. "Gee! I wish I was riding out on that one," said Mike, the first baseman of the Mutual Welfare League.[17] The ball sailed past a watchtower and landed far beyond the center-field wall for the first home run hit over Sing Sing Stadium's center-field barrier. Amazed by the power of the Bambino, even the watchmen in the towers put down their machine guns to applaud. From the warden's box behind home plate, Warden Lawes, just as amazed as everyone else, stood up and cheered. When the ball landed outside the penitentiary, a mad scramble ensued among the children and village's trustees who had camped outside hoping for such a prize.

Ruth took his familiar short, choppy home run trot, but as he headed toward second base, the Mutual Welfare League's second baseman interrupted him with a plea to have his baseball signed. Ruth obliged.

One inning later, Ruth hit another one, this one topping the right-field wall to match Bill Terry's feat. In the top of the fifth, he did it again, his third of the day, another drive to the right field that left the confines.

The game, unsurprisingly a rout in the Yankees' favor, was said to "chiefly be a Yankees ball-signing

Prior to Ruth, the only man said to have hit a home run over Sing Sing's right-field wall was Bill Terry of the Giants on a 1924 visit to the prison.

exercise"[18] rather than a ball game. Throughout the afternoon the inmates interrupted the game's progress by hounding the Yankees for signatures. In the sixth inning, Yankees catcher Ben Bengough was standing on third base when he was approached for an autograph.

Ruth seemed to enjoy himself as much as anybody else, signing throughout the game and exchanging witticisms with the visiting fans while playing first base, his usual exhibition game position. In the bottom of the eighth, Ruth took the mound to pitch the last two innings. When the first batter stepped in, Ruth asked, "Can he hit a hook?" He threw a curveball, which the batter belted to left, but it curved foul. "He can," confirmed Ruth. "I'll try him on a fast one." Before he went into his windup, an inmate left the bleachers and ran to the pitcher's mound, where he pushed a baseball and pen toward Ruth. The Bambino removed his glove, tucked it under his arm, and signed. When play resumed, Ruth threw a fastball that the batter tagged

for a single to center field. "I should have pitched him a knuckler," said Ruth.[19]

In the bottom of the ninth an inmate named Clark tagged a Ruth pitch and sent it over the left-field wall. As Clark rounded the bases, Ruth shouted, "Hey! Are you eligible to sign a contract?"

He's got one now," said a voice from the bleachers occupied by the inmates. "He's a ten year man, Babe."[20]

When the game ended, the manual scoreboard operated by two inmates showed that the Yankees had won, 15–3. The scorebook kept by a trustee from a New York newspaper recorded a 17–3 Yankees win, "If that matters," opted a sportswriter.[21] When the last out was made the inmates immediately surrounded Ruth, forcing him to elbow his way to the dressing room.

Before entering the dressing room, the guards counted each Yankees player, and then they recounted when they had emerged. The guests were then escorted toward the exit. On the way, Ruth took one last look at the prisoners who were lined up and about to head back to their cells. "Goodbye, boys!" Ruth shouted. "And good luck!"

"Goodbye, Babe," said Red Conklin. "Come again, any time. We're always home."[22] ∎

Notes

1. *New York Sun*, August 28, 1929.
2. *New York Sun*, September 6, 1929.
3. *New York Herald Tribune*, August 28, 1929.
4. Ibid.
5. *New York Evening Journal*, September 6, 1929.
6. Ibid.
7. Ibid.
8. *New York Herald Tribune*, September 6, 1929.
9. *New York Evening Journal*, September 6, 1929.
10. *New York Sun*, August 27, 1929.
11. Rud Rennes, "Baseball Behind Bars," *New York Herald Tribune*, September 8, 1929.
12. *The New York Times*, March 19, 1923.
13. *New York Evening Journal*, September 6, 1929.
14. Ibid.
15. Ibid.
16. *New York Herald Tribune*, September 8, 1929.
17. *New York Evening Journal*, September 6, 1929.
18. *The New York Times*, September 6, 1929.
19. *New York Sun*, September 6, 1929.
20. Ibid.
21. *New York Sun*, September 6, 1929.
22. *New York Evening Journal*, September 6, 1929.

Roosevelt Stadium

The Forgotten Ballpark

David Krell

ordering Hoboken—which dubs itself the "birthplace of baseball" because of the legendary 1846 game between the Knickerbockers and the New Yorks at Elysian Fields—Jersey City stands on the edges of the Hudson River and Newark Bay, somewhat obscured by the baseball notoriety of its neighbor to the northeast and the epic annals of baseball history created across the Hudson. Ebbets Field is remembered as a shrine of love for baseball, Yankee Stadium is revered as an example of grandeur, and the Polo Grounds is honored as the home of a baseball reinvention led by John McGraw. Jersey City's Roosevelt Stadium, a jewel of a ballpark boasting a 25,000 capacity within a Ruthian home run of Newark Bay, goes largely unrecognized for its contributions, including being the site of Jackie Robinson's first regular season game in Organized Baseball.

As a member of the Montreal Royals, the Dodgers' AAA team in the International League, Robinson took the field on April 18, 1946, against the Jersey City Giants; he went 4-for-5, including a three-run home run and two stolen bases, to lead the Royals in a 14–1 victory. It was a precursor to glory—the Royals won the Little World Series over the Louisville Colonels of the American Association and Robinson led the

International League in runs scored and batting average. A statue of Jackie Robinson stands outside Jersey City's Journal Square PATH (Port Authority Trans-Hudson) commuter train station.

"There was a lot of fanfare at Roosevelt Stadium," wrote Robinson in his 1960 autobiography, *Wait Till Next Year: The Story of Jackie Robinson*, written with Carl T. Rowan. "Mayor Frank Hague was there, with a lot of school children he had 'liberated' by declaring a holiday. I remember the parades, the brass band's playing 'The Star-Spangled Banner' and the marvelous beauty of this 'day of destiny' for me."[1]

Without a masterful politician, of course, Roosevelt Stadium would not have gone beyond the blueprint stage. Tammany Hall had Boss Tweed; Jersey City had Mayor Frank Hague, who cleared, paved, and smoothed roads to civic projects by pushing buttons of graft, bribes, and political favors.

When Hague died on New Year's Day in 1956, obituaries underscored his impact on New Jersey's second largest metropolis—and his means of maintaining, strengthening, and using power. The *New York Herald-Tribune* wrote, "Mr. Hague ruled his industrial bailiwick in a manner which some described as benevolent despotism, and others dismissed with the term 'Hagueism' which became a sort of epithet. What the city's 3,000-odd municipal employees, forced each year to kick back 3 per cent of their annual stipend for the local party war chest, thought was another matter."[2]

Hague served as mayor from 1917 to 1947, when he stepped down for his handpicked successor; nephew Frank Hague Eggers received an appointment as Jersey City's mayor, but lost the mayoral election in 1949 to John V. Kenny, a former member of the Hague guard. Technology nudged Hague toward City Hall's exit door and away from his infamous desk, which had a compartment facing visitors—Hague could open the compartment with a button, making it easy for those wishing his favor to place the requisite amount of money inside. New Jersey Governor

Jersey City's noted architect Christian Ziegler designed Roosevelt Stadium in the Art Deco style.

Walter Edge mandated the replacement of paper voting ballots with voting machines to lower the likelihood of vote tampering on Election Day.

By even the most generous of yardsticks, Hague's was not a modest existence; he neither hid nor apologized for largesse:[3]

- Occupied a 14-room duplex
- Had a summer home on the Jersey Shore
- Traveled in Europe
- Spent winters in Florida
- Bought $400,000 worth of property in seven years

In Hague's 1956 obituary, *Newark Star-Ledger* reporters Charles Sullivan and Bruce Bailey wrote, "As mayor of Jersey City, Hague's word was undisputed. He gained enough power to declare flatly, 'I am the law,' and that became his trademark.[4]

"Hague's domineering personality reached into every corner of New Jersey and was felt on the national scene when he backed the late Franklin D. Roosevelt for president."

It is President Roosevelt, of course, for whom Roosevelt Stadium was named. Built on the site of the defunct Jersey City Airport in the Droyer's Point section, Roosevelt Stadium belonged to a roster of projects under the umbrella of the Works Progress Administration, established under the Roosevelt presidency in 1935 to create jobs on public projects during the Great Depression and headed by Roosevelt adviser Harry Hopkins. The federal government footed WPA's cost of $11 billion, which funded 8.5 million jobs in the country's infrastructure:[5]

- Roads: 650,000 miles
- Public buildings: 125,000
- Bridges: 75,000
- Parks: 8,000
- Airports: 800

Ending in 1943 because unemployment plummeted when government contractors expanded jobs during World War II, the WPA did more than put laborers to work—it also funded the artistic community:

- Federal Arts Project
- Federal Writers Project
- Federal Theater Project

Two weeks before Christmas in 1935, Hague spoke at the stadium's groundbreaking, heralding Roosevelt's

Roosevelt Stadium debuted in 1937 as a project of the Works Progress Administration. It was demolished in 1985 after years of neglect.

involvement: "We owe to President Roosevelt's efforts the realization of our dream. He has been considerate of Jersey City in giving us this beautiful stadium. Besides the stadium, I am happy that its construction will provide work for nearly 1,000 men and through them hundreds of our citizens will benefit. This is a very happy occasion for all of us."[6]

The United States government made a grant of $1,100,000 for the building costs. Jersey City shouldered $400,000 for costs associated with architect's fees and services, engineering, and construction.[7]

Roosevelt Stadium debuted on April 23, 1937. Though the genesis of government projects goes unsung, for the most part, such was not the case for readers of the *Newark Star-Eagle* the next morning. *Star-Eagle* writer Charles Moran noted Hague's importance in bringing a Giants farm team from to Jersey City. "Politics, it's a wonderful thing," he declared. "It built the handsome Roosevelt Field Stadium [sic] in Jersey City, it materially assisted in bringing the prodigal franchise back to Hagueville; and Mayor Frank Hague fulfilled his promise to [Giants owner] Horace Stoneham and ordered the 'faithful' to appear in droves at the opening."[8]

Hague's partner in developing Jersey City was architect Christian Ziegler. Ziegler, who conceived, among other Jersey City structures, the Margaret Hague Maternity Hospital at the Jersey City Medical Center. Ziegler's predecessor as Jersey City's "architect in chief" was John Rowland, who died in 1945.

Ziegler favored the "Art Deco" approach, described by Jared Goss, former Associate Curator of Modern and Contemporary Art at the Metropolitan Museum of Art, as flourishing during World War I and World War II:

"And so, the Art Deco years were those of the Roaring Twenties, the Jazz Age, the Skyscraper Era, and all their attendant personalities: the flapper, the vamp, and the Rockette; the bootlegger and the gangster." Goss also noted other artistic influences. "But they were also the time of Art Moderne in the English-speaking world, of 'Le Style Moderne' in France, of Nordic Classicism, Swedish Grace and 'Funkis' in Scandinavia, of 'El Noucenstisme' in Spain, of 'Zackenstil' in Germany, of 'Estilo Português Suave'" in Portugal and its colonies—some of the many iterations of Art Deco. Further, it continued through the period of the Crash of 1929, the Great Depression, and the rise of Fascism, an era bracketed at both ends by devastating world wars. Art Deco encompasses and was informed by all of that."[9]

Brian Kelly, Director of the Architecture Program at the University of Maryland's School of Architecture, Planning and Preservation observes, "You cannot talk about the history of American architecture without talking about Art Deco. The style was enormously popular in the 1920s and particularly the 1930s. Instead of ornamental excess, lavish cornices, and intricate columns, you had flat surfaces accentuated by calculated relief that cleverly recalled these features of traditional classical architecture while rendering them by using a more streamlined method. Art Deco buildings were fundamentally traditional, but at the same time, much simpler and more modern in appearance.

"It was a kind of rapprochement between tradition and modernity. The two greatest Art Deco buildings are the Chrysler Building and the Empire State Building. There are repetitive aspects complemented by flourishes of ornament in specific locations. Fundamentally, though, they're stripped down. Some parts of the old Yankee Stadium and Baltimore's Memorial Stadium, where the Orioles used to play, had Art Deco influences."[10]

The "Art Deco" name derives from the 1925 Exposition des Arts Decoratifs in Paris.[11] Art Deco buildings are bold in their simplicity, efficient in their design, and inventive in their execution. From the Space Needle in Seattle to Rockefeller Center in midtown Manhattan, a variety of approaches exist within the Art Deco concept, but the common threads are sleekness, strength, and sustenance. Some examples include:

- Los Angeles City Hall
- Nebraska State Capitol
- Waldorf-Astoria Hotel
- Chicago Board of Trade Building
- Kansas City Power & Light Building
- Buffalo City Hall
- Louisiana State Capitol
- Los Angeles Union Station
- Jefferson County (Texas) Courthouse

Roosevelt Stadium, the great edifice envisioned by Ziegler, propelled by Hague, and supported by a Franklin Roosevelt program, was an Art Deco hallmark of New Jersey's second largest metropolis (second to Newark), as well as a home for the Garden State's baseball enthusiasts. "This was a building that emphasized Jersey City's strength," explains William Neumann, Board Member of Preservation New Jersey, a non-profit dedicated to the advocacy of historic preservation. "Architecture, in a literal sense, cements the ideals, outlook, and faith of a community. When we build stadia, there is an art form with amazing amounts of craft and science behind it. Though it appears simple, architecture can enlighten and entertain."[12]

Indeed, a ballpark's aesthetics in an urban environment can affect the fan's experience in ways that suburban venues cannot. "You are approaching it on a city street, it becomes visible, it rises as you draw near, you pass through the entry threshold and emerge eventually upon a sea of green—ideally with a city skyline beyond," describes Notre Dame University architecture professor Phil Bess. "The most consequential challenge is the design of the ballpark cross-section, because it is there that the problems of ballpark, vertical and horizontal circulation, seating site lines, and proximity to the playing field are determined."[13]

After the Giants left Jersey City for Ottawa in 1950, Roosevelt Stadium's next baseball tenure of importance was hosting 15 Brooklyn Dodgers games in 1956 and 1957. When Dodgers owner Walter O'Malley struck a deal to use Roosevelt Stadium as the home field, it sparked curiosity—and ignited fear in the hearts of fans from Carroll Gardens to Coney Island. Cherished by Brooklynites since its unveiling in 1913, Ebbets Field faced jeopardy. Roosevelt Stadium represented "a step toward the eventual sale of Ebbets Field, possibly within two years. This [Roosevelt Stadium] is the type of setup we would like to have," stated Dodgers assistant general manager Red Patterson.[14]

Instead, O'Malley moved the team 3,000 miles west to Los Angeles.

New decade. New heroes. New opportunities. The future for baseball was brighter than a cloudless July day at the Jersey Shore. Or so thought the fans of Jersey City's latest team. Forced out of Cuba by political strife in 1960 under Fidel Castro, the Havana Sugar

Kings found refuge in Roosevelt Stadium; International League President Frank Shaughnessy told Sugar Kings owner Roberto Maduro that a move was not merely urgent, but necessary. The Associated Press reported, "The message said that an emergency existed in Havana because of tension between Cuba and the United States, and that the safety and welfare of baseball personnel 'is or might be endangered.'"[15] The Sugar Kings played their last game on July 12 in Miami and basked in the cheers of their new hometown fans on July 15 in a parade in Jersey City. One of the fans was Delphine Lisk who, after her boss denied her the opportunity to watch the parade, received the dubbing of Miss Jersey City by the mayor and rode with the team in the motorcade.[16]

An 8–3 loss to the Columbus Jets that night inaugurated a new era for Jersey City baseball that, once again, swept the residents of Hudson County into the joys and sorrows of being fans. The following day augured no better for the team now known as the Jerseys. "Today, the local heroes committed what would have been an unpardonable sin in the eyes of a less hospitable audience," wrote Robert L. Teague in *The New York Times*. "They failed to hold a 2–0 advantage, and finished the contest still under the .500 level for the season and at the .000 mark for their efforts in their new city."[17]

After the following season, the former Sugar Kings moved to Jacksonville and gained a new moniker— Suns.

Rock concerts, high school football games, and drum and bugle corps championships, among other events, took place at Roosevelt Stadium in succeeding years. By the 1980s, however, the neglect was too far gone; Jersey City's City Council okayed demolition of the stadium in favor of housing.[18] A report for the Historic American Buildings Survey noted the disrepair caused by "deterioration and abandonment" of the stadium:[19]

- Baseball scoreboard and light towers collapse
- Seats ripped out
- Windows smashed
- Vandalizing of interior spaces
- Drainage system collapse, causing flooding of dugouts and locker room tunnels

Knocked down in 1985, Roosevelt Stadium exists in the custody of memories, where images, sounds, and stories of its better days echo like a monastery bell. Society Hill at Droyer's Point, an apartment complex, stands on the site that two men, one through political strength and the other through artistic excellence, turned into a source of civic pride, an example of architectural excellence, and a haven for baseball fans in northern New Jersey. ■

Notes

1. Carl T. Rowan with Jackie Robinson, *Wait Till Next Year: The Story of Jackie Robinson* (New York: Random House) 149.
2. "Frank Hague's Career: Absolute Ruler 30 Years," *New York Herald Tribune*, January 2, 1956.
3. Ibid.
4. Charles Sullivan and Bruce Bailey, "Frank Hague Dies at 81," *Newark Star-Ledger*, January 2, 1956. This article was found in the Newark Public Library's microfilm archives of the *Newark Star-Ledger*. Another article references Hague's age at 79.
5. https://www.britannica.com/topic/Works-Progress-Administration.
6. "Stadium Ceremony Attended by 2,000," *Newark Evening News*, December 12, 1935.
7. "Sports Stadiums Near Completion," *The New York Times*, December 13, 1936.
8. Charles Moran, "Record Debut Heartens Jersey Giants," *Newark Star-Eagle*, April 24, 1937.
9. Jared Goss, "What is Art Deco?," http://artdeco.org/what-is-art-deco/what-is-artdeco-by-jared-goss.
10. Telephone interview with Brian 10 Kelly, March 17, 2017.
11. "Art Deco Style 1925-1940," Pennsylvania Historical and Museum Commission, http://www.phmc.state.pa.us/portal/communities/ architecture/ styles/art-deco.html.
12. Telephone interview with William Neumann, March 21, 2017.
13. E-mail from Philip Bess to author, March 22, 2017.
14. "Patterson Likes Roosevelt Set-Up," *Newark Evening News*, August 18, 1955.
15. "Havana Baseball Franchise Goes to Jersey City," Associated Press, *The New York Times*, July 9, 1960.
16. "Events and Discoveries of the Week," *Sports Illustrated*, July 25, 1960.
17. Robert L. Teague, "Jerseys Lose But Fans Love 'Em," *The New York Times*, July 17, 1960.
18. Joseph Malinconico, "Roosevelt Stadium: Glory Fading Fast," *The New York Times*, November 28, 1982.
19. Historic American Buildings Survey No. NJ-819.

From Mexico to Quebec

Baseball's Forgotten Giants

Bill Young

1946

In 1946, 22 major leaguers—11 of whom were under contract to either the New York Giants or the Brooklyn Dodgers—bolted to Mexico in search of greener (base-ball) fields.[1] This article looks at the fate and fortunes of eight members from the 1945 New York Giants who left their New York counterparts to suit up with one of six teams in the Mexican League.

It is worth remembering that the year 1946 was unique in a variety of respects. The war was over, peace and freedom carried the day; military person-nel, young men and women who had sacrificed so much, were returning home, including rafts of ball players itching to get back onto the diamond. Accord-ing to one estimate, nearly a thousand big leaguers and 3,000 minor leaguers were expected to be demo-bilized by early 1946.[2] Suddenly baseball was about to be fun again—except for those major or minor lea-guers who were soon to become expendable as their roles were either turned over to more accomplished players, or were minimized due to some local griev-ance, usually related to money or matters of respect.

For several of them Mexico was the answer.

EIGHT MEN OUT

Mexico certainly was a tantalizing alternative. The Mexican League of the day was offering wealth and opportunity unheard of in major league circles, an op-portunity too good to turn down. And as things turned out, it was everything but.

The *agent provocateur* behind this Latin explosion was Jorge Pasquel, a wealthy Mexican businessman. He was in search of major league players to help raise the profile of the Mexican League to major league level. Although his offers had been rejected by the likes of Ted Williams and Stan Musial, others more vulnerable were willing to take a chance.

Eight members of the war-time Giants were prime targets, beginning with the feisty Danny Gardella. An outfielder/first baseman in 1944 and 1945, his fre-quent spats with manager Mel Ott during spring training—mainly related to dissatisfaction regarding

his $5,000 status quo salary—so frustrated Ott that he eventually booted Gardella off the team, leaving him without a contract.

Without hesitation, Gardella contacted Pasquel, al-ready an acquaintance, offering to make the shift down south. In short order he signed for $8,000 (plus housing allowance), a tidy increase over the Giants offer.

Gardella suited up for Vera Cruz in 1946. But when he was prevented from playing in a game against the Negro Leagues Cleveland Buckeyes in New York the following year, he launched a suit against Major League Baseball, "charging conspiracy to restrain free trade and using the reserve clause to deprive him of his right to make a living. Jumpers Max Lanier, Fred Martin, and (Sal) Maglie filed a similar suit shortly thereafter."[3]

Others following Gardella's lead included pitchers Ace Adams and Harry Feldman, two right-handed hurlers whose six-year tenure with the Giants had pro-duced a combined accumulated record of 76–68; 3.65.[4] Both had such rocky starts in 1946 they side-stepped demotion to the minors by joining Gardella in Vera Cruz.

Seldom-used pitcher Adrian Zabala didn't hesitate when offered $8000 to play for Puebla, plus a $7000 signing bonus. Nor did Cuban-born Nap Reyes, a solid infielder for the 1943–45 Giants, and a stalwart of the winter leagues. He remained in Puebla for three sea-sons before being traded to Mexico City in 1949.

Position players George Hausmann and Roy Zim-merman were especially vulnerable. Hausmann, a light-hitting, smooth-fielding second-baseman 1944–45, was aware his chances with the Giants in 1946 were slight. Rookie Zimmerman had played in only 27 games in 1945 and was dismissed when he sought a cost-of-living raise. Both elected to take the plunge. Hausmann signed first with Torreon, then Monterrey, while Zimmerman joined Nuevo Laredo.

In a bizarre sense, their action influenced Sal Maglie's decision to leave as well. When the duo had sought him out for advice, Giants owner Horace Stoneham assumed erroneously that Maglie was also planning to leave. Angered, the boss summarily "fired" all three, even though they had signed contracts. That rash action so infuriated Maglie that he immediately resolved to join the others and take his chances. Some have called this the best baseball decision he ever made. "I will make as much the first year, including my bonus, as I would in five years at my present rate with the Giants," he said at the time.[5]

The three Brooklyn Dodgers who broke for Mexico were outfielder/third baseman Luis Olmo (only the second Puerto Rican to play in the big leagues), catcher Mickey Owen (he of the dropped third strike), and farmhand Roland Gladu of the Montreal Royals. Olmo remained in Mexico and Venezuela throughout the dark years; Owen's southern sojourn was brief and unhappy, leaving him with no place to play; while Gladu returned to Quebec and built a new career as player, manager, and scout within the province.

SOUTH OF THE BORDER

In the spring of 1945, A.B. "Happy" Chandler—a former Senator and Governor of Kentucky—was named Commissioner of Baseball, filling the position left vacant following the death of long-time occupant, Kenesaw Mountain Landis. Never considered one of the titans of baseball, Chandler nevertheless was immediately faced with two unanticipated and delicate matters, both of which had a profound effect on the game and the men who played it.

In 1945 Brooklyn Dodgers' President and General Manager Branch Rickey signed Negro Leagues infielder Jackie Robinson, formerly of the Kansas City Monarchs, to a contract with the Dodgers' Triple-A farm club Montreal Royals, shattering the color barrier that had beclouded Organized Baseball throughout the twentieth century.

Chandler, in spite of pressure to do otherwise, chose not to interfere, allowing the matter to sort itself out in its own good time.

The other challenge was more complicated; how to deal with those major league players who had fled to Mexico. Here his action was swift and unbending, decreeing that all players who jumped their contracts or violated their reserve status were to be banished from baseball for five years, allowing that this ruling would not apply to players who returned to their teams by opening day.[6]

His rationale was clear. "The question was having the penalty severe enough so that it would deter fellas who might want to do the same thing for quick money...I just made it five years and stopped a whole lot of them."[7]

Danny Gardella, poised in Drummondville.

SOCIÉTÉ D'HISTOIRE DE DRUMMOND

For most of the exiles the experience was an unhappy one, and by 1948 almost all had returned to the United States, slightly wealthier but isolated and with no place to play. The Cardinals' Max Lanier perhaps spoke for the majority when he told author Donald Honig, "Conditions down there weren't too good. Half the time you were so sick you couldn't play, you know problems with the water, the whole thing didn't last very long. I stayed in Mexico about a year and a half... [Jorge] Pascal started cutting everybody. He cut me from $20,000 to $10,000. That's when we started jumping back to the States."[8]

Perhaps the two players with the fewest complaints were Reyes and Maglie. Both adapted readily to their circumstances: Reyes remained in Mexico for the duration, while Maglie learned the language and honed his pitching skills into a fine art. It was his great good fortune to play for Puebla under manager Dolf Luque, a former Giants pitching coach and pilot of Maglie's winter Cuban League team.

"Whatever I am as a pitcher," Maglie said in 1956, "I owe to a great extent to Adolfo Luque, the most accomplished teacher of mound techniques the game has seen."[9] Indeed, as Marshall noted: "Maglie developed an outstanding slider by throwing his curve like a fast ball and went on to win twenty games in each of his two seasons [in Mexico]."[10]

A LOST YEAR

As previously mentioned, by 1948 most of the jumpers had returned home only to learn that baseball's doors were firmly closed to them. Not only was the five-year ban still in effect, the commissioner had now specified that if any of the jumpers surreptitiously played for minor league or other low-level clubs they would be suspended for life.

Left with few choices, Max Lanier formed the Max Lanier All-Stars, a travelling collection of players still considered *personae non gratae*. They included five New York Giants: pitchers Feldman and Maglie, infielders Hausmann and Zimmerman, and outfielder Danny Gardella. Missing were Adams (retired), Reyes (Mexico), and Zabala (Sherbrooke).

Lanier recalls: "We went on the road and played about 80 ball games against college and semi-pro teams…But do you know, we got to where we couldn't get a ball game…We knew we couldn't play in professional ballparks against professional ballplayers but [Chandler] shouldn't have tried to stop us from playing against colleges and semi-pro clubs. But he did."[11]

The team mostly circulated through the South and Midwest, bouncing along in a Trailways Bus emblazoned with the words: "MAX LANIER'S ALL STARS." But they ran out of places to play. Resigned to pumping gas in hometown Niagara Falls, Maglie counted this period among the darkest of his life.[12]

REDEMPTION

In 1948, while the Max Lanier All-Stars were traveling cross country, two other jumpers—Gladu and Zabala—were in Quebec Province exploiting an untouched venue ready to welcome jumpers with impunity, and pay well for their efforts. Called the Provincial League, it was an independent circuit centered in the southwest corner of Quebec that paid homage to no one other than itself.

Long a fixture in the province, by 1948 the proudly autonomous and highly competitive loop was increasingly looking for accomplished players of any stripe. And jumpers were fair game. That spring Gladu was named player/manager of the Sherbrooke club. He knew that he and his counterparts could confidently play in the league, without fear of reprisal, simply because league authorities didn't give a damn. They knew they were beyond censure.

Gladu convinced Zabala to sign with Sherbrooke, the region's metropolis, where he put together a magnificent 18–8 record.[13] Two other jumpers also joined that year: Bobby Estalella (St. Jean), who batted .374 with 27 home runs, and Danny Gardella (Drummondville) a late-season arrival.

If 1948 was prelude, 1949 was the real thing: the exiles' moment of redemption. Various Quebec teams took

on 12 of the original 22 jumpers, including five Giants: Feldman, Gardella, Maglie, Zabala, and Zimmerman.

Nevertheless, these twelve outliers comprised only a fraction of the newcomers discovering the league that year. In spite of—or perhaps because of—its informal status as an Outlaw League, a flood of top-notch talent poured in: young Latin players, veterans of the Negro leagues, wartime fill-ins, and gifted locals. Most fans believed at the time that a select team of Provincials could have defeated the Montreal Royals in a nine-inning game if ever given the opportunity.[14]

About the time the league celebrated Opening Day, Commissioner Chandler was growing increasingly troubled, as suits launched by Gardella, Lanier, Martin, and Maglie were coming before the courts. Gardella, still without a contract, was challenging the Reserve rule—that vulnerable bit of legislation binding a player to his club in perpetuity. Lanier and colleagues, having also registered grievances pertaining to "their right to earn a living," now watched and waited. And equally worrisome for Chandler was the alarming possibility that the Provincial League's success as an independent operation might soon serve as a harbinger for others to follow.

With all of these unsettling factors swirling above his desk, the Commissioner did the only thing he could. He lifted the five-year ban two years before it was to end.

As Marshal puts it: "On June 5, [Commissioner Chandler] announced that the jumpers' bans were being reduced from five years to three and that, in spite of the pending suits against baseball, all of the jumpers were now free to return to the game." Players were entitled to rejoin their clubs for a thirty-day trial period, at which time they would be kept, traded or released.[15]

Roy Zimmerman, who led Cubs in home runs.

SOCIÉTÉ D'HISTOIRE DE DRUMMOND

Interestingly, although most of the jumpers chose to return immediately, a few did not. Of the forgotten Giants, Zabala and Feldman, neither enjoying a bumper strong start in 1949, were the only two to depart.[16] Gardella, Maglie, and Zimmerman, teammates in Drummondville, elected to remain, determined to complete the season.

Zimmerman played 91 games that year, batting .245 with 22 home runs and 77 runs batted in, tops on the club. He started out in brilliant fashion, but as the season progressed, his numbers declined dramatically. The probable cause, according to Drummondville catcher Jerome Cotnoir, was an unknown illness, likely ulcers, that struck early in the summer and hampered his game for the rest of the year.[17]

Gardella was clearly the fan favorite. An unusual soul prone to pranks and outrageous actions, he had a good year both off and on the field, batting .281 with 15 home runs and 59 RBIs. "He would sometimes do a double flip and land right on the plate after a home run," remembers Cotnoir. "Another time he began his homerun trot—by running backwards."[18]

Maglie was the most determined and talented of the three. When asked why he remained behind, he gave several reasons. Partly, it was the money, less than the Giants were offering. Partly, it was conditioning. But mainly it was principle. As he told Cotnoir, "I jumped a team once; I'm not about to do it again."[19]

The season ended well for the Cubs, nicely positioned in first place. They made it to the league finals, a 5 of 9 affair where their opponent was the Farnham Pirates, staffed mostly by Negro Leagues imports. Their heavy hitters were Joe Adkins, future major-leaguer Dave Pope and his pitching-brother Willie—and they were determined to win it all.

In the end, the Cubs were victorious although it took nine games to nail down the Championship trophy. Maglie added to the 18 games he won during the regular season with five more in the play-offs, including the grueling ninth game.

And with that, the up-and-down odyssey these Giant jumpers endured—from travels through Mexico and banishment, to Lanier's Trailways bus, to redemption in Quebec's Provincial League—came to a satisfying end. For it was here their suspensions were lifted, more than a year ahead of schedule, and at a time when this bunch of one-time Giants could still delight in the fun part of playing baseball, and make a bundle of money to boot.

POSTSCRIPT

Although the eight forgotten Giants were all invited

Sal Maglie on the cusp of stardom.

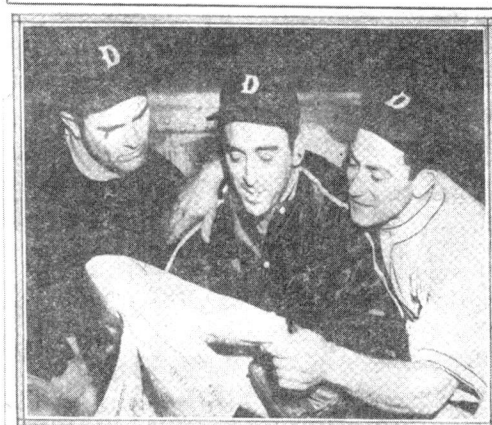

Jumpers Get News From Home

AN ITEM CONCERNING their reinstatement to Organized Ball appears to be of considerable interest to these three ex-major league players who received five-year suspensions in 1946 for jumping to the Mexican League. The players in the uniforms of the Drummondsville club of the Canadian Provincial League are Max Lanier (left), owned by the Cardinals; Sal Maglie, pitcher who is the property of the Giants, and Danny Gardella, former outfielder of the Giants. Lanier and Maglie have asked for reinstatement. Gardella, who has a suit pending against O. B. on anti-trust charges, indicated he has no intention of returning to O. B.

Lanier, Maglie, and Gardella share the good news.

back, little was offered them, apart from Sal Maglie. Ace Adams had retired after one year in Mexico. Harry Feldman settled for two years with the San Francisco Seals. George Hausmann played 16 games with the Giants before joining the Browns' minor league system, playing through 1956. Nap Reyes, after one Giants' at-bat, headed to Jersey City and several different teams through 1954. Adrian Zabala took his 15 games with the Giants in 1949 to the Giants' and Braves' minor leagues, remaining in organized ball until 1956. Roy Zimmerman retired after years with the Oakland Oaks (1950) and Tulsa (1951).

Although Danny Gardella had only one major league at-bat in 1949—before being sent down to Houston and released soon after, pretty well ending his high-minors career—he did come up the big winner on a different front. Major League Baseball, fearing that his legal action might ultimately jeopardize the Reserve Clause, offered to settle for $60,000. Gardella accepted the settlement and split the money with his lawyer.

But it was Sal Maglie who emerged the true star, amassing an enviable record of 119–62, 3.15, over 10 years. He appeared in three World Series, two with the Giants, losing to the Yankees in 1951 and sweeping Cleveland in 1954. In 1956, after being traded to Brooklyn, Maglie defeated Whitey Ford in the World Series opener before later finding himself on the back end of Don Larsen's perfect game, losing 2–0 on five hits. Maglie stepped down in 1958 at age 41, the last of the Giants' forgotten eight to play the game. ■

Notes

1. According to *Baseball Almanac*, MLB's 22 major league jumpers were Ace Adams, Giants; Alex Carrasquel, Senators; Bobby Estalella, Athletics; Harry Feldman, Giants; Moe Franklin, Tigers; Danny Gardella; Giants; Roland Gladu, Braves; Chile Gomez, Senators; George Hausmann, Giants; Red Hayworth, Browns; Chico Hernandez, Cubs; Lou Klein, Cardinals; Max Lanier, Cardinals; Sal Maglie, Giants; Fred Martin, Cardinals; Rene Monteagudo, Phillies; Luis Olmo, Dodgers; Roberto Ortiz, Senators; Mickey Owen, Dodgers; Nap Reyes, Giants; Adrian Zabala, Giants; Roy Zimmerman, Giants.
2. Lee Lowenfish and Tony Lupien, *The Imperfect Diamond: The Story of Baseball's Reserve System and the Men Who Fought to Change It* (New York: Stein and Day, 1980), 125.
3. Charlie Weatherby, Danny Gardella, SABR Bioproject: (SABR, 2014), edited by Bill Nowlin.
4. Baseball-Reference.com: source of all statistical data unless otherwise noted.
5. William Marshall, *Baseball's Pivotal Era 1945–1951* (Lexington, Kentucky, The University Press of Kentucky, 1999), 53.
6. Ibid. 49.
7. Ibid.
8. Donald Honig, "Max Lanier Remembers," *The Armchair Book of Baseball II*, ed. John Thorn (New York: Charles Scribner's Sons, 1987), 184.
9. "Maglie taught how to pitch by Dolf Luque," Daniel, Scripps-Howard staff writer, *The Pittsburgh Press*, September 24, 1956.
10. Marshal, 53.
11. Honig, 184.
12. Judith Testa, *Sal Maglie: Baseball's Demon Barber* (DeKalb, Illinois, Northern Illinois University Press) 81.
13. All statistical information re: Quebec provided by statistician Christian Trudeau.
14. Drummondville starting eight, 1949: Quincy Trouppe, Roy Zimmerman, Stan Bréard, Roger Bréard, Joe Tuminelli, Roberto Vargas, Danny Gardella, Vic Pellot (Power).
15. Marshall, 244.
16. Author conversation with Jerome Cotnoir.
17. Ibid.
18. Ibid.
19. Ibid.

Bats, Balls, Boys, Dreams and Unforgettable Experiences

Youth All-Star Games in New York, 1944–65

Alan Cohen

The summer of 1947 was like few others before it in the annals of New York baseball. The month of August welcomed a heat wave as well as young men (ages 16–18) from all over the United States for two events: the Hearst Sandlot Classic and Brooklyn Against the World All-Stars. Each of the contests was in its second year of existence. Max Kase of the *New York Journal American* had established the Hearst Sandlot Classic in 1946. Hearst papers from 12 cities sent players to face a team of New York's best. That same year, Lou Niss of the *Brooklyn Eagle* invited newspapers from around the country to send players to Brooklyn to face Brooklyn's best.

The initial Hearst Classic was played in 1946 and the New York kids won 8–7 in 11 innings. The second annual Hearst Classic was played August 13, 1947, and produced nine major leaguers. Playing for Ray Schalk's U.S. All-Stars, which won a lopsided 13–2 decision, were three men who would be reunited in the 1960 World Series: Gino Cimoli, Dick Groat, and Bill Skowron. One of the big blows for the visitors was Skowron's eighth-inning inside-the-park homer off Rudy Yandoli, the first home run in the history of the Hearst Classic.

A Classic record 31,232 attended the game which featured Babe Didrikson-Zaharias in a golf and baseball exhibition, and a performance by the Clown Prince of Baseball, Al Schacht, who had also performed at the 1946 Hearst game. Even more notable was an appearance by the game's honorary chairman, Babe Ruth. Ruth took his seat at the start of the third inning of the game and was accorded a standing ovation that stopped the game. His lateness was due to his accepting a series of engagements that would tire the healthiest of men.[1]

The Hearst Newspapers and *The Brooklyn Eagle* were not the first publishing entities to sponsor an All-Star baseball game for the youth of America. With newspapers and periodicals being the dominant form of media, sponsoring baseball events was an attempt to increase circulation. In 1944 and 1945, *Esquire* sponsored All-Star games for 16 to 17-year-old players using an East-West format. The magazine, notorious for its curvaceous "Vargas Girl" caricatures, was seeking to expand into the sports arena.

The August 7, 1944, *Esquire* All-American Boys Baseball Game featured 29 boys from 23 of the then-48 states and was won 6–0 by the East squad in front of 17,803 spectators at the Polo Grounds. The managers in the game were Connie Mack (East) and Mel Ott (West). The dream itinerary included accommodations at the Hotel New Yorker, a visit to the Statue of Liberty, and an Empire State Building tour with former New York Governor and one-time presidential candidate Al Smith.[2] Richie Ashburn from Tilden, Nebraska, caught the final innings and made the game's last out. He was sent east by the *Omaha World-Herald*. Tilden has a baseball diamond with a sign over it that reads: "Tilden Memorial Park–Richie Ashburn Field." Ashburn would return to the Polo Grounds often during his major-league career, covering the expansive center field. In 1962, in his last All-Star appearance, he represented the Mets.

In 1946, the *Brooklyn Daily Eagle* began its "Brooklyn Against the World" competition at Ebbets Field. The forces behind the game were Branch Rickey of the Dodgers and Lou Niss, the sports editor of the *Eagle*. Brooklyn was managed by Leo Durocher, and the World was managed by Hall-of-Famer George Sisler. Henry Tominaga, Lenny Yochim, Roger Breard, Alex Romanchuk, and Joe Della Monica appeared on the "We the People" broadcast on CBS radio.[4] After a performance of *Oklahoma* at the St. James Theater, cast member Beatrice Lynn, who hailed from Flatbush, posed with Chris Kitsos and Joe Torpey of the Brooklyn squad.[5]

The boys woke to rain on August 7. As afternoon turned into evening the rains stopped. At the ballyard, Brooklyn legend Gladys Gooding sang the National Anthem.[6] Also in attendance was Hilda Chester, the most vociferous fan of the Dodgers. Hilda was hard to miss. She came to each game equipped with her cowbells and heckled the opposition with an unmatched fervor. The young "World" players were not

85

spared Hilda's treatment and Brooklyn won the three-game series, 2–1.[7]

Playing right field for Brooklyn in the second game of the series was Ed "Lefty" Ford of the 34th Avenue Boys Club in Astoria Queens and Aviation High School in Manhattan. It was his only appearance in the three games. Ford didn't pitch in BAW but later that summer he would shine.[8] 1946 was the second year for the *Journal-American* Sandlot Alliance championship game. At the Polo Grounds on September 28, pitcher Ford allowed only two hits in 11 innings and struck out 18 batters. He led off the bottom of the 11th inning with a double for his team's first hit, and came around to score the winning run in the 1–0 contest.[9] Ford was awarded the Lou Gehrig Trophy as the game's MVP. A week later, he signed with the Yankees for a $7,500 bonus, and his next game was as a professional. Whitey Ford returned to Ebbets Field to pitch in four World Series and was inducted into the Hall of Fame in 1974.

BAW events would be held in various formats through 1950 and 10 participants—including Ford, Billy Loes, and Joe Pignatano—played in the big leagues. Even more participants found their success elsewhere, fulfilling the vision of men like Lou Niss and his counterpart from the other side of the East River, Max Kase.

Over 100 of the young men from the *Esquire*'s, BAW, and Hearst games made their way to the major leagues. At least one player appeared in the World Series in each year from 1949 through 1975, and in the 1957 World Series, seven participants could trace their starts to these games. There were All-Stars galore, 35 in all. For three consecutive years (1957–59), there were eight alums of the *Esquire*, Brooklyn Against the World, and Hearst programs in each of the All-Star games. And there was at least one alum in every All-Star Game from 1951 through 1978.

Max Kase of the *New York Journal American* created the Hearst Sandlot Classic in 1946. That year, it was known as the Hearst Diamond Pennant Series. Former ballplayer "Rabbit" Maranville directed the *Journal-American* Sandlot Alliance, and managed the *Journal-American* All-Stars. The All-Stars, selected from tryouts held in the leagues that comprised the Alliance, were opposed by the U.S. All-Stars. The visitors were selected by Hearst newspapers in 12 cities from coast to coast, and included representatives from each of the cities. In the first two years, they were managed by Ray Schalk, but Oscar Vitt took over in 1948. For 14 years, Vitt was the lifeblood and face of the U.S. All-Stars. Each year an MVP was selected to receive the Lou Gehrig Award. Five players from these games

(including two New Yorkers) would be selected for enshrinement at Cooperstown. Many of the players from around the country would become part of the fabric of big-league ball in New York. Fifteen played for the Mets, 11 for the Yankees, and two went on to lead New York teams to championships in the World Series.

The inaugural Hearst game was played on August 15 and each visitor spent a week in New York, staying at the Hotel New Yorker. The first few days included a Yankees-Red Sox game, a trip to Long Island's Jones Beach, a reception at Gracie Mansion, the residence of New York's Mayor, and an evening show at Radio City Music Hall, where the movie *Anna and the King of Siam* was on the big screen. On Tuesday, there was a trip around Manhattan Island by boat, which included a view of the Statue of Liberty, followed by a Broadway show—that year it was *Showboat*. On the eve of the game, the boys travelled to West Point and dined on steak at the Bear Mountain Inn. The final highlight: U.S. All-Stars played in front of major league scouts and got to meet with major league players. The game was won, 8–7, in eleven innings by the New Yorkers in front of 15,289 fans.

Billy Harrell, from Troy, New York, was the first black player to appear in the Hearst Classic, playing in 1946 and 1947. In 1946, he starred at the All-Star game held at Albany's Hawkins Stadium on June 15, with three singles and a double in six at-bats, driving in two runs.[10] When he played in the Hearst Classic for the first time, heavyweight champion Joe Louis bought 1,000 tickets for the game, and these tickets were distributed by *The Amsterdam News* to children in Harlem.[11] After playing in the Hearst Classic, he attended Siena College, starring on the basketball court as well as the baseball diamond. Harrell was signed by Hank Greenberg of the Indians in 1952, and played with the Tribe in parts of the 1955, 1957, and 1958 seasons.

Baseball lost Babe Ruth on August 16, 1948, and the Hearst game on August 26 was played in his memory. Joe DiMaggio stepped in as honorary chairman, and each of the players received an autograph from the Yankee Clipper. Dick Groat's one vivid memory of his two games in New York was standing outside in the rain across from St. Patrick's Cathedral during Ruth's funeral on August 19.

There were three Hall-of-Famers in the history of the Hearst Classic. In 1951 Al Kaline set the standard for excellence. He had completed his sophomore year of high school, and at age 16 years, 7 months, and 20 days was one of the youngest players to play in the Hearst Classic. He was accompanied to New York by *Baltimore News-Post* writer Frank Cashen, who would go on to orchestrate the ascendance of the New York Mets during the 1980s. Kaline went 2-for-4 in the Hearst Classic with a single and an inside-the-park homer that sailed over the center fielder's head. In the field, he was equally adept, making five good plays and gunning down a runner at third base.[12] In 1960, long time U.S. All-Star manager Ossie Vitt said, "I could tell he was one of the best prospects I'd ever seen the first time I saw him. He had those wrists with a snap in them, the poise, hustle, and attitude, and how he could throw and run."[13]

Ron Santo was the starting catcher for the U.S. team in 1958, and his hitting display in the practice leading up to the game was beyond impressive. Four of his first five swings were for homers. After starring as an infielder in his early years of high school, he caught as a senior. That fall, Santo was signed for a bonus estimated at $25,000 by the Chicago Cubs. One of their scouts, Dave Kosher, had been watching Santo since his sophomore year in high school, and, with Cubs head scout Roy "Hardrock" Johnson, corralled Santo. After signing with the Cubs, Santo was converted back to third base in his Texas League days. He made his major-league debut with the Cubs in 1960, less than two years after playing in the Hearst Classic, and had a 15-year major league career. He was named to nine All-Star teams, and batted .277 with 342 home runs. He was elected to the Hall of Fame in 2011.

Joe Torre played in the 1958 Hearst game. Torre was a bona fide hitter for the Brooklyn Cadets, but he was significantly overweight and was not considered major league material at either first or third base. His older brother Frank convinced him that his only way to the majors would be as a catcher, and he made the switch. Within a year, he was signed by the Milwaukee Braves. In 1961, he batted .278 and finished second in the rookie-of-the-year balloting. The Braves traded him to St. Louis in 1969, and he had an MVP season in 1971. At the end of his playing career he took over the managerial reins of the Mets as player-manager before switching to managing full time. After several mostly disappointing years managing the Mets, Braves, and Cardinals, he joined the Yankees in 1996. During his 12 years in the Bronx, his teams made it to the postseason every year, winning 10 divisional championships, six American League pennants, and four World Series. He left the Yanks after the 2007 season and managed the Dodgers to Divisional

Championships in 2008 and 2009. On December 9, 2013, he received word that he had been elected to the Hall of Fame.

Davey Johnson, who would manage the Mets to the World Series in 1986, first attracted scouts at San Antonio's Alamo Heights High School. He had just completed his first year at Texas A&M when he played in the 1961 Hearst game. In the regional game in San Antonio he had earned his way to New York with a fielding gem and a line-drive single. He was very highly thought of by Assistant Manager Buddy Hassett who commented, "I like his wrist action and the way he whips the bat around so fast."[14] After the Hearst game, he went back to Texas A&M for his sophomore year, where he played shortstop for "the greatest coach in the world, Tom Chandler, a real classic who taught me real respect for the game, and gave me an opportunity to show what I could do."[15] He signed with Baltimore after his sophomore year. He went on to appear in four World Series, was named to four All-Star teams, and won three Gold Glove Awards.

Tommy Davis won two National League batting titles and batted .302 with 16 homers and 73 RBIs in 154 games for the Mets in 1967. He was listed as Herman Davis from Brooklyn's Boys High School when he played in the Classic in 1955. Hurricane Connie put a damper on things and the game was stopped after 4½ innings with the New Yorkers winning, 4–3. He signed with Brooklyn, but when Davis was ready for the big leagues, the Dodgers were in Los Angeles. In 1962, with the Dodgers, he returned to the Polo Grounds on Memorial Day, when 55,704 fans saw Davis's Dodgers sweep the Mets in a doubleheader. In the first game, Davis went 2-for-5 with a pair of RBIs. A knee injury in 1965 set him back, and the knee would continue

1957 Hearst Sandlot Classic. Mantle and DiMaggio partook in a pre-game home run hitting contest (with Willie Mays). The boys between DiMaggio and Mantle are Thomas Hollman and Frank Heinicke of Pittsburgh.

to give him problems for several years. However, he reemerged as a Designated Hitter in 1973 with Baltimore.

Tony Kubek represented Milwaukee in 1952. His father had played with the Milwaukee Brewers during the 1930s. Tony did not sign right away, as he was only 16 when the game was played in 1952. He gained great experience playing sandlot ball, and caught the eyes of scouts, including Lou Maguolo of the New York Yankees.[16] Kubek's first spring training with the Yankees was in 1954. Five years after appearing in the Hearst game, Kubek was the American League Rookie of the Year.

There were many stars in the 1962 Hearst game which was stopped by curfew after 11 innings and over four hours of play, tied 4–4. It was the only tie in the history of the series. The game's MVP, New York shortstop Joe Russo, made some sparkling plays in the field. He went on to graduate from St. John's University and served as the school's baseball coach for 23 years.

Ron Swoboda got to visit the Mets clubhouse at the Polo Grounds in 1962. In the Hearst game, a very nervous Swoboda went 0-for-4. The following summer Ron was on a Baltimore team that finished second in the All-American Amateur Baseball Federation championship game in Johnstown, Pennsylvania.[17] After the game in Johnstown, Swoboda was signed by Pete Gebrian, a scout for the New York Mets.[18] He made his major-league debut in 1965. He spent nine seasons in the big leagues and is best remembered for his game-saving catch in the ninth inning of the fourth game of the 1969 World Series.

The 1969 Mets also featured a man who had represented San Antonio in the 1961 game. During the week leading up to the 1961 Hearst Game, Jerry Grote roomed with fellow San Antonian Davey Johnson. Johnson remembers sitting on Grote's shoulders while the future Mets catcher was doing pushups to strengthen his arms. Grote signed with Houston in 1962 for a reported bonus of $20,000 and was traded to the Mets in one of a series of trades that would lead the Mets to glory in 1969. He played twelve seasons in Queens, was named to two All-Star teams, and has a rightful place in the Mets Hall of Fame.

Most of the players did not make it to the majors, but their stories are compelling just the same. Howie Kitt of Oceanside, New York, was all over the local papers as a kid. In 1960, Kitt, who had just completed his freshman year at Columbia University, was the starting pitcher for the *Journal-American* All-Stars. In his three innings of work the left hander allowed no hits. His seven strikeouts (six of them were consecutive) set a Hearst record. After five minor league seasons in the

Yankees organization, he left baseball behind him with no regrets and forged a career as an economist. His career took him to the top echelons of antitrust and trade regulation matters.[19]

Over the years, between tryouts, elimination games, and the big events in New York, over one million boys participated in these programs. ■

Sources

In addition to the sources in the notes, the author used Baseball-Reference.com and the following newspapers:
Baltimore News-Post
Milwaukee Sentinel
San Antonio Light

The author also interviewed the following persons for this story.
Dick Groat: 5/21/3014
Billy Harrell: 1/22/2014
Jim Henneman: 07/07/2014
Davey Johnson: 03/10/2015
Howie Kitt: 05/19/2016
Tony Kubek: 5/23/2014
Jim McElroy: 06/06/2014
Joe Russo: 01/22/2015 and 05/27/2017
Ron Swoboda: 1/07/2014

Notes

1. Edgar C. Greene, "Babe Still 'Do as I Please' Guy," *Chicago Herald-American*, August 14, 1947: 24.
2. Bill Leiser, "As Sports Editor Bill Leiser Sees It," *San Francisco Chronicle*, August 3, 1944: 1-H.
3. Mark Kram, "Welcome to Tilden Nebraska: Ashburn grew up in a Quiet, Safe, and Friendly Place, and It Hasn't Changed," *Philadelphia Daily News*, July 26, 1995.
4. "Boro, World Pilots Announce Starting Lineups Tomorrow," *Brooklyn Daily Eagle*, August 5, 1946: 10.
5. "Brooklyn Born and Bred," *Brooklyn Daily Eagle*, August 6, 1946: 13.
6. James Murphy, "Brooklyn All-Stars Seek 2nd Win Tonight," *Brooklyn Daily Eagle*, August 8, 1946: 1, 15–16.
7. "Array of Notables See Brooklyn Triumph," *Brooklyn Daily Eagle*, August 8, 1946: 15.
8. Fay Vincent, *We Would Have Played for Nothing* (New York, Simon and Schuster, 2008), 149–50.
9. "34th Avenue Nine Takes Met Crown with 1–0 Victory: Ed Ford Outstanding Star of 11 Inning Test at Polo Grounds," *Long Island City Star Journal*, September 30, 1946: 12.
10. Dick Walsh. "District's Stars Rally in 10th for 10-7 Victory," *Albany Times-Union*, June 16, 1946: B-7.
11. "Negro on Hearst Sandlot Nine; Louis Tix for Free," *The Amsterdam News*, August 3, 1946: 10.
12. Al Jonas, "U. S. Stars Defeat New York Team in Sandlot Classic," *The Sporting News*, August 15, 1951: 28.
13. Morrey Rokeach, "Vitt Picks Hearst Stars: Kaline, Loes Among Grads of Sandlot Tilts," *New York Journal-American*, August 14, 1960: 29.
14. Rokeach, "Vitt Impressed by Star Nine's Power, Speed," *New York Journal-American*, August 19, 1961: 15.
15. Edward Kersch, "Davey's Destiny," *Cigar Afficionado*, September, 1999.
16. Joseph Wancho. "Tony Kubek" SABR Bio-Project.
17. L. D. McReady, "Brooklyn Cadets top Baltimore in AAABA Title Tilt," *The Sporting News*, August 31, 1963: 39.
18. Len Pasculli. "Ron Swoboda" SABR Bio-Project.
19. "Antitrust and Trade Regulation Specialist Howard Kitt Joins CRA International's New York Office; Founder of NERA's Antitrust Consultancy Offers Wealth of Experience," *Business Wire*, June 2, 2005.

The Remaking of Casey Stengel

Marty Appel

Until the Dodgers and Giants come to their senses and return home to New York, Casey Stengel remains the only figure in history to have worn the uniform of these four New York City teams: the Dodgers, Giants, Yankees, and Mets. The coincidence of this was no small thing to Casey, who died in 1975, but who was aware of the distinction and was occasionally introduced that way at Old Timers gatherings he attended. During his playing days he earned a reputation as one of baseball's clown princes. Who could have predicted that during a long tenure as skipper of the Yankees he would build a reputation as a managerial genius? He could have rested on those laurels all the way into the Hall of Fame, but when the chance to manage the expansion Mets came along, Casey risked his hard won reputation in a return to clown prince status.

The scope of his career includes six different decades, spanning such a long period that he went from the days of John McGraw to the days of Tug McGraw. He chased down fly balls hit by Babe Ruth and platooned Ron Swoboda in left field. He played for the Brooklyn Superbas (later Robins) 1912–17 and the New York Giants 1921–23. He coached for the Brooklyn Dodgers in 1932–33, and managed them 1934–36. He managed the Yankees 1949–1960 and then the Mets 1962–65.

Thirty years of New York baseball in his 54-year career. He batted against Christy Mathewson and sent Cleon Jones up to pinch-hit. When Sandy Koufax no-hit his Mets in 1962, he was asked after the game if Koufax might be the "best he'd ever seen."

"Oh no," he replied without pausing, "that would be Grover Cleveland Alexander."

Casey's path to the majors was relatively swift. He began with the Kankakee Lunatics in 1910. Yes, the Lunatics. Technically they were called the Kankakee Kays, but as their ballpark was located next to an asylum for the insane, the newspapers couldn't resist. So Casey started off as a Lunatic and went from there.

The next year "Dutch" (not yet Casey) was playing for Aurora, Illinois, which by good fortune was a short and direct train connection to Chicago. Brooklyn scout Larry Sutton took a train and watched Stengel play a few games.

"I was always partial to boys with blonde hair and blue eyes," said Sutton. "That combination is always a fighter."

Thanks to the easy train ride, and Stengel enjoying a few good days, he got a Brooklyn contract, and by September 1912 was in the big leagues.

He arrived by train at Penn Station, and took a small hotel room in Times Square. It was his first day ever in New York City, and it would take him several hours by public transportation to find his way to Washington Park in Brooklyn, where he hung his clothes on a nail and shyly introduced himself around.

His teammates (hardly "illustrious"), generally ignored him, as was the fashion with rookies. It even took several days for them let him take batting practice, and to recommend an apartment in Brooklyn (The Fulton Arms near Borough Hall) where some of them lived.

In his very first game, the left-hand hitting prodigy went 4-for-4 and then had the audacity to switch to the right side of the plate for his fifth plate appearance (he walked). He had never been a switch-hitter, and here he was pulling off this stunt in his debut game. The 4-for-4 with two RBIs and three stolen bases remains one of the best debut games in major league history.

He wound up playing in the final game in Washington Park, and the first game in Ebbets Field, hitting the first home run in Ebbets Field.

Casey's time with the Dodgers was very much defined by his relationship with the team's high-profile manager, Wilbert Robinson. Casey was never sure if "Uncle Robbie" liked him or not. He thought Robinson was a lot of fun to play for and Casey's .316 season in 1914 seemed to make him an elite player, but the following year, nursing a shoulder injury, he plunged to .237, one of the lowest batting averages in the league. It did not help his standing when, during spring training of 1915 (the .237 season), he participated in a stunt in which Uncle Robbie was to catch a baseball dropped from an airplane flying over the practice field in Daytona Beach. It turned out it wasn't a baseball, but a grapefruit, which exploded on Robbie's chest, causing him to yell "I'm killed! I'm killed!"

Many blamed Stengel for the stunt gone bad, because by 1915, it seemed like a Stengel thing to do. (He may have been an instigator but was likely not on the plane himself.)

"When you are younger you get blamed for crimes you never committed," he said. "And when you're older you begin to get credit for virtues you never possessed. It evens itself out." If we take him at his word, Casey's later managerial prowess could have been a canny case of letting the press draw their own conclusions from his team's success. But if Casey was a clown, he was a class clown in the school of baseball, learning from every manager he played for and often excelling on the field. Had there been All-Star Games in those days, he would likely have been chosen for two or three.

In 1916, Brooklyn won its first pennant of the twentieth century, losing to Babe Ruth's Red Sox in the World Series. Casey went 4-for-11 (.364) in the Series. In 1917, his final season with Brooklyn, he mastered the right field wall at Ebbets Field, recording 30 outfield assists, a total bettered only five times since. Up until the arrival of the "Boys of Summer" in the late 1940s, Casey would have been in the conversation of notable

Casey Stengel, shown here in 1916, mugging for the camera in Brooklyn's short-lived "checkerboard" uniform (only worn in 1916–17).

outfielders in franchise history. He was certainly a fan favorite, a matter enhanced when he made his return to Ebbets Field after being traded to the Pirates and famously doffed his cap to the crowd, releasing a stunned sparrow he had retrieved in the bullpen between innings. The "giving the fans the bird" incident came to exemplify his zany and colorful persona.

His "time" served in Pittsburgh included World War I military service—back at the Brooklyn Navy Yard, where he got his first real taste of managing. He managed the shipyard team against incoming sailors from other ships. "Play 'em the first day they've landed," he strategized, "before they get over their sea legs." It wasn't Casey's first time in a managerial role, however. A fact rarely mentioned in his career recaps his stint as an assistant manager for the Ole Miss baseball team through a Kansas City connection.

Casey hated playing in Pittsburgh and was even more miserable when they traded him to the Phillies in August 1919. He refused to report, went home, and organized a barnstorming tour. If there had been a commissioner of baseball, this probably would have gotten him kicked out of Organized Baseball. He finally reported in 1920, and was lying on the training table in July 1921 when he was told he'd been traded to the New York Giants. He bolted from the table, ran onto the field, and celebrated by running the bases, sliding into each one. So much for whatever injury had him on the training table. He was going back to New York!

New York was truly the center of the baseball universe. Often four of the sixteen teams were in New York, some days as many as six, and all would socialize in the evenings at select watering holes in Manhattan. Casey, extroverted as he was, came to know everyone in the game.

Happy as he was to be returning to the city he had come to love, it was going to be a very different experience for him. Playing for John McGraw was not like playing for the jolly Uncle Robbie, where rules seemed meant to be broken. McGraw was strict, but Casey also learned a lot about the game under his tutelage. Just sitting in the dugout, listening to McGraw grumble about some botched play was an education. He marveled at how much McGraw knew.

But McGraw saw him mostly as a wiseguy and told him so.

Because of his now advancing age, and the Giants being laden with star players, Casey didn't play as often as he would have liked. Although he'd often been swapped with Joe Riggert and Hy Myers against left-handers in his Robins days, being a part-time player now was his role. Casey would eventually become famous as a master of platoons as a manager himself. McGraw saw the managerial potential in Casey, often letting him coach first base and making him a frequent guest at the McGraw home for late night strategy sessions. One spring McGraw assigned him to coach sort of a "B squad" that trained 200 miles away from the San Antonio "big league" camp. Casey wasn't ready to quit playing for coaching and he let McGraw know he resented it. He "fired" himself and returned to the big camp.

"That's another smart-aleck thing you've done," said McGraw.

Yes, the kid from Kansas City, who used to throw snowballs at men with pipes in an effort to dislodge them, was still a rascal.

Despite not playing every day, Casey was part of Giants championship clubs of 1921, 1922, and 1923. In the 1923 World Series—the first played in Yankee Stadium—he hit an inside-the-park home run to win the first game, and hit one into the right field bleachers to win game three, with a risqué thumb of his nose at the fans as he circled the bases. (Yankees owner Colonel Ruppert wanted him reprimanded; Judge Landis demurred).

Casey's lifetime World Series batting average for 12 games was .393.

And then he was done.

After those Series heroics, McGraw traded him to the hapless Boston Braves.[1] His playing career was nearly over, his professional managing career about to begin—first at Worcester (1925) and then at Toledo (1926–31), until the Depression left the team—and the Stengels—broke.

He leaped at an offer to become a Brooklyn Dodgers coach in 1932–33, and then succeeded Max Carey as the club's manager in 1934. This was a low-budget team going nowhere, and after three second-division seasons, he was fired and paid not to manage in 1937. It was his only year out of uniform between 1910 and 1960. And all he did in that year off was invest in a Texas oil field that made him a rich man.[2]

Signed to manage the Boston Bees in 1938, Casey stayed for six lackluster years with four seventh place finishes. His final year, 1943, began with his being run over by a car in Kenmore Square before opening day and missing almost three months of work.

He followed that with five more seasons of minor league managing, including the Yankees farm club in hometown Kansas City in 1945. At Oakland, 1946–48, he managed a colorful group of veterans (and a very young Billy Martin), and won the Pacific Coast League championship in 1948 as the Yankees were disposing of their manager, Bucky Harris.

In a surprise hiring, the Yankees named him Harris's successor, handing him the most coveted managing position in the game (along with Harris's number 37).

"They hired a clown," screamed the multitudes, feeling him a most un-Yankee-like choice.[3] His record as a manager was certainly lackluster to that point. But the screaming abated after he won the 1949 world championship (despite more than 70 team injuries), during which time he perfected his version of platooning (it helped to have a lot of talent on the bench and various injuries forced him to be creative to great effect) and Stengelese—his unique brand of doubletalk which would enable him to circle around a question until he felt he had avoided or answered it. The writers—"my writers" he called them—found it amusing. Casey had found a way to take his "clown prince" mantle and wear it to shrewd advantage.

The '49 championship erased all doubts about his managing prowess. By the time he had rolled off a fifth straight world championship, not only was he no longer a "clown," he was on his way to Cooperstown. Although the Joe McCarthy-era Yankees like Joe DiMaggio and Phil Rizzuto never quite warmed to him, his own players—notably Yogi Berra, Whitey Ford, and Mickey Mantle—were carving out their own Hall of Fame careers under his leadership.

Casey rode championship after championship through the '50s, losing only to oil partner Al Lopez's 1954 Cleveland Indians, and Lopez's 1959 Chicago White Sox. When the Yankees fired him after he lost a seven-game World Series to Pittsburgh in 1960 ("I'll never make the mistake of being 70 again," he said), the Baby Boomer generation had lost a father figure. But all things must pass. The Yankees felt Casey mismanaged the pitching rotation in the '60 World Series, but they also did not want to lose manager-in-waiting Ralph Houk, who was being pursued by both Detroit and Boston.

At that point in his career, Casey could have hung up his jersey for good. He would no doubt have been remembered as a colorful but astute mastermind of the game and a Hall of Fame shoo-in. But after sitting out 1961 in Glendale, largely to work on his autobiography, he allowed the expansion New York Mets to pluck him out of retirement and bring him back to New York. He and his wife Edna (neé Lawson) would continue to reside at the Essex House on Central Park South, as they had done throughout his Yankee years, even after the Mets moved to Shea Stadium in 1964 and the taxi fare to Flushing soared to six dollars! But first would come two seasons at the Polo Grounds, where he had played for the Giants, where he had met Edna, and where he had butted heads with McGraw.

The Mets got a lot right immediately—the name, the announcers, the logo, the team song, the mascot, the uniform, the fans chanting "let's go Mets," and hiring a legend as manager.

But Casey was a different manager with the Mets. The year off from baseball and the realization that he was now in his 70s seemed to take a lot of the fire from his belly. Even late in his Yankee career, he was deeply engaged in the games, thinking three innings ahead, pushing the right buttons. With the Mets, he more or less turned over daily control to his coaches, Cookie Lavagetto and Solly Hemus, and let center fielder Richie Ashburn run things on the field. Casey (or the coaches), could still platoon, but now it involved sending in bad players to replace bad players. The Mets had done so many things right except build a talented roster. Realizing this, Casey's best managerial move was to steer attention away from this horrible, 40–120 team, and onto the power of his personality. As it turned out, that was the winning move. The writers loved having him and admired his longevity and wit, and his ability to touch history.

While Casey became the face of the franchise, his coaches would work the pitching rotation, do the lineup, "suggest" pinch-hitters and defensive replacements. Roger Craig, his leading pitcher, was influential in evaluating pitching prospects, perhaps just as much as coaches Red Kress and Red Ruffing.

"Ain't like the old days," he whispered to Gene Woodling in the dugout one afternoon, winking. Woodling had been with the Yankees for the five straight; now, he was playing out his career with Casey at the Mets.

Yes, Casey might occasionally doze off in the dugout, but his old Yankee boss George Weiss (now the Mets president), and Joan Payson and M. Donald Grant (ownership) did not seem to mind. The team was considered an immediate hit, even though they averaged a mere 9,000 fans a game against the seven teams who were not the Dodgers and Giants. The

illusion of success was strong, and Casey, once the "clown," also proved to be an illusionist of sorts.

By the time the team moved to Shea in 1964, even some of his writers were thinking the Stengel era had run its course; it was time to shake up this now dull franchise. Even Casey was running out of jokes to distract from the bad play.

It ended for Casey in 1965 when he broke his hip in a fall that no one saw after an Old Timers party in mid-season. He was, at 75, the oldest man in uniform and one of the oldest managers in history. Hall of Fame induction would be speeded up to include him the following year, and he would spend the remaining ten years of his life living the good life in Glendale, but ever a presence on the baseball scene, whether in spring training, at banquets, in Cooperstown, or at Old Timers gatherings. ∎

Select Bibliography

Allen, Maury. *You Could Look it Up*. New York. Times Books. 1979.

— *Now Wait a Minute, Casey!*.Garden City, N.Y. Doubleday. 1965

Appel, Marty. *Casey Stengel. Baseball's Greatest Character*. New York. Doubleday. 2017.

Bak, Richard. *Casey Stengel: A Splendid Baseball Life*. Dallas. Taylor. 1997.

Creamer, Robert. *Stengel: His Life and Times*. New York. Simon and Schuster. 1984.

Durso, Joseph. *Casey: The Life and Legend of Charles Dillon Stengel*. Englewood Cliffs NJ. Prentice-Hall. 1967.

Goldman, Steven. *Forging Genius. The Making of Casey Stengel*. Dulles, VA. Potomac Books, 2005.

Graham, Frank Jr., *Casey Stengel: His Half-Century in Baseball*. New York, John P. Day Co. 1958.

Howard, Arlene with Ralph Wimbish. *Elston and Me: The Story of the First Black Yankee*. Columbia, MO. University of Missouri Press. 2001

Koppett, Leonard. *The New York Mets: The Whole Story*. New York. Macmillan. 1970.

Stengel, Casey and Harry Paxton. *Casey at the Bat*. New York. Random House. 1962.

Stengel, Edna. Unpublished memoir. 1958.

Vecsey, George. *Joy in Mudville*. New York. McCall. 1970.

Notes

1. McGraw did bring Casey back in a Giants uniform for a European tour after the 1924 season, which doubled as a Stengel honeymoon.

2. A player, Randy Moore, whose father had invested in an oil well, got Casey and Al Lopez into a small group backing it, and the well came in. It made Casey a rich man for the rest of his life. That well is still pumping oil.

3. Forty-eight years later, "Clueless Joe" Torre, a longtime unsuccessful National League manager, received much the same greeting in New York.

Brooklyn, The Dodgers...and The Movies

Rob Edelman

As major league ballyards across America were celebrating the 2013 baseball season's Opening Day, a high-profile new film about a deceased player from a bygone team came to movie theaters. That film was *42*—a biopic charting the life and legend of Jackie Robinson of the beloved Brooklyn Dodgers.

While addressing the crowd at Cooperstown's Doubleday Field during Hall of Fame weekend later that summer, Thomas Tull, the film's producer—whose credits range from *The Dark Knight* to *The Hangover* to *Ninja Assassin*—observed that *42* is "the most important film I'll ever do." And he added: "After making *Batman*, *Superman*, and other superhero movies, the greatest 'superhero' movie that could be made is about Jackie Robinson."[1]

Yet this recent Jackie film is not the first.[2] Way back in 1950—63 years earlier—the ballplayer's struggles were depicted in *The Jackie Robinson Story*. That film may cover essentially the same territory as *42*, but the earlier version is a mirror of its era and a valuable social history. Beyond the rare pleasure of seeing the real number 42 playing himself and reciting his lines, the scenario deals with issues that transcend singles, doubles, and dingers. *The Jackie Robinson Story* dates from the dawn of the civil rights movement; when it was released, 21-year-old Martin Luther King Jr. had recently received his B.A. from Morehouse College and was a second-year student at Crozer Theological Seminary. *Brown v. Board of Education* was four years in the future and the signing into law of the Voting Rights Act would be 15. No one could foretell the scope of the demand by black Americans to embrace equal rights with white Americans, but Hollywood, after years of marginalizing black characters, was belatedly acknowledging its biased depiction of African-Americans; previously, the industry consistently had trivialized them as stereotypical mammies and janitors, train porters and shoeshine boys whose eyes popped out of their heads while they fractured the English language.

The Jackie Robinson Story put forth the idea that for every exclusionary bigot in America, there is a man who is fair and humane, a man who would judge Jackie solely on his performance between the foul lines. In other words, for every racist, there is a Branch Rickey. *The Jackie Robinson Story* heralded a new, refreshing—and, by 1950s standards, radical—celluloid depiction of black Americans and racism American-style. Plus, its star was not the lone future Hall of Famer appearing onscreen. Dick Williams, then a twenty-year-old Brooklyn minor leaguer, is in two sequences, playing two different roles. "First, I was a second baseman," he recalled. "They shot that in one day. The next day, they needed a pitcher. So I did that, too."[3] In the film, there is extensive footage of Williams as the Jersey City hurler who pitches to Jackie in his first minor league game.

Of course, not all Brooklyn-centric baseball films highlight Jackie Robinson, or even the Dodgers. *Rhubarb* (1951) is a slapstick about a tough, spirited alley cat who is taken in by the eccentric millionaire owner of the big-league Brooklyn Loons. Upon his master's demise, Rhubarb becomes the principal heir, inheriting $30-million—not to mention those lovable Loons. Baseball also plays a small but significant role in *The Chosen* (1982), an adaptation of the Chaim Potok novel. The setting is World War II and the story opens with boys playing ball in a Brooklyn schoolyard. One team is consists of Americanized Jews while the other is made up of Hasidic Jews; their competition illustrates their collective assimilation into the American mainstream at a time when those left behind in Europe were being slaughtered by Adolf Hitler.

But films like *Rhubarb* and *The Chosen* are the exceptions. Prior to the Dodgers abandoning Brooklyn for the California orange groves, the borough and its big league nine were inexorably linked by Hollywood. On occasion, they were united in entire films, while other storylines only featured Dodgers references or sequences. As a whole, however, these films capture the flavor of baseball Ebbets Field-style, with the wear-your-emotions-on-your-sleeve enthusiasm of the Dodgers diehards.

Perhaps the quintessential Brooklyn baseball film is one that is little-seen and barely remembered.

Though the names of Hall of Famers Christy Mathewson, Walter Johnson, Dazzy Vance, Grover Cleveland Alexander, and Tony Lazzeri are casually dropped into the script, neither the Dodgers nor Ebbets Field are cited by name. Still, *It Happened in Flatbush* (1942) embodies the essence of the borough during a long-ago era. Though the on-screen image is that of the Brooklyn Bridge, the opening credits feature a soundtrack of "Take Me Out to the Ball Game."

The scenario charts what happens when Frank Maguire (Lloyd Nolan), a washed-up ex-ballplayer who "used to be shortstop for Brooklyn," is resurrected as the team's skipper. Upon his hiring, the team's owner tells Maguire: "See you in New York"—and he is quick to respond: "Not New York. Brooklyn." The woman who eventually inherits the club is no baseball fan. We know this because she resides in Manhattan, whose residents are referred to as "foreigners." And Brooklyn is labeled "the best baseball town in America," with its residents loudly, endlessly arguing—and not just about sports. But bats and balls are at the core of the story. One fan even rushes onto the field to belt an umpire, while another proudly declares: "Baseball belongs to the people, and the Brooklyn team belongs to us."

The Dodgers are cited by name in other period titles. *Once Upon a Honeymoon* (1942) stars Ginger Rogers as a Brooklynite who came of age near Ebbets

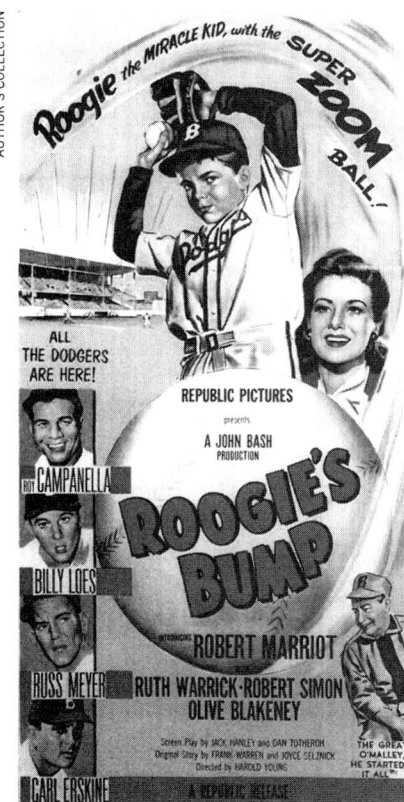

AUTHOR'S COLLECTION

Roogie's Bump is a 1954 kiddie film featuring appearances by real-life Brooklyn Dodgers Roy Campanella, Billy Loes, Russ Meyer, and Carl Erskine. No explanation is necessary for the line that appears in the bottom right-hand corner: "The Great O'Malley, He Started It All."

Field and who quips: "Foul balls used to light in my backyard" before sighing "Dem lovely Bums." The opening sequence in *Arsenic and Old Lace* (1944) features loudmouthed Dodgers fanatics and brawling players at Ebbets Field. The *It Happened in Brooklyn* (1947) scenario stresses that every genuine Brooklynite knows that the Ebbets address is "Bedford and Sullivan"; upon arriving home after four years in the military, Brooklynite Frank Sinatra immediately spots a poster advertising a ballgame ("Game Today Ebbets Field Dodgers vs. Cubs"). The musical *The West Point Story* (1950) includes a "Brooklyn" production number, one of whose lines is: "They know my shield from Ebbets Field to Cheyenne..." The Dodgers first—and lone—World Series title is acknowledged in *The Man in the Gray Flannel Suit* (1956), the tale of a stressed-out suburbanite (Gregory Peck) who travels into Manhattan by train every workday. On one occasion, the man sitting beside him dourly declares: "There's no use trying. I just can't get used to it." "Used to what?" he asks. His fellow commuter responds: "The idea of the Brooklyn Dodgers as world champions."

Big Leaguer (1953) was made two years after Bobby Thomson's shot-heard-round-the-world resulted in the Dodgers' embracing defeat yet again. Though the film is New York Giants-centric—with Edward G. Robinson playing "Hans" Lobert, an ex-big leaguer who runs a Giants' Melbourne, Florida tryout camp—the finale features a game between the Giants prospects and Dodgers rookies. The Brooklynites are leading, 7–4, in the ninth inning when Carl Hubbell, on hand to evaluate Lobert's players, offers insight into the heart of baseball by observing: "The game's now getting interesting."

Among all the actors who've played fans of all stripes, the one who embodies the essence of the baseball zealot is William Bendix. Certainly, Bendix's role in baseball movies extends way beyond his characterization of The Bambino in *The Babe Ruth Story* (1948)—arguably one of the worst-ever baseball biopics. For indeed, during World War II, one of the character types found in a typical military unit in a typical Hollywood war movie is played most memorably by Bendix: the energetic Brooklynite, a lovable "woiking class" Joe who endlessly blabs on about Dem Bums while bullets from the guns of the heinous "Japs" and "Krauts" zip by overhead. For after all, weren't our boys in uniform battling Hitler, Tojo, and Mussolini to preserve baseball as much as mom's apple pie and the red, white, and blue?

In *Guadalcanal Diary* (1943), Bendix plays Taxi Potts, an affable jokester and Brooklyn cabbie-turned-US Marine. The film opens with Potts and his fellow

GIs on board a transport somewhere in the South Pacific, heading for a Japanese beachhead. "If I was back home, I wouldn't be on no boat…," he quips. "Ebbets Field. That's for me. Watchin' them beautiful Bums… Just leadin' the league… That's all, just leadin' the league… You got any dough which says the Yanks'll take the Bums in the Series?" (The year is 1942 and, later on, the marines listen to a World Series radio report in which the Bronx nine faces off against… the St. Louis Cardinals!) But Potts's Dodgers devotion is endless. Just before landing at Guadalcanal, he admits: "…times like these kinda make me wish I was back in Brooklyn, drivin' my cab with the fast meter and keepin' an eye on them Bums." While digging a fox-hole, he notes: "Maybe if we dig deep enough, we'll come up somewhere around Ebbets Field."

Not all of Bendix's Borough of Churches characters are in the military. In *Lifeboat* (1944), he plays Gus Smith, a stoker on a freighter destroyed by a German U-boat. "What a day for a ballgame," he feverishly declares while struggling to maintain his sanity on the lifeboat. The Cardinals may be "the team to watch this year" because they "got hitters… Stan Musial's been clubbin' 'em," but he adds: "If the Dodgers only had a guy like Ernie Bonham, or even Johnny Humphries." He then conjures up a fictional game between Brook-lyn and Pittsburgh. The pitching matchup will "probably be [Whitlow] Wyatt for the Dodgers, [Rip] Sewell for the Pirates. I think I'll take Rosie (to) Ebbets Field. It's gonna be a good game this afternoon."

The actor also portrays a baseball-loving Brook-lynite in a trio of Hal Roach "streamliners": films with lengths between that of a short subject and feature. Their titles are *Brooklyn Orchid* (1942); *The McGuerins from Brooklyn*, also known as *Two Mugs from Brook-lyn* (1943); and *Taxi, Mister* (1943), all of which chart the misadventures of Tim McGuerin (Bendix) and Eddie Corbett (Joe Sawyer), the rough-hewn but affa-ble co-owners of a Brooklyn taxi company.

The McGuerins from Brooklyn may have been ad-vertised as a comedy in which Bendix and Sawyer "…Bat Out Laughs Like the Dodgers Bat Out Runs," but baseball is most prevalent in *Taxi, Mister*. The sce-nario has McGuerin pitching on a sandlot ball team; Corbett is the catcher; their nine is named for one of the most celebrated Brooklyn neighborhoods: Flat-bush. A mobster plots to do in McGuerin during a game but, in a sequence which ends in a free-for-all, the pitcher's ability to throw a wicked curveball allows him to knock out the bad guy.

On other occasions, real-life Dodgers show up on-screen. *Whistling in Brooklyn* (1943) stars Red Skelton

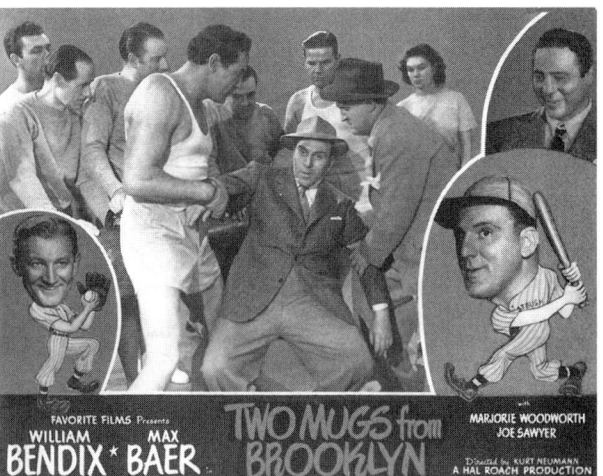

Two Mugs from Brooklyn (also known as *The McGuerins from Brooklyn*) is one of three World War II-era "streamliners" featuring William Bendix and Joe Sawyer as baseball-loving Brooklynites.

as a popular radio sleuth who is involved in off-the-air murder and mayhem; he comes to Ebbets Field and mixes with Leo Durocher, Arky Vaughan, Ducky Med-wick, and Billy Herman, among others. Plus, as Herman comes to bat, who should appear on-camera but the inimitable Hilda Chester, Dodgers fan extraordinaire. (Hilda, Leo, Pee Wee Reese, Pete Reiser, Eddie Stanky, and Red Barber appear in *Brooklyn, I Love You*, a Para-mount short subject spotlighting the Dodgers' 1946 campaign.) Billy Loes, Carl Erskine, Russ Meyer, and Roy Campanella play themselves in *Roogie's Bump* (1954), a *Rookie of the Year* precursor involving a little boy who, via the maneuvering of Red O'Malley, a de-ceased Dodgers pitching star, becomes the "miracle kid with the super zoom ball" who fires horsehides with the "speed of light." Walter O'Malley is not to be seen but his influence is obvious, as hurler O'Malley is noth-ing less than saintly, and even is patronizingly referred to as the "Great O'Malley."

Three years later, the Dodgers abandoned Brook-lyn and O'Malley no longer was "great"—at least in the souls of Brooklynites. *Sweet Smell of Success* came to theaters in June 1957, scant months before the team's Brooklyn swan song. In the film, slimy press agent Sidney Falco (Tony Curtis) tells the secretary of ruthless newspaper columnist J.J. Hunsecker (Burt Lancaster): "Don't try to sell me the Brooklyn Bridge. I happen to know it belongs to the Dodgers." But Falco was of course dead-wrong. This repartee is contrasted to another Tony Curtis film: *Some Like It Hot* (1959), which is set in Chicago in 1929. The following dia-logue may be lost on twenty-first-century viewers who are neither baseball, movie, nor American history savvy, but it resonated with then-contemporary movie-goers. At one point, saxophonist Joe (Curtis) queries his pal Jerry (Jack Lemmon), a double-bass player: "Jerry boy, why do you have to paint everything so black?... Suppose the stock market crashes. Suppose Mary Pickford divorces Douglas Fairbanks. Suppose the Dodgers leave Brooklyn..."[4]

For decades after their departure, Brooklyn Dodgers nostalgia permeated American movies. In *Kramer vs. Kramer* (1979), a father (Dustin Hoffman) who hails from the borough tells his son (Justin Henry) about his childhood: "We listened to the radio... We didn't have diet soda. We had egg creams... We didn't have the Mets, but we had the Brooklyn Dodgers. And we had the Polo Grounds. And we had Ebbets Field. Oh boy, those were the days." Fact and fiction merge in *Simple Men* (1992), featuring a central character who was the Dodgers' all-star shortstop during the 1950s— and who is decidedly not Pee Wee Reese. After his playing career ended, the ballplayer (known as "Dad," played by John MacKay) became an anarchist who allegedly tossed a bomb at the Pentagon during the late 1960s, killing seven people. But in no way is his baseball career marginalized. "I saw your father play with the Dodgers back in '56," a cop tells one of his sons. "He was the greatest shortstop who ever lived, no matter what anyone says about him."

Brooklyn (2015), based on Colm Tóibín's novel and set in the early 1950s, is the story of Eilis Lacey (Saoirse Ronan), a shy Irish lass who leaves her smalltown home, sets off for America, and settles in the title borough. Once there, Eilis is pursued romantically by Tony (Emory Cohen), a blue-collar Brooklynite of Italian extraction who lives and breathes Dodger-blue. At one point, Eilis is told that she will "have to go to Ebbets Field if you want to see (Tony) in the summer." She then asks Tony: "They're that important to you?" And he responds: "Put it this way, if our kids end up supporting the Yankees or the Giants, it would break my heart."

A far less misty-eyed take is found in *Smoke* and *Blue in the Face* (both 1995), based on works by Newark, New Jersey native and longtime Brooklyn resident Paul Auster, which offer portraits of the borough pre-gentrification. At one point, one of its characters, who is old enough to recall the Dodgers in Brooklyn, tellingly explains: "If there was probably a childhood trauma that I had, other than the Dodgers leaving Brooklyn which, if you think about it, is a reason why some of us are imbued with a cynicism that we never recovered from. Obviously, you're not a Mets fan and you can't possibly be a Yankee fan. So baseball is eliminated from your life, because of being born in Brooklyn." And he concludes: "Maybe I don't like baseball because the Dodgers aren't here anymore..."

The title character in *The Angriest Man in Brooklyn* (2014) is no grouchy golden ager who also misses Dem Bums. He is Henry Altmann (Robin Williams), a perpetually enraged (not to mention terminally-ill) individual. Altmann is surrounded by hostile, endlessly kvetching Brooklynites; however, a once-upon-a-happier-time is represented in a black-and-white photo of two Dodgers jacket-clad boys posing with their father in Ebbets Field.[5]

Finally, during the 2016 presidential race, *My X-Girlfriend's Wedding Reception* (1999), an otherwise obscure low-budget throwaway, became a hot online ticket. The reason: Playing a rabbi named Manny Shevitz—remember, this *is* a comedy—is none other than Bernie Sanders. He is billed as "Congressman Bernie Sanders" and his yarmulke-clad character addresses the wedding guests by observing: "Today we celebrate life: a very sacred part of life." That's fair enough, coming from a rabbi. But then Rabbi Manny, after declaring that he, like the man who plays him, was born and bred in Brooklyn, goes on a riff about the tragedy of the Dodgers leaving the Borough of Churches. Then, as if addressing a convention of sports fans rather than a wedding party, he segues into a criticism of baseball free agency. ∎

Notes

1. http://wamc.org/post/rob-edelman-now.
2. Robinson also is the central character in two made-for-TV movies. Andre Braugher plays him in *The Court-Martial of Jackie Robinson* (1990), involving his plight upon refusing to move to the back of a bus while in the US Army during World War II. Blair Underwood plays him in *Soul of the Game* (1996), centering on his interaction with Satchel Paige and Josh Gibson at the time of his signing by Branch Rickey. In *Blue in the Face* (1995), Keith David appears as the ghost of Jackie Robinson. And in Spike Lee's *Do the Right Thing* (1989), Mookie the pizza delivery guy (played by Lee) comes to work garbed in a number 42 jersey. But Jackie is missing from another TV movie: *It's Good to Be Alive* (1974), a Roy Campanella biopic.
3. Rob Edelman. "The Jackie Robinson Story: A Reflection of Its Era," *NINE: A Journal of Baseball History & Culture*, Fall 2011, 40–55.
4. A link between Brooklyn past and present is found in *Captain America: The First Avenger* (2011), which is written up in detail in "More Baseball in Non-Baseball Films," published in the Spring 2015 issue of the *Baseball Research Journal* (76–82). To summarize: The time is World War II and Brooklyn-born 90-pound weakling Steve Rogers (Chris Evans) has been transformed into the muscular title character. At one point, he hears a Dodgers-Phillies game broadcast on the radio from Ebbets Field. Only there's a problem. The scenario may be set during the war, but this particular contest was played pre-Pearl Harbor: in May, 1941. He knows this because he was in the stands; the fictional Steve Rogers was one of the 12,941 fans on hand that day. Something is amiss... and this knowledge on Rogers's part further propels the plot.
5. Pictured in the 1955 photo is five-year-old Phil Alden Robinson (the director of *The Angriest Man in Brooklyn* as well as *Field of Dreams*), his older brother, and their father.

Remembering Earl—Not George—Toolson

The Plaintiff Who Took the New York Yankees to the US Supreme Court

Ed Edmonds

On November 9, 1953, the United States Supreme Court issued a one paragraph opinion in *Toolson v. New York Yankees, Inc.*[1] The decision affirmed three lower federal court decisions that turned aside lawsuits challenging the Court's 1922 ruling regarding the application of the nation's antitrust laws to Organized Baseball.[2] The concluding sentence succinctly declared that "without re-examination of the underlying issues, the judgments below are affirmed on the authority of *Federal Baseball Club of Baltimore v. National League of Professional Baseball Clubs*…so far as that decision determines that Congress had no intention of including the business of baseball within the scope of the federal antitrust laws."[3] Although the majority opinion was challenged by a much lengthier and strenuously argued dissent by Justices Harold H. Burton and Stanley Reed, the *Toolson* decision reinforced baseball's exemption from antitrust challenge.

Nearly two decades later in *Flood v. Kuhn*, the Court revisited the question again, ultimately determining that "with its reserve system enjoying exemption from the federal antitrust laws, baseball is, in a very distinct sense, an exception and an anomaly. *Federal Baseball* and *Toolson* have become an aberration confined to baseball….Accordingly, we adhere once again to *Federal Baseball* and *Toolson* and to their application to professional baseball."[4] The decisions in all three cases are frequently criticized, but they are still legally important. In the past few years, the reach of baseball's antitrust exemption was a critical factor in two cases reaching conflicting conclusions in cases dealing with broadcast blackout restrictions and franchise relocation.[5]

The life and baseball career of the plaintiff at the heart of the 1953 *Toolson* case is largely unknown. In fact, he is almost always identified as George Toolson, his given first and last names, or his complete name, George Earl Toolson, used in the legal documents surrounding the case. Because George Earl Toolson's father was also named George, the son was known by family and teammates by his middle name Earl. This article will address the life of the very real man behind one of baseball's major legal challenges against its

business practices. Rather than focus on the federal court decisions, this article will review Earl's early years in Burley, Idaho, his college years at Willamette, his military service during World War II, his minor league career, and the reasons behind his decision to file a lawsuit against the New York Yankees.

EARL'S EARLY LIFE

Earl Toolson was born in Burley, Idaho, on September 30, 1922, the second son of George H. and Ella Matthews Toolson. Burley is primarily located on the southern side of the Snake River in Cassia County in the south central part of the state adjacent to the path of the Oregon Trail. The town was founded in 1905, just 15 years after Idaho gained statehood, incorporated in 1909, and named for Oregon Short Line Railroad Company passenger agent David E. Burley.[6]

Earl's parents were married in Salt Lake City on February 24, 1920. George, Earl's father, was a dentist. The family first lived on Miller Avenue where Earl's older brother Tom was born on January 27, 1921. Earl's sister Margaret arrived in 1925, and William ("Bill") followed a little over two years later. The burgeoning family moved to Conant Avenue, and Earl's youngest brother James Richard ("Dick") was born in 1934.[7] George displayed an early interest in baseball, helping to organize games and teams in the young city. He later managed American Legion teams that included Tom and Earl. Earl's prowess emerged at an early age; as a 15-year-old he pitched for the Burley team in the Northwest Regional Legion Junior Baseball Championship on August 13, 1938. Unfortunately, he was "erratic" on the mound and his team's six errors contributed to a 14–2 loss to the Postoffice Pharmacy team from Portland, Oregon.[8] The following year, Earl pitched and led his Burley team to a 16–15 victory over Twin Falls to take the Idaho south-central district championship by striking out 18 and batting 3-for-4 with a three-run homer.[9] During the summer of 1940, Earl also pitched for the Idaho Falls Tigers in the Idaho semi-pro tourney.[10] Earl starred in baseball, basketball, and track at Burley High School.

WILLAMETTE UNIVERSITY

After graduating from high school, Earl enrolled at Willamette University in Salem, Oregon, where he starred in both baseball and basketball for the Bearcats. He also participated in track and earned letters in all three sports. As a freshman, Earl started Willamette's initial game of the 1941 baseball season, a 10–0 victory over the Greys, a team composed of inmates at the state penitentiary. Described as "the widely heralded Idaho youngster," Toolson hurled "smoothly despite nervousness, striking out six, walking three, and allowing but two hits."[13] On April 12, 1941, "Big" Earl tossed a 6–0 shutout, scattering nine hits while striking out 11 to defeat the University of Oregon Ducks.[14] Earl, a right-handed pitcher, was often described as big. He was variously listed during his career at either six feet or 6-foot-1 and weighing 195–208 pounds (with an excellent curve ball).

Earl pitched the first game of the Northwest Conference championship series against Whitman College on May 22, 1941. Despite Toolson recording 11 strikeouts, Whitman defeated Willamette 8–3 at the Blues diamond in Walla Walla, Washington.[15] Whitman relied on six errors in the first two games to capture the championship.[16] Earl led the Silverton Red Sox semi-pro team to the Oregon state championship during the summer of 1941.[17] During the 1942 Willamette season, Toolson dropped a "well pitched ball game" to the Oregon State Beavers 4–3, when the Corvallis nine scored twice in the ninth to earn a come-from-behind triumph.[18] The Oregon Ducks prevailed over Toolson in the second game of a doubleheader on April 4, pushing across three unearned runs in the eighth inning for a 5–2 win.[19] The following year the Bearcats avenged their 1941 loss to Whitman by capturing the Northwest Conference title on May 23, winning the first game 6–0 while Earl lost the second game, 2–1, a 7-inning decision to the Blues despite giving up only two hits.[20] With fellow pitchers Bill Hanauska and Jack Richards, Earl formed Willamette coach Spec Keene's "The Big Three." In 1942, all three signed minor league deals.[21]

1942

Soon after the completion of Willamette's season, Earl signed with Boston Red Sox scout Ernie Johnson for a $2,500 signing bonus. He was assigned to Boston's Greensboro, North Carolina, franchise to begin his minor league career.[22] The B-level Greensboro Red Sox won the Piedmont League crown during the playoffs after finishing the year functionally tied for first place, mere percentage points ahead of the Portsmouth Cubs with a 78–53 record.[23] Hall of Famer Heinie Manush was the Red Sox manager. Earl posted a 2–5 record with a 4.86 ERA in 11 games. In 63 innings, Toolson surrendered 58 hits and 46 runs with 34 of those runs earned. Earl displayed a career-long issue by issuing 48 walks for the Red Sox. In an era before WHIP was an acknowledged statistic, Earl checked in at 1.683 for the season. In the fall, Earl returned to Willamette, where he noted in an interview with *Statesman Journal* columnist Al Lightner that many of his appearances were in relief because Manush "didn't want to take any chances with the rookies" while the team battled Portsmouth for the league crown.[24]

1943

In 1943, Earl was promoted to the Double-A American Association Louisville Colonels. He appeared in the Colonels' May 5 opening day 7–4 loss to Columbus, entering the game in the fourth inning with Louisville trailing, 5–3. *Louisville Courier-Journal* writer Tommy Fitzgerald described Earl as "a boy from Idaho who can throw the potato" and noted that in $3\frac{2}{3}$ innings, the young hurler surrendered only one hit to Emil Verban.[25] Four days later he won a complete game 1–0 shutout against the Toledo Mud Hens when Colonels scored in the bottom of the ninth inning. Fitzgerald noted, "Toolson's control was perfect. He didn't issue a walk and turned back six batters on strikes."[26]

On May 15, Toolson's control deserted him as he issued three walks, threw two wild pitches, and balked once in a 5–2 loss to the Milwaukee Brewers.[27] In his next outing against the Kansas City Blues on May 20, Earl, "a rookie whose previous efforts had merited the plaudits of the mob, didn't have his stuff and was rapped rather vigorously" for four runs and six hits in $1\frac{2}{3}$ innings.[28] Four days later, Toolson was tagged with another loss when three of the four batters that he walked scored in a 4–2 Minneapolis victory.[29] Earl's next starting assignment was on June 12, and "for five innings…[he] had the Millers feeding from the palm of his pitching hand. He shut them out with only two hits." However, in the sixth inning a two-run, pinch-hit home run by Joe Vosmik produced a 5–1 Minneapolis win.[30] A few days later Toolson suffered a knee injury, and he would not return to action until July.[31] Earl was ineffective in his relief efforts in August and September. For the season Earl appeared in 24 games winning three of his eight decisions with a 5.33 ERA.

1944–45: MILITARY SERVICE

After the 1943 season, Earl enlisted in the Marines reserves but was granted a medical discharge. He subsequently joined the Army Air Corps, where he arrived for enlistment on February 14, 1944, on crutches due to knee surgery, and he was assigned to Williams Field in Higley, Arizona.[32] While serving as a cadet, his athletic prowess was recognized, and he spent most of his military time as a physical training (PT) instructor while playing basketball and baseball for the Williams Field team. While serving in the military, Toolson married Pasadena native Lucile Chisholm on March 17, 1945.[33] Earl spent many years working offseasons in the Hollywood film industry. Toolson completed his military service on November 2, 1945.

1946

Earl returned to the Louisville Colonels for the 1946 season, and he helped his team capture the American Association pennant. The Colonels had moved up to the AAA level, and Earl won five and lost three while posting a 3.88 ERA in 58 innings. After being used infrequently early in the season, Toolson notched his first win on May 17, a three-hit, five-walk, 6–5 complete game effort over the Milwaukee Brewers. In early July, the hurler was sidelined by a cyst on his hip that ultimately required surgery.[34] He returned to the mound on August 23, picking up the loss in an 8–6 Toledo victory.[35]

1947

In 1947, Toolson posted some of the top numbers of his career with 11 wins against six losses, a 3.19 ERA, and 125 hits in 127 innings.[36] Toolson's ERA ranked eighth amongst American Association pitchers who logged 45 or more innings. Prior to the season, Earl was fearful that he would not be able to pitch because of the pain in his left leg and hip near the area where the cyst had been removed.[37] Although Earl did not pitch during the month of March, Colonels manager Nemo Leibold still felt that Toolson would be able to contribute to the team's efforts and named him as one of the 12 pitchers for his staff coming out of spring training.[38]

On May 5, Earl entered a 5–5 game against Minneapolis and won the game despite loading the bases with walks, including two intentional passes. Jim Gleeson's "brisk grounder" went through the Miller shortstop's legs to tally the winning run in the ninth.[39] On May 12, Toolson surrendered a bases-loaded single in the tenth inning of a wild 12–11 loss to Kansas City.[40] On May 25, Toolson was granted a win in a 1–0 victory over Toledo when he relieved "hard luck" Jim Wilson—who suffered a broken leg when struck by a blast off his left shin, putting Wilson "out of commission...for possibly two months."[41] In the second game of a May 30 Memorial Day doubleheader in Indianapolis, Toolson was locked in a scoreless pitching duel with Indians starter Ken Gables before the home team erupted for four seventh-inning runs, paving the way to a 4–0 loss for Earl and his Colonels teammates.[42] On June 23, Earl, pitching "probably his best ball of the season" against the Columbus Red Birds, threw eight strong innings before giving way to Al Widmar in a 2–1, 14-inning Columbus win.[43]

Earl surrendered two runs in the first inning against Kansas City on July 18, but he settled down to strike out ten Blues before running into trouble in the bottom of the ninth after his teammates scored four times in the top half of the inning. Reliever Clem Dreisewerd locked down the 6–4 win, but only after the two runners that he inherited from Toolson scored to narrow the Colonel lead.[44] On July 24, "Toolson turned the Brewers into complete submission" with a 6–1 complete game victory, and he "would have had a shutout but for Chuck Koney's error in the ninth."[45] On August 3,

TEAM PHOTO, PUBLIC DOMAIN

Earl Toolson with the 1949 Oakland Oaks. Earl appears in the center of the top row, to the right of Billy Martin.

Earl captured a 4–2, seven-inning win against Milwaukee in the second game of a doubleheader when he was aided by a sixth inning three-run rally.[46]

One week later, Earl pushed his season log to 9–5 with "distinctive seven-hit ball" in a 4–2, complete-game win over the Minneapolis Millers in the second game of a doubleheader.[47] During the playoffs on September 11, Colonels shortstop Billy Goodman unleashed two throwing errors that propelled the Minneapolis Millers to a 13-8 win that hung a loss on Earl.[48] At the end of the 1947 season, Toolson's record demonstrated his persistent battle with wildness, and his 67 walks pushed his season WHIP to 1.512. The Colonels finished the season in second place.

1948

The Louisville Colonels dropped to last place in the American Association in 1948, and Earl's career took a step backwards as well. He won only four of his 14 decisions despite turning in a career high with 140 innings pitched. However, he allowed 160 hits, 64 walks, with a 5.21 ERA.

During spring training Earl pitched in a 12–6 exhibition game loss to Kansas City in Bradenton, Florida, on April 6 with Baseball Commissioner Happy Chandler in attendance. Tommy Fitzgerald quipped in the *Louisville Courier-Journal*, that the executive "refused to nullify the victory on the ground the conduct of the Blues was detrimental to baseball in Louisville."[49]

On April 27, "Toolson's lack of control got the Colonels off to a disadvantage. Three passes and a couple of singles...spotted the home team [Minneapolis Millers] a pair of runs." In three innings, Earl was responsible for five Miller runs in a 9–5 loss; Bill Elbert relieved him.[50] On May 4, "Toolson gave a reasonably good account of himself for five periods and then weakened in the sixth for three extra base wallops and as many runs" in a 6–4 loss to the Milwaukee Brewers.[51]

Earl picked up one of his four wins in relief against the St. Paul Saints on August 1. The Colonels scored seven runs in the seventh and eighth innings to pull out an 8–4 decision.[52] On August 8, Earl nearly caused a bench-clearing brawl in the second game of a doubleheader with Kansas City. Blues outfielder Bill Sinton, a former Louisville player, broke Colonels catcher Russ Rolandson's nose in a collision at home plate while tying the score at 3–3 in the seventh inning. When Toolson's first pitch to Sinton in the eighth was inside, the Kansas City player headed "toward the mound with bat in hand." Earl ultimately lost a 5–4, 8-inning decision.[53]

The Colonels spent much of the year trading players in search of a winning formula. Earl and fellow pitcher Bill Elbert had been strong contributors in 1947 only to slip badly during the 1948 campaign. Although they lasted the entire 1948 season with the Colonels, that situation was remedied in early October when the pair was traded to Kansas City—the New York Yankees farm team in the American Association—for pitcher Bob Alexander and "an unstipulated amount of cash."[54]

1949

In mid-April 1949, before Earl could pitch a single game for the Blues, the Yankees engineered a swap from Kansas City to their other Triple-A affiliate, the Newark Bears.[55] Toolson started 11 of his 12 games for the woeful Bears, a club destined to finish the season in last place. He won one-half of his ten decisions with a 4.74 ERA. On July 22, the Yankees, attempting to bolster their big league relief corps, shipped Earl and cash to the Oakland Oaks of the Pacific Coast League for 38-year-old veteran Ralph Buxton.[56]

On July 24, Earl pitched in his first game for the Oaks against the San Francisco Seals, giving up two hits and one earned run in three innings of relief in a 5–2 Oaks loss.[57] Emmons Byrne, a writer for the *Oakland Tribune*, wrote that the Oaks "did introduce an effective new pitcher in the sixth when Earl Toolson, who reported two days ago from Newark...A right hander, he's big and he's strong. His curve ball certainly baffled the Seals."[58]

Earl Toolson notched his first PCL victory on July 29 in a 6–3 Oaks win over Seattle, helping himself at the plate with two RBIs.[59] However, Earl soon became ineffective due to a recurrence of his hip ailment and a sore back. The Oaks placed him on the disabled list in August and the Yankees were later forced to assign pitcher Ernie Groth as additional compensation for Buxton's acquisition.[60]

1950

On February 8, 1950, *The Statesman* (Salem, OR) reported that general manager Bill Mulligan of the Portland Beavers had purchased Earl's contract from the Oakland Oaks on a 30-day conditional basis.[61] Toolson never pitched for the Beavers. As he recovered from his injuries, the Yankees decided in May to outright his contract to the Class-A Binghamton Triplets in the Eastern League. When Earl refused the assignment, he was placed on the ineligible list. While his status was being considered, he was actually allowed to accept a conditional assignment from Binghamton to the San Francisco Seals, where Seals manager Lefty O'Doul, "needing pitching help," took a chance that Earl's "sore arm has been cured."[62] Unfortunately, Earl pitched very ineffectively in three games for the Seals, giving up 10 earned runs, 15 hits, and seven walks in six innings. After the season ended, the Seals returned Toolson's contract to Binghamton.

1951

After the 1950 season, Earl sought advice from boyhood friend Howard Parke, now an attorney in Santa Barbara, California.[63] Working with Parke's colleagues Gene Harris and Harry Ross, the group decided to file a lawsuit in the Southern District Court of California on May 1, 1951, challenging the continued viability of the Supreme Court's 1922 *Federal Baseball* decision.[64] On November 6, Judge Ben Harrison rendered his opinion based upon his determination that "the simple issue of this case is whether the game of baseball is 'trade or commerce' within the meaning of the Anti-Trust Acts, and whether the structure known as 'Organized Baseball' is engaged in such trade or commerce."[65] Laying out a traditional view of the role of a federal court judge, Harrison turned aside Toolson's claim:

> Plaintiff seeks to have this court disregard an adjudication made thirty years ago by the Supreme Court. I am bound by the decision of the Supreme Court. It is not my function to disregard such a decision because it is old. If the Supreme Court was in error in its former opinion or changed conditions warrant a different approach, it should be the court to correct the error.[66]

The case was appealed to the Ninth Circuit Court of Appeals.[67] On December 12, 1952, that court affirmed Judge Harrison's decision in a one sentence per curiam opinion.[68] Toolson's legal team appealed their case to the United States Supreme Court.

MOTIVATION FOR THE LAWSUIT

On February 19, 1970, during the Curt Flood litigation, Rube Samuelsen, the long-time *Pasadena Star-News* sports writer and editor, published an article based on an interview between Earl and Eddie West. Toolson, at that time the president of Mortgage Correspondent, Inc., provided one answer to his motivation in bringing his lawsuit: "I had suffered a spinal injury, a ruptured disc, much like Charley Keller's. It was a baseball injury, no question of that. The Yankees refused to assume any responsibility for my injury. They wanted me to go to Binghampton (sic), a minor league affiliate, and work my way back to the big club. I refused. They put me on their suspended list. For that matter I'm still on it."[69] During a 2007 interview with

Earl's brother Bill and son Pete, they noted that Earl was also upset that they wanted to cut his salary due to his demotion from Triple-A to an A-level team. Earl felt that the Yankees should honor the salary in his contract.[70]

Earl was first stricken with cancer in 1982 and had his kidney removed. He died on November 27, 1987.[71] *Orange County Register* writer Keith Sharon noted that "for the most part, Toolson was far removed from his baseball past. He spent much of his time in pain. Mrs. Toolson said her husband underwent 17 surgeries since his playing days."[72] ■

Notes

1. 346 U.S. 356 (1953).
2. Toolson v. New York Yankees, Inc., 200 F.2d 198 (9th Cir. 2 1952), Kowalski v. Chandler, 202 F.2d 413 (6th Cir. 1953), Corbett v. Chandler, 202 F.2d 428 (6th Cir. 1953)
3. 346 U.S. at 357.
4. 407 U.S. 258, 282, 284 (1972).
5. City of San Jose v. Office of the Commissioner of Baseball, 776 F.3d 686 (9th Cir. 2015); Garber v. Office of the Commissioner of Baseball, 120 F. Supp. 3d 334 (S.D.N.Y. 2014).
6. Valarie K. Bowen and the Cassia County Historical Society, *Cassia County* (Charleston, SC: Arcadia Publishing, 2009), 38; Cassia County History, CassiaCounty.org, http://www.cassiacounty.org/about-cassia-county/history.htm.
7. Brief History of George H. Toolson, Father of William E. Toolson, FamilySearch, https://familysearch.org/photos/artifacts/7295384.
8. Ron Gemmell, "Postoffice and Shelton Left To Fight for Regional Crown," *Oregon Statesmen* (Salem, OR), August 14, 1938.
9. "Burley Legion Team Defeats Twin Falls," *Post Register* (Idaho Falls, ID), July 25, 1939.
10. "Aupperle's Strong Nine Enters Preston Tourney," *Post Register*, July 18, 1940.
11. "Bearcats vs. Packards In Hoop Bill Tonight," *Oregon Statesman*, December 6, 1940; "'Cat Hoopsters Hard at Work," *Oregon Statesmen*, November 17, 1940 (Toolson listed as a freshman); "Bearcats Stop Whitman, 54–43; Top Circuit," *Statesman Journal*, February 5, 1941; Fred Zimmerman, "Skits and Scratches," *Capital Journal* (Salem, OR), March 22, 1941.
12. "Letter Award Assembly for WU Athletes," *Oregon Statesman*, May 21, 1942.
13. "Keene Quiet As 'Cat Chuckers Stop Greys, *Oregon Statesman*, March 30, 1941.
14. "Willamette Bearcats Blank Oregon Webfoots, 6–0," *Register 14 Guard* (Eugene, OR), April 13, 1941.
15. "Whitman Takes First Game From Bearcats," *Capital Journal*, May 23, 1941.
16. "Bearcats Lose to Whitman in Playoff," *Capital Journal*, May 24, 1941; "Bearcats Win Over Whitman Nine, 11–1," *Capital Journal*, May 26, 1941; Fred Zimmerman, "Skits and Scratches," *Capital Journal*, May 27, 1941.
17. "Silverton Takes State Semi-Pro Championship," *The Observer* (La Grande, OR), July 14, 1941.
18. "Bearcats Lose to Beavers By 4–3 Score," *The Capital Journal*, March 31, 1942.
19. Al Lightner, "Webfoots Hand Bearcats Double Baseball Dunk at Waters Park, 7–3, 5–2, *Oregon Statesman*, April 5, 1942.
20. "Bill Hanauska Hurls 'Cats to Ball Title," *Oregon Statesman*, May 24, 1942.
21. Al Lightner, "From the Bleachers," *Oregon Statesman*, May 30, 1942.

22. *Who's Who in the American Association*, 1948 Edition, 35. The bonus information was obtained from official card maintained by the Boston Red Sox and Al Lightner, "From the Bleachers," *Oregon Statesman*, June 4, 1942; Fred Zimmerman, "Skits and Scratches," *The Capital Journal*, June 1, 1941.

23. J. Chris Holaday, *Professional Baseball in North Carolina: An Illustrated City-by-City History, 1901–1996*, 77.

24. Al Lightner, "From the Bleachers," *Oregon Statesman*, September 22, 1942.

25. Tommy Fitzgerald, "Colonels Lose In Opener By 7 to 4," *Louisville Courier-Journal*.

26. Tommy Fitzgerald, "Toolson Hurls Shutout As Colonels Ruffle Hens 1–0, 4–3," *Louisville Courier-Journal*, May 10, 1943.

27. Tommy Fitzgerald, "Brews Bunch 9 Blows With Toolson's Wildness to Win 5–2," *Louisville Courier-Journal*, May 16, 1943.

28. Tommy Fitzgerald, "Cols Get Only 5 Hits In 16 Innings 28 And Bow to Blues By 8–1, 3–1," *Louisville Courier-Journal*, May 21, 1943.

29. Tommy Fitzgerald, "Colonels Break Even—But Not Financially," *Louisville Courier-Journal*, May 24, 1943.

30. George Barton, "Vosmik's Homer Beats Kens 5–1," *Louisville Courier-Journal*, June 13, 1943.

31. Tommy Fitzgerald, "Tired Colonel Hurlers Gain Split; Help to Come As Rebel Traded," *Louisville Courier-Journal*, June 21, 1943.

32. *Who's Who in the American Association*, 1948 Edition, 35.

33. Ibid.

34. Tommy Fitzgerald, "Cols Win, Gain But Limp Away," *Louisville Courier-Journal*, July 27, 1946; Bob Hooey, "American Association: 15 Wins on Road Put Colonels on Top," *The Sporting News*, August 21, 1946.

35. Sam Levy, "American Association: Braves Take Over Brewers October 1," *The Sporting News*, September 4, 1946.

36. Earl Flora, "Dreisewerd, Lanky Lefty, A. A. Pitching Pace-Maker," *The Sporting News*, December 10, 1947.

37. Tommy Fitzgerald, "McDermott and 20 Pounds My Be Great Combination," *Louisville Courier-Journal*, March 16, 1947.

38. Tommy Fitzgerald, "Buffalo Defeats Louisville 2 to 0," *Louisville Courier-Journal*, March 29, 1947; Tommy Fitzgerald, "Colonels May Be Minus Genovese," *Louisville Courier-Journal*, April 1, 1947.

39. Tommy Fitzgerald, "Errors In Ninth Bring Colonels Victory By 6–5," *Louisville Courier-Journal*, May 6, 1947.

40. Ernie Mehl, "Colonels Get 5 in 9th, Lose to Blues By 12–11 In 10th," *Louisville Courier-Journal*, May 13, 1947.

41. Tommy Fitzgerald, "Wilson Breaks Leg to Mar Pair of 1–0 Colonel Wins," *Louisville Courier-Journal*, May 26, 1947.

42. Les Koelling, "Cols, Despite Fine Fielding, Bow to Hoosiers 4–3, 4–0, *Louisville Courier-Journal*, May 31, 1947.

. Tommy Fitzgerald, "Wild Pitch Wins For Clark In 14th," 43 *Louisville Courier-Journal*, June 24, 1947.

44. Tommy Fitzgerald, "Colonels Rally for 4 In ninth And Whip Kansas City by 6–4," *Louisville Courier-Journal*, July 19, 1947.

45. Red Thisted, "Toolson Scores Over Brews 6–1," *Louisville Courier-Journal*, section 3, July 24, 1947.

46. Tommy Fitzgerald, "Goodman Is Hero Again As Colonels Capture Two," *Louisville Courier-Journal*, August 4, 1947.

47. Tommy Fitzgerald, "Ostrowski, Toolson Hurl Cols To 3–0, 4–2 Wins Over Millers," *Louisville Courier-Journal*, August 11, 1947.

48. Tommy Fitzgerald, "5 Gift Runs in 8th Beat Cols By 13–8," *Louisville Courier-Journal*, September 12, 1947.

49. Tommy Fitzgerald, "Blues Club Elbert for 6 Runs In 5th as Chandler Watches, *Louisville Courier-Journal*, April 7, 1948.

50. George Barton, "Cols Score 5 in 9th But Kels Win 9–5," *Louisville Courier-Journal*, April 28, 1948.

51. Amos Thisted, "Brewers Down Cols 6–4; Toolson Weakens in 6th," *Louisville Courier-Journal*, May 5, 1948.

52. Tommy Fitzgerald, "Himes Enslaves Us Again to Give Saints Split," *Louisville Courier-Journal*, August 2, 1948.

53. Tommy Fitzgerald, "Rolandson's Nose Broken In Plate Play That Leads Almost to Riot in Twin Loss," *Louisville Courier-Journal*, August 9, 1948.

54. "Colonels Trade Elbert, Toolson for Alexander," *Louisville Courier-Journal*, October 3, 1948.

55. "Deals of the Week Majors-Minors," *The Sporting News*, April 20, 1949.

56. John Drebinger, "Raschi Gains 15th Victory, 5 to 3, As Bombers Take 5½-Game Lead," *The New York Times*, July 22, 1949; Al Wolf, "Ignited Seraphs Burn Stars Again," *Los Angeles Times*, July 23, 1949.

57. "Oakland Blanks Seals, Then Loses Nightcap," *Los Angeles Times*, July 25, 1949.

58. Emmons Byrne, "Oaks Divide With Seals, Capture Series," *Oakland Tribune*, July 25, 1949.

59. Emmons Byrne, "Toolson Hurls Oaks to 6–3 Victory," 59 *Oakland Tribune*, July 30, 1949; "Toolson Twirls Oaks 6–3 Win," *Los Angeles Times*, July 30, 1949.

60. Emmons Byrne, "The Bullpen," *Oakland Tribune*, April 17, 1950; John B. Old, "It's Stars' Hurling vs. Padres Batting," *The Sporting News*, April 26, 1950; "Oaks Get Hurler." *Oakland Tribune*, August 24, 1949. In the February 7, 1951, issue of *The Sporting News*, Oakland owner Brick Laws complained that the Yankees were supposed to provide a "good pitcher" in the Buxton deal, "but they sent us Earl Toolson. He pitched only ten or 12 innings for us and we let him go. Naturally, I let out a growl to the Yanks about it." Jack McDonald, "Laws Duels With Devine on Yank Aid," *The Sporting News*, February 7, 1951.

61. "Portlands Buy Earl Toolson," *Oregon Statesman*, February 8, 1950. A similar article appeared on February 7 in the *Oakland Tribune*. "Toolson to Bevos," *Oakland Tribune*, February 7, 1950.

62. John B. Old, "Attendance Below Last Year's Rate," *The Sporting News*, July 12, 1950.

63. Keith Sharon, "Challenger to Baseball Reserve Clause Dies at 65: Yankees Pitcher Lost Case in Supreme Court," *Orange County Register*, December 24, 1987.

64. "Baseball Player Asks $375,000 in Damage Suit," *Los Angeles Times*, May 2, 1951; "Game's Reserve Clause Under Fire From Two Angles," *The Sporting News*, May 9, 1951.

65. Toolson v. New York Yankees, Inc., 101 F. Supp. 93, 94 (S.D. Cal. 1951).

66. 101 F. Supp. at 94–95.

67. "Supreme Court Test of Clause Is Probable," *Binghamton* (NY) *Press*, November 8, 1951, at 26, col. 3.

68. Toolson v. New York Yankees, Inc., 200 F.2d 198 (9th Cir. 1952).

69. Rube Samuelsen, "Reserve Clause Was Tested With Little Luck by Yankee," *Honolulu Advertiser*, February 19, 1970.

70. Interview with William "Bill" Toolson and George "Pete" Toolson, Las Vegas, Nevada, June 16, 2007.

71. Sharon.

72. Ibid.

The Dodgers–Giants Rivalry During "The Era"

The Dark-Robinson Incident

John J. Burbridge, Jr. and John R. Harris

Roger Kahn coined the phrase "The Era" to represent New York City baseball from 1947 through 1957.[1] During this era the Yankees won nine AL pennants and seven World Series, the Dodgers won six NL pennants and one world championship, and the Giants won two NL pennants and one World Series. While this success certainly contributed to "The Era," another major factor was the intensity of the rivalry between the Dodgers and Giants. Perhaps no rivalry in the history of baseball created the level of ill feeling towards the opposing team as that between Giants and Dodgers fans and players, feelings which peaked during "The Era."

One particular event deserves our attention: a lightly publicized incident at Ebbets Field on April 23, 1955, between Jackie Robinson and Alvin Dark. In retaliation for close pitches by Sal Maglie, Robinson collided with Davey Williams at first base. Williams suffered a major injury to his back. Dark, the Giants captain, retaliated later in the same game. The relationship between Robinson and Dark did not end with the incident but carried into the 1960s when Dark became embroiled in a controversy over remarks concerning black and Spanish-speaking players.

THE RIVALRY

What intensifies a baseball rivalry? One factor is the proximity of the rivals, and being located in two boroughs of the same city made the distance between the Dodgers and Giants functionally zero. Dodgers and Giants fans rubbed elbows in a variety of venues throughout the latter part of the nineteenth century and half of the twentieth century. Imagine the arguments that took place in watering holes in both Brooklyn and Manhattan. One Dodgers fan killed a close friend and wounded another in a barroom in Brooklyn after being "ribbed" about the Dodgers.[2]

While the cities of Boston, Philadelphia, Chicago, and St. Louis also had two franchises for much of the same period, the distinctiveness of Brooklyn and Manhattan and what they represented created a more intense environment. Brooklyn was an independent city until 1898 when it became a borough of New York City. There was the natural divide of the East River but also a political and cultural divide. The Giants had among their fans Manhattan's elite while Dodgers fans were mainly composed of Brooklyn's working class.

In addition, the Dodgers and Giants were both in the National League while the other cities with two teams had a franchise in each league who rarely, if ever, met outside of exhibitions. The Dodgers and Giants played each other 22 times per year. Many of these regular season games were played with the intensity and emotion more usually found in a World Series. The rivalry dated all the way back to 1889 when the Brooklyn Bridegrooms won the American Association title and played the National League winner, the Giants, in the World Series.

Brooklyn then joined the NL in 1890 and promptly won the pennant. They also won pennants in 1899 and 1900. The Giants had to await the arrival of John McGraw as manager in 1902 to begin experiencing success. In addition to McGraw, several of his Baltimore Orioles teammates also joined the Giants. The Giants proceeded to win NL pennants in 1904, 1905, 1911–13, and 1917. The Dodgers struggled during this period until Wilbert Robinson was named manager in 1913.

Robinson and McGraw had been good friends since they were both with the Orioles. When McGraw went to New York, Robinson became the manager of the Orioles but his tenure was short-lived. In 1909 he rejoined his old friend John McGraw as pitching coach for the Giants. However, their friendship ended in 1913 when they were both critical of each other's performance while drinking beer at the conclusion of the season. After dousing McGraw with beer, Robinson walked out of the gathering and became manager of the Dodgers in 1913.[3] The rift between McGraw and Robinson certainly contributed to the intensity of the rivalry. Robinson led the Dodgers to the NL pennant in 1916 and 1920 but the Giants responded with pennants in 1921–24.

The 1930s saw Bill Terry become a player-manager for the Giants. During this decade the Giants were successful on the field while the Dodgers struggled. However, the rivalry escalated as a result of a comment made by Terry in January of 1934. When asked by a reporter about the Dodgers, Terry replied, "I haven't heard much about the Dodgers. Are they still in the league?"[4] This comment became a rallying cry for the Dodgers as they proceeded to eliminate the Giants from pennant contention, beating their rivals in the final two games of the year and giving the pennant to St. Louis.

The 1940s saw the fortunes of the two franchises change. Larry MacPhail became executive vice president of the Dodgers in 1938 and hired Leo Durocher to manage the Dodgers after the 1938 season. Durocher led the Dodgers to the NL pennant in 1941. MacPhail resigned his position in 1942 to accept a commission in the US Army and was replaced by Branch Rickey. Rickey retained Durocher as manager. During the war years the Dodgers were competitive and just missed the 1946 NL pennant, losing to the Cardinals in a playoff. The Giants under Mel Ott as manager struggled.

"THE ERA"

1947 was a turning point in the history of major league baseball because Jackie Robinson made his debut, breaking the "color barrier." Durocher, still the Dodgers manager, was suspended for the year supposedly for actions detrimental to baseball. Under Burt Shotton, the Dodgers won the NL pennant while the Giants, finishing fourth, set a major league team record by hitting 221 home runs.

Durocher returned to the Dodgers in 1948 but with a slow start extending into June, Rickey was wondering whether Durocher could be the problem. Meanwhile, Giants owner Horace Stoneham was contemplating a managerial change and contacted Rickey to inquire whether he could get Durocher from the Dodgers to replace Ott. Durocher did indeed leave the Dodgers to become manager of the Giants. With the skipper jumping ship, the rivalry was sure to escalate.[5]

Durocher was not satisfied with the Giants' roster. The players could hit home runs but lacked speed and fielding finesse. Durocher spent most of 1948 and 1949 trying to convince Stoneham that significant changes had to be made. Finally, during the 1949 offseason, the Giants made a blockbuster trade with the Boston Braves. They sent sluggers Sid Gordon and Willard Marshall, shortstop Buddy Kerr, and pitcher Red Webb to Boston in exchange for shortstop Alvin Dark and second baseman Eddie Stanky, two players who fit the Durocher mold.[6]

Stanky had previous played for the Dodgers 1944–47. He was not a great hitter but had an uncanny ability to get on base and was hard-boiled and competitive. He was supposedly bitter at the Dodgers and Durocher due to his contract negotiations in 1947.[7] Rickey had shipped him to Boston. Dark, a former LSU all-star football player and Rookie of the Year in 1948, was also a fierce competitor and was coveted by Durocher.

While the Dodgers won pennants in 1949, the Giants were undergoing more changes. The Giants had acquired Negro Leagues players Monte Irvin and Hank Thompson. In addition, Sal Maglie was allowed to rejoin the Giants in 1950 with the lifting of the ban that kept former Mexican League players from playing in the major leagues.

In 1950 the bitterness of the rivalry increased. When Durocher had managed the Dodgers, he accused Carl Furillo—a Dodgers outfielder and right-handed hitter—of not being able to handle outside pitches and often platooned him.[8] The animosity between the two men heightened with Durocher now the Giants manager. In a 1950 game Sheldon Jones, a Giants pitcher, hit Furillo in the head with a pitch. Furillo claimed that both Durocher and Giants coach Herman Franks had threatened him with beanballs the day before. Jones later admitted he was directed by Durocher to throw at Furillo.[9] Furillo's dislike of Durocher intensified after the beanball.

1951 saw the Giants get off to a slow start. As a result, they called up Willie Mays from their Minneapolis farm team. The Dodgers, on the other hand, were playing exceptional baseball at the beginning of the year and had early success against the Giants, sweeping them in two successive series. Don Newcombe was quoted as saying, "Me and Ralph Branca used to bang on that door after we beat them and holler, eat your heart out Leo, eat your heart out."[10] That door was the thin door that separated the visitors and home team clubhouses in center field of the Polo Grounds. After the Dodgers won on August 9, the Giants could once again hear the Dodgers singing, "Roll out the barrels. We've got the Giants on the run."[11]

Unfortunately for the Dodgers, the Giants made them regret such shenanigans by winning 37 of the last 44 games, erasing a 13½ game lead and forcing the three-game playoff that culminated in Bobby Thomson's "Shot Heard 'Round the World." His three-run home run in the bottom of the ninth gave the Giants the 1951 pennant. (Later the Giants were found to have used a telescope from their center field clubhouse, possibly tainting their victory, although

Thomson denied getting information on Branca's pitches.[12])

The Dodgers rebounded, winning pennants in both 1952 and 1953, but a Labor Day weekend game on September 6, 1953, illustrated the hostility between Furillo and Durocher. Furillo, after going 4-for-4 in the previous game, was hit by Giants pitcher Reubén Gómez. As he was going to first base, Furillo heard Durocher heckling him and charged the Giants dugout, getting Durocher in a chokehold that caused Leo's face to change colors.[13] As Furillo and Durocher were separated, a Giants player stepped on Furillo's hand, breaking a bone. Furillo was out for the season but still won the batting title.

1954 was a Giants year as they won the pennant and then swept the Cleveland Indians in the World Series. Leo had finally managed a team to a world championship.

THE DARK-ROBINSON INCIDENT

As the 1955 season began, the Giants and Dodgers were both favorites to contend for the National League pennant. On Saturday, April 23, the Dodgers were playing the Giants at Ebbets Field with Maglie pitching for the Giants and Carl Erskine for the Dodgers. True to form, the "Barber" Maglie began the game pitching inside to Dodgers hitters and then following up with an outside curveball, his best pitch. In the second inning, Maglie threw a pitch behind Jackie Robinson's head. When Robinson returned to the dugout Pee Wee Reese instructed Jackie, "When you come up, drop one down the first base line and dump him on his butt."[14]

As the Dodgers came to the plate in the bottom of the fourth, Roy Campanella was the first batter and Robinson second. Campanella was a strikeout victim after being knocked down by an inside Maglie pitch. Robinson decided to take Pee Wee's advice and lay down a bunt up the first base line intending to either knock Maglie down while fielding the bunt or, if Maglie covered first base, knock him down there. However, Maglie knew very well of Robinson's intentions.[15] Maglie let Whitey Lockman, the Giants first baseman, field the bunt. Davey Williams, the second baseman, headed to first to record the putout. Williams took a rather circular route to first, arriving in time to field Lockman's throw but putting him directly in Robinson's path as he crossed the base. Robinson charged into Williams, knocking him to the ground. Giants players rushed to the site of the collision and Alvin Dark, the Giants captain and shortstop, ran directly to Robinson and can be seen yelling at Robinson in a news photo of the aftermath.[16]

NATIONAL BASEBALL HALL OF FAME, COOPERSTOWN, NY

Hostility between the teams put Alvin Dark and Jackie Robinson on a collision course.

After the inning, while the Giants were in the dugout, Durocher, the coaches, and the Giants players were in agreement that they had to retaliate. There are several versions of what occurred in the dugout. One version is that Durocher was concerned how his black ballplayers felt about going after Robinson. Supposedly, he polled Monte Irvin and Hank Thompson and they told Leo to go get Robinson, he had hurt a teammate.[17] Another version has Alvin Dark, the Giants captain, vowing revenge for Robinson's role in the collision.[18]

Dark would bat third in the fifth inning. The first two batters made out and then Dark hit a line drive into the left-field corner of Ebbets Field for a sure double. But Dark didn't stop at second base. Dark, a former football player at Louisiana State University, headed to third base at full speed knowing that Robinson, the Dodgers third baseman and also a former football player, would have the ball well before he could arrive. Dark was determined to barrel into Robinson in retaliation for the earlier collision, also hoping to jar the ball loose. The collision occurred and Dark successfully upended Robinson and the ball did come loose for a Robinson error. Dark was safe at third.

All 32,482 spectators and the Giants and Dodgers players wondered how Robinson would react.[19] Jackie got up off the ground, collected the ball, and told Dark he would get even with Dark at shortstop. Herman Franks, the Giants third base coach, commented to Dark that he was crazy to do something like that while playing in the Dodgers' home ballpark, Ebbets Field.[20] The game continued. Dark was stranded at third base and the Giants lost, 3–1. The significant casualty was Davey Williams whose back was further damaged by the collision. He retired at the end of the 1955 season. Maglie was criticized for not covering first base and later refused to discuss the incident.[21] Robinson expressed some remorse and questioned why such hatred between two teams should exist.[22]

The remainder of "The Era" belonged to the Dodgers as they won both the pennant and World Series in 1955 and the National League pennant in 1956. Leo Durocher left the Giants at the end of 1955. Durocher's exit as Giants manager removed a major target of the Dodgers' hostility. During the 1956 season Alvin Dark was traded to the St. Louis Cardinals in a blockbuster deal. At the end of the 1956 season, the Dodgers then traded Jackie Robinson to the Giants for Dick Littlefield but Robinson retired. The end of "The Era" was rapidly approaching.

NINE YEARS LATER

After refusing to become a Giant, Jackie Robinson joined Chock-Full-O-Nuts as a Vice President. Dark was finally reunited with the Giants at the end of the 1960 season after playing for both the Chicago Cubs and Philadelphia Phillies. Dark was then named manager for the 1961 season.He led the Giants to the pennant in 1962. But 1963 was a disappointment, as the Giants finished third and the beginning of 1964 was no better. In a trip east to play the Mets in August 1964, Stan Isaacs of *Newsday* asked Dark about the Giants' troubles and he supposedly said, *"We have troubles because we have so many Negro and Spanish-speaking players on this team. They are just not able to perform up to the white players when it comes to mental alertness."*[23] On the Giants roster were Willie Mays, Willie McCovey, Orlando Cepeda, Felipe Alou, Matty Alou, and Jose Pagan, all of whom contributed significantly in the pennant-winning year of 1962. Obviously, such a statement caused significant controversy, but guess who came to Dark's defense? Jackie Robinson. Robinson was quoted as saying, "I have known Dark for many years and my relationships with him have always been exceptional. I have found him to be a gentleman and, above all, unbiased."[24] This was somewhat surprising given that Dark and Robinson were not close friends. Since the incident in 1955, they probably only saw each other at charity golf events.

Regardless of Robinson's words of support, Dark's days as the Giants skipper were numbered. Stoneham fired Dark at the end of the 1964 season. Dark weathered the controversy and later helmed the Cleveland Indians, San Diego Padres, and the Athletics in both Kansas City and Oakland.

CONCLUSION

The intensity of the Giants-Dodgers rivalry between 1947 and 1957 was possibly greater than any other in the history of baseball. Leo Durocher leaving the Dodgers in 1948 and joining the Giants intensified the

rivalry. Sal Maglie's fiery personality and penchant for pitching inside was another contributing factor. The feud between Durocher and Furillo which began in Brooklyn and erupted on several occasions illustrated the animosity between the teams. This hostility between the two franchises came to a head in the collisions of April 13, 1955. But given Durocher's resignation at the end of 1955, Robinson's retirement, and the subsequent moves of the Giants and Dodgers to the West Coast, the feelings that sustained the rivalry diminished. "The Era" had come to an end. ∎

Notes

1. Roger Kahn, *The Era 1947–1957 When the Yankees, Giants, and Dodgers Ruled the World* (Lincoln, Nebraska: University of Nebraska Press 1993), 1.
2. "Man Slew Friend in a Baseball Row," *The New York Times*, July 14, 1938.
3. Alex Semchuk, SABR Bioproject Biography of Wilbert Robinson, http://sabr.org/bioproje/person 5536caf5
4. Fred Stein, SABR Bioproject Biography of Bill Terry, http://sabr.org/bioproj/person/4281b131
5. John Drebinger, "Durocher to Manage Giants; Ott Quits; Shotton to Dodgers," *The New York Times*, July 17, 1948.
6. https://www.baseball-reference.com/leagues/MLB/1949-transactions.shtml
7. Leo Durocher with Ed Linn, *Nice Guys Finish Last* (Chicago & London: The University of Chicago Press, 1975) 273–77.
8. Roger Kahn, *The Era 1947–1957 When the Yankees, Giants and Dodgers Ruled the World* (Lincoln, Nebraska; University of Nebraska Press 1993), 228.
9. Roger Kahn, *The Boys of Summer* (New York, Harper and Row, 1972), 338–39.
10. Jim Caple, ESPN Classic, "1951 was a season for the ages," October 8, 2001, http://espn.go.com/classic/s/2001/0927/1255904.html
11. Ibid
12. Joshua Harris Prager, "Was the '51 Giants Comeback a Miracle, or Did They Simply Steal the Pennant," *Wall Street Journal*, January 31, 2001, https://www.wsj.com/ articles/sb98089644829227925
13. Roger Kahn, *The Era 1947–1957 When the Yankees, Giants and Dodgers Ruled the World* (Lincoln, Nebraska: University of Nebraska Press, 1993), 314.
14. Judith Testa, *Sal Maglie* (DeKalb, Illinois: Northern Illinois University Press, 2007), 245–46.
15. Judith Testa, *Sal Maglie* (DeKalb, Illinois: Northern Illinois University Press, 2007), 246–247.
16. Joseph M. Sheehan, "Dodgers Defeat Giants, 3–1," *The New York Times*, April 24, 1955, S1.
17. Judith Testa, *Sal Maglie* (DeKalb, Illinois: Northern Illinois University Press, 2007), 248.
18. Alvin Dark & John Underwood, *When in Doubt, Fire the Manager* (New York: E.P. Dutton, 1980), 49.
19. Joseph M. Sheehan, "Dodgers Defeat Giants, 3-1," *The New York Times*, April 24, 1955, S1.
20. Alvin Dark & John Underwood, *When in Doubt, Fire the Manager* (New York: E.P. Dutton, 1980), 50.
21. Judith Testa, *Sal Maglie* (DeKalb, Illinois: Northern Illinois University Press, 2007), 247.
22. John P. Rossi, *A Whole New Game: Off the Field Changes in Baseball 1946–1960* (Jefferson, NC: McFarland, 1999), 152.
23. Steve Travers, *A Tale of Three Cities: The 1962 Baseball Season in New York, Los Angeles and San Francisco* (Washington, D.C.: Potomac Books, 2009), 213.
24. James S. Hirsch, *Willie Mays The Life, The Legend* (New York: Scribner, 2010), 420.

A Pioneer for the New York Mets

Joan Whitney Payson

Leslie Heaphy

In late May 1957, the National League owners voted unanimously to allow both the Brooklyn Dodgers and the New York Giants to move out west, leaving a hole in the hearts of New York fans and in the market. Talks quickly developed about who might move in to take over the National League vacancy. A unique result came about when the winning group included Joan Whitney Payson among its shareholders. Mrs. Payson became the first female owner of a major league ball club who did not inherit a team but used her own money to buy the club. A lifelong sports fan, Mrs. Payson helped bring National League baseball back to New York and remained with the game until she died in 1975. During her tenure, the New York Mets went from the worst to the best. They started at the bottom of the league but won the World Series in 1969 and made the playoffs in 1973. So who was Joan Payson and how did she end up as the owner of the Mets, taking her place in history with a small number of female owners?

The number of female owners in baseball is slim. One has to go back to the early 1900s to find the first, Helene Hathaway Robison Britton of the St. Louis Cardinals. Britton became the owner of the Cardinals in 1911, inheriting the team after both her father and uncle passed away. She held the reins for six years, finally selling the ball club for a handsome profit to a group of local investors headed by Sam Breadon, who became club president. After Helene Britton, the next female owners include Phillies secretary Mae Nugent and widow Laura Baker who were left 500 shares of stock when Baker's husband died in 1930. James Dunn's wife inherited his fortune upon his death in 1922 and that included the Cleveland Indians though she did not get involved in the day-to-day operations. Barney Dreyfuss's widow Florence passed on the running of the Pittsburgh Pirates to their son-in-law, Williams Benswanger in 1932. Grace Comiskey took over principal ownership of the Chicago White Sox in 1939 following the death of her husband and held the position until her death. After her mother's death in 1956, Dorothy Comiskey served as owner of the

White Sox until 1959 when the reins passed to Veeck's syndicate and her brother Chuck kept his minority share after a legal battle.

Next in the annals of female owners is Effa Manley, owner of the Newark Eagles in the Negro Leagues in the 1940s, a team that also won a World Series in 1946. She owned the team with her husband Abe and was involved in all the daily affairs of the team. She even served as the league's unofficial secretary/treasurer.

When Mrs. Manley sold the Eagles in 1948 there would not be another significant female owner until the 1960s when the National League expanded, creating the Houston Colt .45s and the NY Mets. Since then, Jean Yawkey, Joan Kroc, and Marge Schott have all been in ownership positions. Joan Whitney Payson is a pioneer within this small group, becoming principal owner of the expansion Mets by buying the franchise with her own money.

Joan Whitney was born in New York in February 1903 to a family with an impressive lineage. A few examples follow. Her father, Payne Whitney, came from a family line that included a democratic senator from Ohio in the 1880s and his own father, William C. Whitney, who served as secretary of the navy during the administration of Grover Cleveland and owned a streetcar line. His uncle, Colonel Oliver Payne, left his fortune to his nephew when he died in 1917. Her mother, Helen Hay Whitney (from Cleveland), was the daughter of John Hay. Hay began his career as assistant private secretary to President Abraham Lincoln and went on to serve as secretary of state to both Presidents McKinley and Roosevelt. Joan clearly came from a family of prestige, privilege, and wealth. How did she end up involved in baseball, a sport of the masses?

Both Joan's parents were involved in various sporting endeavors. Her father crewed while at Yale (as his father did before him) and owned a number of stables and breeding operations. Helen loved horseracing and took over the tracks and breeding in 1927 when her husband died. Helen Whitney made a name for herself in the racing world with her horses running and

NATIONAL BASEBALL HALL OF FAME, COOPERSTOWN, NY

Before the existence of the Mets, New York philanthropist and socialite Joan Whitney Payson tried to convince Horace Stoneham to let her buy the Giants rather than move them to the West Coast. He refused.

winning in the Kentucky Derby twice: In 1931 with Twenty Grand and in 1942 with Shut Out. She was often referred to as the "Grand Lady of the Tracks." Helen also loved baseball and often took Joan to see the Giants play as a child, starting as early as age six. Helen remained an avid fan until her death in 1944.

While her family had multiple residences, Joan spent most of her time at their home in Manhattan, on Fifth Ave between 78th and 79th Streets. She attended an all-girls school, Miss Chapin's School, and then went to Barnard for a year. She also took a course or two at Brown's business college. Since her family owned stables, she learned to ride as a child and spent lots of time at the races in NYC and Saratoga.

Just before her nineteenth birthday, Joan's parents threw her a debutante ball at "The Plaza" and then when she turned twenty-one they announced her engagement to Yale graduate Charles Shipman Payson. Payson also came from a long and distinguished American family line. Their marriage at Christ Church was a huge social event in 1924, uniting two old-time wealthy families. During the course of their marriage they had five children: three girls and two boys. Their son Daniel died at the Battle of the Bulge.

As the wife of a wealthy and successful businessman, Joan played out her role as a social hostess. Their homes hosted many large balls and soirees over the years. They had at least five residences where they spent considerable time, though her favorites were in Manhattan and on the Greentree estate in Manhasset, Long Island: 600 acres of sprawling countryside, described as "unarguably one of the grandest residences in America."

Mrs. Payson did not just spend her time raising her children and throwing parties. She had a number of her own businesses and philanthropic ventures as well. For example, she and friend Josephine Kimball

started a bookstore in Manhattan in 1929, just before the stock market crashed. The store survived and remained in business, growing to include more than just children's books. With her brother, Jock, Joan got involved in the newly emerging film industry, investing in scripts they read and enjoyed. The real opportunity they found there was buying the film rights for *Gone with the Wind* for an original investment of $50,000 with Selznick International Pictures, where Jock served as Chairman of the Board.

In 1943 Joan created the Helen Hay Whitney Foundation to honor her mother. The foundation supported research in the biomedical sciences. She also donated land and money to a number of hospitals that today bear her name in various wings and endowments. She donated her time and money to the Women's National Republican Club and party. Joan not only inherited millions from her parents, she also added to her fortune through her own business ventures and investments.

Joan's real loves after her family seemed to settle around art, horses, and baseball. In 1950 she bought a single share of stock in the New York Giants. Over the course of the decade her stockbroker, M. Donald Grant, bought ten percent of the Giants' stock for her. This became a dilemma for her when the Giants moved to San Francisco and she sold her shares after trying to convince Horace Stoneham to let her buy the Giants and keep them in New York. He refused.

Initially she helped fund a team in a third major league suggested by New York attorney William Shea, the Continental League. She invested with three friends (M. Donald Grant, G. Herbert Walker Jr., Pete Davis) in this New York team, and when the Continental League fell apart, the National League awarded them a franchise. Warren Giles, president of the National League, agreed to the franchise because Mrs. Payson was the majority stockholder and not Branch Rickey and his group. She paid an initial $1,000,000 for her controlling interest in the team.

In May 1961, Payson hosted a gathering at her Manhattan home to name the new club. According to some of those present, Payson's personal favorite was the Meadowlarks but the New York Mets was chosen. The name was announced at the Savoy Hilton on May 8, 1961, by Payson herself. She had a huge interest in baseball and when she became involved with the Mets she was not a silent observer but lived and breathed the ball club's successes and failures until her death on October 4, 1975.

From the beginning of her involvement with the Mets, the press sought her out and she often obliged in talking with them briefly. She was never known as a publicity seeker and in fact preferred to stay in the background. She did not call attention to herself by her clothing and style or by her actions. This did not mean she avoided the team or the stadium—in fact quite the reverse was true. She was often found in the owner's box and when she was not in town she often sent her chauffeur, Arthur Desmond to sit in her place behind first base and send her the scorecards after the games. She carried a portable radio with her when she went to the race track and even in her purse at social events so she could stay abreast of what was happening. She kept score in her own unique style when she attended games and knew all the players and their successes and failures. It was her idea to bring in Casey Stengel to manage the ball club because he brought experience. She called his wife Edna and asked for her help in securing Casey's services for the Mets.

To her ballplayers Mrs. Payson was the friendly mom/grandmother many of them missed. She took care of them and watched out for them. She sent gifts for special occasions like the birth of a baby or deaths, marriages etc... Ron Hunt's wife Tracy kept the sterling silver Tiffany set Mrs. Payson gave them when their daughter was born. She rewarded her players with small tokens for their successes on the field as well—roses, tickets, etc.—for a game-winning hit, a home run and the like. She hosted parties and trips for the entire ball club—players, management, and other personnel. She also wore her affiliation to the Mets proudly, on her hats, her car license plates, and even redecorated some of her homes with Mets memorabilia.

To the fans she was a congenial, happy owner who loved to chat with them, wave, and sign autographs. She was an important face for the Mets in their early years, a key contrast to the stern president, George Weiss, and the less-than-trustworthy chairman of the board, Donald Grant.

Given her interest in the team, it is not surprising to note that she got involved in some of the decision-making, or at least voiced her ideas and opinions on trades such as Ron Hunt's to the Dodgers, or the effort to get Willie Mays to join the team in 1972 and keep him on the payroll after he retired the following year. She also said on many occasions that she promised never to interfere directly in the team decisions. She did, however, visit the players in the locker room after they clinched first place in 1969, promptly sending them all scrambling to get dressed because that had never happened before.

As with many involved in the baseball world, she was a bit superstitious as well. One of her biggest

Joan Payson was a devoted owner who often attended games, keeping score in her own unique style. When she couldn't be at the ballpark because she was attending some social function, she was known for carrying a transistor radio in her purse to keep abreast of the team's doings.

concerns was not moving from her seat when the team went ahead until they either won or fell behind. Likewise, if she moved from her seat and the club went ahead, she had to stay where she had gone. Another quirk was to turn her back on certain players when they came to the plate so she would not have to watch them. This usually started when she was turned away and something big happened and she would take to repeating the action. She also had a bad habit of crossing her fingers when the Mets were behind and would not uncross them til they went ahead. Some speculate this led to her later arthritis.

When the Mets finally moved out of the cellar and ascended to the pinnacle with their World Series win in 1969, no one was happier than Joan Payson. After enduring many agonizing years, she was happy to see the losing at an end.

After her death, her son John gave away most of her art collection, mainly Impressionist and Post-Impressionist works, to the Portland Museum of Art (1991) and her daughter Lorinda took over her role as President of the Mets. When Payson's family later sold the Mets to the Doubleday group in 1980, she became one of the first two members of the Mets Hall of Fame, along with Casey Stengel. Her legacy continues to live on today in a variety of hospitals and schools that bear her name or which house collections of her artwork. For example, St. Andrews School (DE) hosts a lecture series called the Payson Art History Lecture Forum because her granddaughter graduated from the school in 2005. Just this past year her great-grand-daughter, Zoe Morgan Haydock, got married in New York City and the lengthy write-up in *The New York Times* mentions Joan and her role as the "founder of the NY Mets." Yogi Berra was quoted after her funeral as saying simply, "She was a great baseball fan and a great woman." She was the face of the Mets for so many in those early tough years. ∎

Bibliography

"A Sentimental Journey." *The Sporting News*, April 18, 1962.

Allen, Maury. *After The Miracle: The 1969 Mets Twenty Years Later.* New York: Franklin Watts, 1989.

—. *Now Wait a Minute, Casey!* New York: Doubleday and Company, Inc., 1965.

"Baker's Last Will Provided against Sale of Phillies." *Pittston Gazette*, December 11, 1930.

Dempsey, David. "Says Mrs. Payson of the Mets, 'You Can't Lose 'Em All.'" *The New York Times Magazine*, January 23, 1968.

Durso, Joseph. *Amazing: The Miracle of the Mets.* Boston: Hoguhton Mifflin, 1970.

—. "Mrs. Payson Elected President of the Mets, Succeeding Devine." *The New York Times*, February 7, 1968.

Frederick Trask File. National Baseball Hall of Fame and Library. Cooperstown, New York.

"The Gilded Age Billionaires, Part II." New York Social Diary, http://www.newyorksocialdiary.com/node/750, accessed March 2012.

"Good Eye." *Portland Monthly*, (May 2010).

"In the Beginning for the NY Mets." *New York Daily News*, April 14, 2012.

Joan Payson File. National Baseball Hall of Fame and Library. Cooperstown, New York.

"Joan Whitney Payson." Whitney Research Group Archives, 1999 and 2006.

"Mets Board Names Joan Payson President." *St. Petersburg Times*, February 7, 1968, 1C.

"Mets Owner Caught Up in Championship Effort." *Sarasota Journal*, October 10, 1969.

"Mets Owner Finally Gets Big Winner." *Pittsburgh Press*, June 3, 1968.

Mizell, Hubert. "Roulet's Philosophy…Win…Win… Win." *St. Petersburg Times*, March 10, 1979, 1C, 7C.

Moran, Sheila. "Players are First: Joan." *Schenectady Gazette*, October 17, 1969.

Montgomery, Paul. "Diverse Friends of Joan Payson Fill Church for Last Goodbyes." *The New York Times*, October 8, 1975.

Thomas, Joan M. "Joan Payson." SABR Biography Project, http://sabr.org/bioproj/person/88dc3fa9, accessed February–April 2012.

"Zoe Haydock, Daniel Millen." *The New York Times*, June 10, 2011.

The Turbulent '70s

Steinbrenner, the Stadium, and the 1970s Scene

Tony Morante

Anyway you look at it, the 1970s was a decade of upheaval and change everywhere in the country, but particularly in New York City. The "police action" of Vietnam ended and an era of urban decay began. The personal computer arrived, the Twin Towers of the World Trade Center became the world's tallest buildings, and Watergate was front page news. President Ford to NYC: "Drop Dead." The "Son of Sam" terrorized the City. The NYPD went on strike. There was a blackout of the entire city's electrical power. Arson was shown nationwide during the World Series. All of this to the strains of "disco fever" emanating from the infamous Studio 54.

I witnessed all of it from the Bronx, where I had been working for the New York Yankees since 1958. Talk about a decade of change: I'd started as an usher in the original Yankee Stadium and by the end of the 1970s I was the renovated Stadium's official tour guide. Yankee Stadium was well on the way to becoming the mecca for outdoor events in the United States, but the stark realization was beginning to sink in that nearly five decades of wear and tear since Ruth's day was taking a toll on the superstructure. Furthermore, "Yankee Village," the neighborhood surrounding the Stadium, was in decline. "The realistic truth is that people won't go there anymore because it is not a nice place to go," claimed Dick Young of the *New York Daily News*.

If it weren't for Mayor John Lindsay, the 1970s might have been the final decade of the Yankees in the Bronx. Other sites were proposed for a new stadium. New Jersey lured Stadium tenants the New York Giants football club to the Meadowlands, where a new home for them opened in 1976. But Mayor Lindsay struck a deal with New York City to perform a major renovation: it would cost around $28 million and require the team and the offices to temporarily relocate to Shea Stadium, home of the Mets, for two years.

Of course a major player in the renovation deal was the newly minted owner of the Yankees, Mr. George M. Steinbrenner. As Sam Roberts of *The New York Times* reported, "Mr. Arthur R. Taylor, president of CBS, unloaded the New York Yankees in 1973. He oversaw the sale of CBS's share of the Yankees to a group of investors led by George M. Steinbrenner for $10 million. CBS had purchased 80 percent of the team for $11.2 million in 1964." In 1966, the team finished last in the American League for the first time since 1912, and the team struggled, rarely ranking higher than fourth by the time CBS sold its share.

A highly decorated WWII veteran (OSS agent, Navy Cross and the Silver Star), CBS vice president Michael Burke had been instrumental in purchasing the Yankees for CBS through his friendship with Yankees co-owner Dan Topping. Although Burke was promised the president's role to stay on with the team, a buttoned-up Steinbrenner was not appreciative of his appearance, putting Burke on a slippery slope to his ouster. Burke was gone by April 1973, manager Ralph Houk and general manager Lee MacPhail by the end of the year.

Perhaps the greatest acquisition of the Steinbrenner era was not, as one might think, a great ballplayer, but a savvy baseball veteran of over four decades, Indians general manager Gabe Paul. Shortly before he left Cleveland to come to the Yankees, he traded Graig Nettles to the Yankees for a few nondescript players. After coming to the Yankees he brought in Chris Chambliss, Dick Tidrow, and Oscar Gamble from his former club. He also got Dock Ellis from the Pirates, Bucky Dent from the White Sox, and acquired key players Lou Piniella, Mickey Rivers, Ed Figueroa, Willie Randolph, and Ken Brett. Another major upheaval of the decade: the introduction of free agency to major league baseball. On New Year's Eve of 1974, Paul signed Catfish Hunter, who had been declared a free agent in arbitration by Peter Seitz. Paul also signed free agent Reggie Jackson in 1976.

The face of the game had also changed with the controversial 1973 adoption of the designated hitter rule by the American League, and as it happened the first appearance of the DH era was made by a Yankee, Ron Blomberg. The Stadium was such a locus of change that two Yankees players, Fritz Peterson and Mike Kekich,

NATIONAL BASEBALL HALL OF FAME, COOPERSTOWN, NY

Reggie Jackson's big bat and big personality brought pennants and controversy to the Bronx.

swapped wives and lives. The two left-handed starters were close friends and roommates on the road, and both men became enamored with each other's wives. The subject of changing partners came up late in 1972 at a party in writer Maury Allen's house. Six months later the deal was consummated as the two pitchers literally exchanged lives, kids, houses, and all, with each man moving into the other family's home.

But as all that was occuring, the renovation of the Stadium loomed. What fans referred to as the Stadium's "aura and mystique"—the lingering light of the great ballplayers, the great personalities, and the great events that were held here—would end for good on September 30, 1973, with the final game of the season.

The closing of the Stadium's doors opened another door in our pop culture: collectibles. Everybody wanted a piece of this historic edifice! Gabe Paul offered a token of appreciation to the approximately 6,000 season ticket holders by giving them actual Stadium chairs which were removed by the Invirex Demolition Co. Only around 4,000 ticket holders' chairs were accounted for. The rest were put on sale to the public. Department store E.J. Korvette managed to get a boatload of the chairs and sold them at $7 each. A few hundred also made their way to War Memorial Stadium, a minor league ballpark in Greensboro, North Carolina, where the seats were in use until that stadium was renovated in the early 1990s. In one case of appreciation for Stadium memorabilia, collector-author Bert Sugar signed two checks, each $1,500, made payable to the New York Yankees to appropriate some of the artifacts that were left behind. In a very short time some of the removed artifacts, including the chairs, were selling for thousands of dollars.

With reconstruction completed, the Yankees returned to their newly refurbished Stadium in 1976. The major renovations included a cantilevered support

system which required 106 cables that surrounded the Stadium, replacing the obstructive girders that supported the mezzanine and upper level. The hard wooden seats were replaced with softer plastic seats. A new mercury-vapored lighting system replaced the banks of lights that had been installed in 1946.

In 1975, Steinbrenner felt that the more genteel nature of manager Bill Virdon had to give way to the fiery Billy Martin, who had been fired by the Texas Rangers. Steinbrenner and Martin were two ego-centric personalities headed for much volatility. Martin's ensuing multiple firings and re-hirings became a soap opera unto itself.

Volatile as the personalities at the top were, talent pushed the Yankees to the top of the league in 1976. "After so many years without postseason play, the '76 pennant was an enormous relief," recalled Marty Appel, then the team's public relations director. "But after the World Series loss to Cincinnati, there was a greater determination than ever to finish the job. Mr. Steinbrenner had instilled a winning attitude that extended even to the front office. We were going to be all-in for 1977. Eyes on the prize." Chris Chambliss's dramatic home run against the Kansas City Royals had brought the Yankees back from anonymity after a 12-year-long hiatus from the postseason and had made a prophet out of Mr. Steinbrenner. Unfortunately, they ran into a hot Cincinnati Reds team—a.k.a. the Big Red Machine—that swept them in four games. All through this season, Thurman Munson, catcher and the newly named captain of the Yankees, continued to cement his position as the backbone of the team. He was awarded the AL MVP honors. But Munson's position as clubhouse top dog was about to be challenged. In November of 1976, Reggie Jackson was added to the already combustible mixture of characters with a five-year contract worth $2.96 million. The Boss cavorted all around the Big Apple with Reggie for three weeks. Munson was none too happy to hear the details of the contract; after all, he had been told that he would be the highest paid Yankee by Mr. Steinbrenner.

In May 1977 an interview with Jackson appeared in *Sports Illustrated* with the infamous quote, "I'm the straw that stirs the drink, Munson thinks that he can stir the drink, but he can only stir it bad." Munson took it badly. Teammates rallied to Munson as he was respected as the heart and soul of the team. Relations were strained all around.

Murray Chass of *The New York Times* tells the tale: "After Martin had benched Jackson a couple of times bigger trouble followed. Matters continued to deteriorate when it all exploded in Fenway Park on June 18th.

When Jackson seemingly loafed after a hit to right field Billy Martin sent Paul Blair out to replace him. This was a great embarrassment to Jackson who felt that Martin never liked him in the first place. After Jackson reached the dugout the two antagonists continued to berate each until they were separated by Elston Howard and Yogi Berra. All of this occurred while the game was being nationally televised giving the audience a taste of what was going on in Yankee-land. The Boss was irate!"

Across town, the Mets showed they were not immune to drama, either. The greatest ballplayer in the Mets' young 15-year history—pitcher Tom Seaver, who was called "The Franchise" by the Mets' chairman of the board, M. Donald Grant—become embroiled in a contract dispute. Grant felt that Seaver's demand for a salary of $250,000 was nothing but greed. Seaver was traded to Cincinnati for four nondescript ballplayers. Mets fans were heartbroken.

Despite daily brush fires with the Boss, Martin, and Jackson, the Yankees won the pennant, once again beating Kansas City, then bested the Dodgers in six games in the World Series. In the clincher, Reggie electrified the Stadium crowd by hitting three home runs on three consecutive pitches off three different pitchers. He won MVP honors for the Series. The victory was followed by a tickertape parade up the "Canyon of Heroes" (Broadway) which was thrilling for me to be a part of.

The drama didn't end there. Reliever Sparky Lyle had been instrumental in the 1977 Yankees' success, capped off with the Cy Young award, the first American League relief pitcher to achieve that distinction. The month after the parade, Mr. Steinbrenner picked up the hottest reliever on the free agent market in Goose Gossage—an embarrassment of riches and a crushing blow to Lyle. Lyle would spend a season playing an unhappy second fiddle to Goose and then was traded to Texas on November 10, 1978. Another major loss was occurring at this time. The architect of the Yankees' success, Gabe Paul, resigned after the 1977 season and departed for Cleveland. Steinbrenner claimed Paul was getting too much of the credit for the player moves and the team's success.

Opening Day 1978 started with another unforgettable event. Before Reggie ever came to the Yankees he had made a statement, "If I ever played in New York they would name a candy bar after me," perhaps thinking that "Baby Ruth" bars had been named for Babe Ruth. Well. In a promotion with Curtis Candy Mfg., over 40,000 candy bars called "Reggie Bars" were issued to the fans entering the Stadium. In pure theatrical fashion, Reggie stepped up to the plate with two men on board and hit a home run. All of a sudden, the candy bars became missiles and they were launched from every part of the Stadium. It took the grounds crew half an hour to clean the field.

The main story line in 1978 was Ron Guidry's great pitching. He won 13 games in a row from the start of the season, and on June 17, as he pitched against the California Angels, Guidry began to pile up strikeouts with his vicious slider. By the fifth inning fans started to rhythmically clap whenever he put two strikes on a batter, exhorting him to strike the batter out. Guidry, who was dubbed "Louisiana Lightning" by Yankees announcer Phil Rizzuto, wound up with 18 Ks on the day. The "two-strike clap" practice became commonplace at the Stadium after that.

Other than Guidry's great performance, the team was really struggling. They had fallen 14 games behind the league-leading Boston Red Sox when the high drama returned. On July 17, Reggie—who had recently been made DH by Martin, and not too happy at all by it—disobeyed an order by failing to heed a sign by the third base coach. He was taken to task by Martin and suspended for five games. But Billy was also hearing it from The Boss, and blurted to a reporter, "He's a born liar. The two of them deserve each other, one's a born liar, the other's convicted." Martin appeared physically and emotionally drawn.

Martin decided to resign before being fired. His replacement was Bob Lemon, who had been fired from the White Sox. But five days after his tearful farewell, Billy and Steinbrenner engineered a moment of pure spectacle at the Old Timers Day Game. During pregame introductions by public address announcer Bob Sheppard, Billy was squirreled away in the bowels of Yankee Stadium, ready to make a surprise appearance. Sheppard then delighted the crowd with the announcement that Martin would be returning as manager

Billy Martin's complex relationship with owner George Steinbrenner would define the Yankees in the 1970s and beyond.

Relief ace Sparky Lyle won the Cy Young Award in 1977, the first American League relief pitcher to do so.

Thurman Munson was considered the heart and soul of the team by many fans and teammates who felt an era came to an end with his death in an August 1979 plane crash.

starting with the 1980 season "and hopefully for many years after that." This was followed by a seven-minute standing ovation.

Boston started to tail off as the Yankees mounted a comeback. By early September the gap was down to four games with a four-game series at Fenway on the slate. In what came to be known as "The Boston Massacre," the Yankees swept all four games, outscoring the Red Sox, 42–9. By season's end both teams were tied in the standings, prompting a one-game playoff at Fenway. Many people call the Boston Red Sox/New York Yankees the "greatest rivalry in professional sports" because of moments like this one: Yankees shortstop Bucky Dent hit a three-run homer in the seventh inning to put the Yankees on top. Guidry ran out of gas and was replaced by Gossage who sealed Boston's fate. The Yankees then beat the Dodgers again in six games to win the World Series.

In 1979, the decade drawing to a close, the Yankees were lingering around fourth place for most of the season. Another comeback was not in the making. A series of minor injuries and ailments to key players including Nettles, Jackson, Gossage, and especially to their captain, Thurman Munson, contributed to the mediocrity, but none could predict the tragedy that would strike.

As reported by Marty Appel in his book *Munson: The Life and Death of a Yankee Captain*, Munson's career as a catcher was probably winding down by 1979, injuries having taken their toll. Munson had never spent a day on the disabled list. When a plane crash claimed his life on August 2, it really closed a chapter on the Yankees' decade, a decade in which Munson went from Rookie of the Year to captain of a world champion ballclub. The appreciation of what he meant to the resurgent Yankees only grew over time. He had led them to the top of the baseball world, and had reconnected them to the team's past glories, proudly taking his place in the lineage of great Yankee catchers. The team's first captain since Lou Gehrig, he was firmly tied forever to Yankee heritage, and he remained an old school symbol of playing the game right. The fans saw through his gruff exterior to the soul of a champion. All these years later, his image still invokes grit and determination, a time when leadership was on display daily as he pushed his teammates towards glory.

Isn't it fitting that peace came to Yankee Stadium on October 2 with a Catholic mass? Pope John Paul II celebrated mass with 80,000 faithful followers, wrapping up the raucous decade. ■

Bibliography

Appel, Marty. *Munson: The Life and Death of a Yankee Captain*, Anchor, 2010.

Appel, Marty. *Pinstripe Empire*, Bloomsbury, 2014.

Durso, Joseph. *Yankee Stadium; Fifty Years of Drama*, Houghton Mifflin, 1972.

Lyle, Sparky and Peter Golenbock. *The Bronx Zoo*, Crown Publishing, 1978.

Pepe, Phil. *Talkin' Baseball: An Oral History of Baseball in the 1970s*, Ballantine Books, 1998.

Stout, Glenn and Richard Johnson. *Yankees Century*, Houghton Mifflin, 2002.

Sullivan, Neil J. *The Diamond in the Bronx*, Oxford University Press, 2001.

Yankee Stadium-The Official Retrospective. Pocket Books of Simon and Schuster.

A Hall-of-Fame Cup of Coffee in New York

Steven Glassman

I was inspired to write this article by Jonah Gardner's Sports-Reference.com post "Remembering Mike Piazza's 8 Amazing Days with the Florida Marlins," about Hall-of-Famer Piazza's short 1998 Florida Marlins stint before getting traded to the New York Mets.[1] New York City's major league teams have a storied history but I was curious: how many Hall-of-Famers had "cups of coffee" of this type with them? For purposes of this article I defined a "cup of coffee" as a single-digit number of games for a player. The names I found give an interesting glimpse into New York big-league baseball in the twentieth century. For each I will provide position, year, and method of induction to the National Baseball Hall of Fame in Cooperstown, as well as the year and positions played for the "cup of coffee" team.

YOGI BERRA, C (1972 BBWAA)
New York Mets (1965), C-PH: Four Games

I chose to start this list with no less a fixture of New York sports than Yogi Berra, who of course is best known as a Yankee, but had a brief playing stint with the Mets. Berra was fired as Yankees manager on October 16, 1964.[2] Less than a week later, he spoke to Casey Stengel about joining the Mets. He "signed a two-year [deal] with the Mets at a reported $35,000 per year" as a player-coach on November 17 at Shea Stadium's Diamond Club.[3] Berra notified the Yankees he was signing with the Mets the day of the news conference, during which he told the press he had received offers from "several clubs including the Senators and Cardinals. He refused to name any of the others."[4] The Sporting News reported that in addition to coaching, "he will also take a shot at coming back as a player. His physical condition after spring training will determine that. Stengel would like to have him as a pinch-hitter and spot player for catching and outfielding."[5,6] Even though now with the Mets, Yogi kept uniform number eight.[7]

Berra was thirty-nine years old and had not played in a game since October 5, 1963. He was concerned about getting his timing back. He went hitless as a pinch-hitter in his first Mets spring training game versus the St. Louis Cardinals in St. Petersburg on March 13, 1965. He caught Warren Spahn the next day versus the Cardinals.[8] Spahn said, "I don't know if we're the oldest battery, but we sure are the ugliest."[9]

Berra said he would still catch but not as a regular. "Maybe 20–30 games would be okay....My legs would never stand it."[10] Berra was "strictly listed as a coach, and when he's put on the playing roster, it won't happen until the last possible moment before the start of the regular season."[11]

Even though Berra got off to a slow spring training start, Stengel was not worried: "It's too early now. You've got to give Yogi a chance to keep swinging. In batting practice, I've seen him get off some long shots. Once he gets his eye on the ball, he'll probably do the same thing in a game."[12] Stengel added about Berra's catching workload, "All I would want of this fella would be to work in some spot games. I don't expect him to be my regular catcher. That job belongs to Cazonara [Chris Cannizzaro]."[13,14] Altogether, Berra went hitless in eight spring training at-bats in six games played (one start).[15]

Cardinals manager Red Schoendienst believed that Berra could contribute: "You're darned right he'll help the Mets. It's hard to find a real good pinch-hitter. He's aggressive with that bat and he's been around. He'll win some ball games over there."[16] Sports Illustrated

Yogi Berra followed in Casey Stengel's footsteps from the Bronx to Queens for a short-lived stint as a Mets player, followed by a long tenure as a coach, eventually becoming Mets manager himself in 1972.

reported that "Yogi will not catch many full games, but it seems likely that when Casey needs a left-handed bat late in the game the ex-Yankee manager will be the one."[17] SI also noted Berra's other use—draw at the box office: "[They] will go on filling Shea Stadium—especially when the battery of Spahn and Berra is announced—and if Spahn pitches back to his form the Mets may nudge the Astros out of ninth place."[18,19]

Yogi was activated to play on April 27 when Kevin Collins went on the disabled list. Berra's reaction: "'Sure, I'm glad. It's like a shot in the arm.'"[20] About his slow spring: "When you've laid off for a year, you gotta come back slowly. But I've been taking a lotta batting practice and I've also been throwing and my arm is pretty good. Sure, I didn't throw too good in Florida, but I wasn't gonna cut loose until my arm was strong. Now it's strong."[21] Stengel also viewed Berra as another left-handed pinch-hitter and late-inning catcher. Until then, first baseman Ed Kranepool and outfielder Johnny Lewis were the Mets' only left-handed hitting options. "It wasn't written in my contract to play, too," Yogi told the press, "but, [Weiss and I] talked about it when I signed."[22] Weiss hoped that adding Berra would help. "Sure I had that in mind when I put Yogi on the playing roster. He could be a big help if he's anything like his old self."[23]

Berra made his Mets debut on May 1 versus the Cincinnati Reds. Down 8–2 in the top of the eighth and pinch-hitting for relief pitcher Jim Bethke, Berra grounded out to first baseman Gordy Coleman to end the inning. On May 4, Berra singled twice and scored a needed run in a 2–1 home win versus the Philadelphia Phillies. Berra led off the bottom of the seventh with a single and scored two batters later on Roy McMillan's single.

He also caught Al Jackson who set a career-high and a then-team single-game record, striking out 11 Phillies.[24] On May 5, pinch-hitting for Cannizzaro in the bottom of the eighth, Berra grounded out to Dick Stuart, who threw it to Jim Bunning to end the inning and left Ron Swoboda at second base. He and Jackson did not fare well together on May 9 at home versus the Milwaukee Braves. Berra struck out three times in four at-bats versus Tony Cloninger while Jackson lasted only 2⅓ innings, allowed five runs on nine hits (including two home runs), committed a balk, and hit a batter in the 8–2 loss.

Two weeks after being activated, on May 11, Berra announced his retirement as a player. The Mets were making a series of moves and they needed to meet the 25-player roster limit on May 12. It was also the day before his fortieth birthday. "After each game, I was aching," Yogi said. "It got me in the back more than in the legs. The worst of it was that I could not follow the ball at bat. My reflexes were slow."[25] He reflected about his comeback attempt when he was voted into the Hall of Fame in 1972. "It was a mistake....Tony Cloninger threw the fastball right by me and I knew I'd had it. I was always a fastball hitter. I told Casey Stengel right after the game I was through."[26]

DAN BROUTHERS, 1B (1945 OLD-TIMERS)
New York Giants (1904), 1B-PH: Two Games

Playing in his first full professional season since 1897, Brouthers won the 1904 Hudson Valley batting title (.373) at the age of 46 for Poughkeepsie, and was also the team's captain. After Poughkeepsie's season was over, Brouthers was reunited with his former teammate and manager at the time, John McGraw.[27] McGraw "sent out invitations to two retired [sic] veterans to suit up and play one more big league game in front of the home crowd at the Polo Grounds."[28] He sent out invitations to Orator Jim O'Rourke (1885–89,

Dan Brouthers won the Hudson Valley batting title in 1904 at age 46, and then played a few games with John McGraw's Giants.

1891–92 Giants) and Brouthers, who did not previously play for the Giants. Brouthers got his opportunity on October 3 versus the Cardinals. He went hitless in four at-bats and fielded six chances successfully while playing first base at the age of 46 in the 3–1 victory. Brouthers went hitless in a pinch-hitting appearance on October 4 in a 7–3 loss to the Cardinals in game one of a doubleheader, and started in the second game, which was forfeited by the Giants in the fourth inning. After the season ended, McGraw organized an exhibition game between the 1889 champion Giants and their 1904 counterparts, and Brouthers again donned a Giants uniform, substituting for an absent member of the 1889 squad.[29]

MORDECAI BROWN, RHP (1949 OLD-TIMERS)
Brooklyn Tip-Tops (1914): Nine Games

Brown started the season as playing manager of the Federal League's St. Louis Terriers but was replaced by Fielder Jones on August 22, 1914, after a 50–63–1 (.442) start. By that point they were in seventh place, 12½ games behind the Indianapolis Hoosiers.[30] Brown said that he was not notified that he would be fired by St. Louis management and he would not play for the new manager. He added that he also might retire from baseball.

Brown's $10,000 contract was bought by the Brooklyn Tip-Tops from the Terriers on September 1. Miner Brown was given a warm reception by the Brookfeds on his arrival at Buffalo.[31] He made his first appearance in relief on September 2 in the second game of a doubleheader versus Buffalo. Manager Bill Bradley summoned Brown in the bottom of the eighth inning with the Tip-Tops leading, 5–4. He pitched five innings, struck out six, and allowed three hits; however, he allowed the tying run in the bottom of the ninth and the two teams finished tied at five after 12 innings.

Brown made his Tip-Top home debut—and first start—versus the Pittsburgh Rebels in game two of a doubleheader on September 7. Brown received an ovation by the fans at Washington Park. However, after retiring Pittsburgh in order in the first inning, the Rebels knocked him out of the game, scoring five runs on five hits and a walk.[32] The September 12 *Brooklyn Daily Eagle* noted that he "is suffering from a boil on his leg, and it gives him no little pain, so that his recent work must not be taken as a sample of what may be expected of him when he is right."[33] Brown went deeper in his next start—versus his former team, St. Louis—but took a loss, allowing six runs (two earned) on five hits in seven innings. Altogether, the Tip-Tops lost four straight starts by Brown. He finally

won his first Brooklyn start on October 2, allowing an unearned run in the ninth inning in a 3–1 win over the Baltimore Terrapins. Brown helped himself with a single and a run scored in a three-run fifth inning. He struck out Jimmy Walsh with the bases loaded in the ninth inning to end the game.

Brown won his second straight start, striking out five in eight innings, in a 10–4 road rout at Buffalo on October 7, then made his final Tip-Top appearance on October 10 in game two of a doubleheader at Baltimore. Brown pitched his fifth complete game in six starts, but lost 1–0 on an eighth-inning run. Walsh singled, stole second, and reached third on catcher Yip Owens's second error of the game. Harry Swacina's "sacrifice fly" scored the only run.[34] Brown won two games and completed five of his eight starts (nine games) for Brooklyn. Meanwhile, during a restructuring of the Brooklyn Federals, Mordecai's contract was put on the trading block.[35] On March 4, Mordecai returned to Chicago as a player after a two-year absence.[36]

JOE GARAGIOLA, C
(1991 FORD C. FRICK AND 2014 BUCK O'NEIL AWARDS)
New York Giants (1954), C-PH: Five Games

Although technically not a Hall of Famer (he is a recipient of the Ford C. Frick Award for broadcasters), Joe Garagiola's cup of coffee in New York is a tale worth telling. Garagiola informed the Chicago Cubs during the season that he would retire after the 1954 season and join the Cardinals as a broadcaster. He was acquired on waivers by the Giants on September 8, 1954. After having been promised by the Cubs that he wouldn't be traded, Garagiola was shocked by the move.[37] Giants manager Leo Durocher said that no one from the Cubs organization notified them about Garagiola's impending retirement plans. Garagiola submitted his case to Commissioner Ford Frick, who made the Cubs take him back for the waiver price [$10,000] at the end of the season.[38] Until then, though, Garagiola was a Giant. He joined a catching corps that already included veteran Wes Westrum and rookie Ray Katt.

In his first start, in game two of a doubleheader versus those same Cubs on September 9, he singled in the ninth inning.[39] He fouled out in pinch-hitting appearances (September 10 and 17 versus Cincinnati and Philadelphia, respectively). His final major league start came in game one of a doubleheader at Philadelphia on September 24. Garagiola walked once in four plate appearances in the 1–0 win. Two days later came his rather thrilling final game. On September 26 at Philadelphia, he pinch-hit for Jim Hearn in the seventh inning and tied the game at two on a sacrifice fly off

Robin Roberts. Garagiola remained in the game and doubled and scored the winning run in the 11th for a 3–2 victory.

Ineligible to play in the World Series because he was acquired after September 1, Garagiola received a $1,000 share after the Giants swept Cleveland. He described being there as "like a contest winner who has written in 25 words or less 'Why Henry Thompson Is My Favorite Player' and got an all-expenses paid trip to the World's Series."[40] He officially announced his retirement on October 18 and embarked on his broadcasting career.

TOMMY LASORDA, LHP (1997 VETERANS AS A MANAGER)
Brooklyn Dodgers (1954–55): Eight Games

Lasorda was selected by the Dodgers' Nashua farm team from Schenectady in the Minor League Phase of the Rule Five draft on November 22, 1948. He was promoted to the Dodgers' top minor league affiliate in Montreal (International League) for the 1950 season. Lasorda spent four seasons there and was added to the Dodgers' 1954 spring training roster after winning 17 games and posting a 2.81 ERA and an appearance in the 1953 Junior World Series.[41] He did not make the opening day roster but won 14 games for Montreal, including his last nine straight. The Dodgers called Lasorda up on August 1. He warmed up in the bullpen the following night versus the Braves but was not used in the 2–1, 13-inning victory.

Lasorda did not have an auspicious debut versus the Cardinals on August 5.[42] He started the fifth inning in relief of Erv Palica with the Dodgers losing, 8–2. Altogether he allowed three runs, a walk, and six hits, in three innings pitched.[43] He finished the season with four relief appearances.[44]

Lasorda made the opening day roster in 1955. He left his only start—versus the Cardinals on May 5—after one inning due to an injury. Although Lasorda struck out two, he walked two, threw three wild pitches, and allowed a run. He was spiked by Wally Moon on his knee while covering home plate on his third wild pitch.[45] Lasorda also did not fare well in his first game back from injury on the road versus the Pirates on May 24. He entered the game in the bottom of the sixth with the Pirates leading, 10–1. Lasorda allowed five runs, four hits, two walks, and a hit batter.[46] He pitched scoreless outings on June 5 and 6 versus the Cardinals. Lasorda was sent back to Montreal on June 8 to make room on the roster for Sandy Koufax. "'They never gave me a chance to pitch. I knew I could win in the big leagues,' Lasorda said. 'I never reached a level of success as a pitcher, but, I felt that maybe I would be a success some other way.'"[47]

RAY SCHALK, C (1955 VETERANS)
New York Giants (1929), C: Five Games

Schalk spent the first fifteen years of his career as the White Sox catcher (1912–26) and the next two as playing manager (1927–28).[48] He was signed by the Giants to a one-year contract on November 12, 1928, as player and assistant head coach to manager John McGraw.[49] Schalk was also responsible for handling the catchers and pitchers.[50] His first game and only Giant start was on "Ray Schalk Day" at Wrigley Field on June 3. The Cubs gave him a golf bag and traveling bag. He caught Carl Hubbell for three innings and went hitless in his only plate appearance in an 8–1 Giants victory.[51] Schalk appeared in both ends of a road doubleheader versus the Phillies on June 30 and struck out in his final at-bat versus Claude Willoughby in game two. He was a defensive replacement for Bob O'Farrell in a 14–8 home win versus the Pirates in game one of a doubleheader on August 24. Schalk made his final appearance on the road catching the bottom of the eighth with Jack Scott in a 6–4 loss at the Cardinals on September 15. He and Bert Niehoff did not work well together. Their contracts were not renewed on November 1 and they were replaced by Dave Bancroft and Emil Meusel, respectively.[52] Schalk coached with the Cubs for the 1930 and 1931 seasons. ∎

Ray Schalk spent 1912–28 with the White Sox before going to the Giants as a player-coach. His lone start came when the Chicago Cubs fêted him at Wrigley Field on "Ray Schalk Day."

Notes

1. Jonah Gardner, "Remembering Mike Piazza's 8 Amazing Days with the Florida Marlins," Sports Reference Blog, July 21, 2016, accessed December, 2016, http://www.sports-reference.com/blog/2016/07/remembering-mike-piazzas-8-amazing-days-with-the-florida-marlins.
2. The Yankees hired Johnny Keane on October 20, 1964. Keane managed the Cardinals to the 1964 WS title versus the Yankees, their first since 1946.
3. Barney Kremenko wrote in a November 28, 1964, article in *The Sporting News* ("Lure of Uniform Prompted Yogi To Accept $35,000 Mets' Post") that "Berra already had signed a two-year pact with the club [Yankees] to serve as General Manager Ralph Houk's helper ['special field consultant'] at $25,000 per annum. However, it had an escape clause in it, permitting him to go elsewhere whenever he so pleased. It had another clause which gave Yogi $25,000 'severance pay' outright, no questions asked."
4. Ibid.
5. Ibid.
6. Berra entered the 1965 season with 1,697 games caught, 260 in the outfield (149 in left and 116 in right field), and 216 games as a pinch-hitter.
7. Cannizzarro originally wore number eight with the Mets and switched to five.
8. Spahn was sold to the Mets by the Braves on November 23, 1964, six days after Berra signed with the Mets. Berra and Spahn were battery-mates for the first three innings of this spring training game. It was the only game they worked together.
9. David Pietrusza, Matthew Silverman, and Michael Gershman. "Yogi Berra." In *The Biographical Encyclopedia of Baseball* (Kingston: Total Sports Publishing, 2000), 85.
10. Barney Kremenko, "Yogi Can't Bear Duty as Mets' Mittman," *The Sporting News*, March 27, 1965, 8.
11. Ibid.
12. Ibid.
13. Ibid.
14. Cannizzaro caught 112 games for the 1965 Mets.
15. Berra also caught an exhibition game versus the Mets' AAA minor league affiliate Buffalo Bisons (IL) on March 27, 1965. He went hitless in two at-bats.
16. Dick Young, "Young Ideas," *The Sporting News*, March 27, 1965, 18.
17. William Leggett, "New York Mets," *Sports Illustrated*, April 19, 1965, 58.
18. Ibid.
19. The Mets finished the season 10th for the fourth straight season, the Astros finished ninth for the third consecutive campaign.
20. Barney Kremenko. "Player Again—Yogi Hails News As 'Shot in Arm,'" *The Sporting News*, May 8, 1965, 29.
21. Barney Kremenko. "Weiss Sizes Up Mets As 'Too Righthanded,'" *The Sporting News*, May 15, 1965, 22.
22. Ibid.
23. Ibid.
24. Jackson broke the record of 10 previously held by the following: Jay Hook versus the Pittsburgh Pirates on July 19, 1962 (game two) and May 8, 1963 versus the Philadelphia Phillies, Dennis Ribant versus the Pirates on August 17, 1964, and Tracy Stallard at the San Francisco Giants on September 16, 1964.
25. Barney Kremenko. "Bitter Blow to Met Hopes: Hunt Likely Out for Season," *The Sporting News*, May 22, 1965, 17.
26. Jack Lang, "Sandy, Yogi, Early Make the Grade," *The Sporting News*, February 5, 1972, 31.
27. Brouthers and McGraw were teammates for the 1894–95 National League Baltimore Orioles.
28. Roy Kerr, Big *Dan Brouthers* (Jefferson: McFarland and Company, 2013), 146.
29. Ibid.
30. Jones was originally hired on August 14, but, could not officially take over as the manager until he resigned as the Northwestern League president.
31. "Brooklyn Feds Lose and Tie," *The Brooklyn Daily Eagle*, September 3, 1914, 12.
32. Despite Brown's shortest start of the season, the Tip-Tops came back and won, 12–11.
33. "Federal League Notes," *The Brooklyn Daily Eagle*, September 12, 1914, 18.
34. The article mentioned sacrifice fly—40 years before it became a statistic separate from the sacrifice bunt.
35. Christy Thomson and Scott Brown, *Three Finger: The Mordecai Brown Story* (Lincoln: University of Nebraska Press, 2006), 142.
36. Ibid.
37. W.G. Nicholson, "Garagiola Downplays Diamond Career." *The Baseball Research Journal*,15, No. 1 (1986), 15.
38. Ibid.
39. Garagiola caught John Antonelli who struck out 10 in a 3–0 loss at the Polo Grounds.
40. Bob Broeg, "Joe Garagiola: From Mask to Mike," *The Sporting News*, November 24, 1954, 14.
41. Lasorda was purchased by the Browns on February 21, 1953, but sent back to the Dodgers on March 26.
42. In his autobiography, *The Artful Dodger*, Lasorda and co-author David Fisher incorrectly wrote that his debut was versus the Reds. He faced the Reds in his *third* major league game on September 16 in a blowout loss, but not in the sequence described in the book.
43. His debut was his longest outing in his Dodger career.
44. Lasorda's only ejection as a major league player was in a game he did not play. On September 19 at Pittsburgh, he was ejected by home plate umpire Frank Secroy with one out in the bottom of the eighth for bench jockeying.
45. Lasorda and Fisher incorrectly wrote that Ken Boyer was at bat during his third wild pitch. Boyer's first at-bat was in the second inning and did not face Lasorda in this game.
46. Lasorda and Fisher incorrectly wrote that Tom Saffell hit a home run off of him. Saffell singled off of Lasorda.
47. Joe Resnick, "Lasorda remembers being replaced by Koufax," Associated Press, June 7, 2005.
48. He was forced to resign as White Sox manager in July 1928.
49. Bert Niehoff was also hired. He played seven games for McGraw in 1918.
50. Schalk replaced Roger Bresnahan who was on the coaching staff from 1925 to 1928.
51. It was his first game at catcher since July 4, 1928, which was also the last day he managed for the White Sox.
52. Even though their ERA increased from 1928 (3.67), the Giants led the NL in ERA (3.97) for the first time 1922.

Additional Books

Cooper, Brian E. *Ray Schalk: A Baseball Biography* (Jefferson: McFarland and Company, 2009), 253–56.

Lasorda, Tommy and David Fisher. *The Artful Dodger* (New York: Arbor House), 1985), 50–56.

Overfield, Joseph M. "Dennis Joseph (Big Dan) Brouthers." *Baseball's First Stars*, edited by Frederick Ivor-Campbell, Robert L. Tiemann, and Mark Rucker. (Cleveland: The Society for American Baseball Research, 1996), 11–12.

Additional Periodicals

"Brooklyn Feds Win And Lose," *The Brooklyn Daily Eagle*, September 4, 1914, 20.

"Chicagos Take Lead in Fed Race Through Johnson's Great Pitching," *The Brooklyn Daily Eagle*, September 26, 1914, 18.

Daniel, Daniel M., "Cubs Must Refund $10,000 If Garagiola Retires in '55," *The Sporting News*, September 29, 1954, 27.

Davids, L. Robert. "Altrock, at 57 Oldest to Play in Major Game," *The Sporting News*, August 25, 1962, 1.

Drebsinger, John, "Giants Get Schalk To Assist McGraw," *The New York Times*, November 13, 1928, 40.

"Feds End Season With Even Break," *The Brooklyn Daily Eagle*, October 11, 1914, 33.

"Garagiola Hangs Up Mask and Pad to Pitch Quips Over Microphone," *The Sporting News,* October 27, 1954, 11.

"Great Rally By The Brooklyn Feds Puts Them In Third Place Again," *The Brooklyn Daily Eagle*, September 8, 1914, 20.

Holmes, Tommy, "Dodger Hill Staff Totters," *The Brooklyn Daily Eagle*, August 1, 1954, 37.

"Hoosiers Make It Five In A Row And Quit Brooklyn In First Place," *The Brooklyn Daily Eagle*, September 19, 1914.

"John McGraw Signs Bancroft As Coach," *The Sporting News*, November 7, 1929, 1.

"Miner Brown Joins The Brooklyn Feds," *The Brooklyn Daily Eagle*, September 1, 1914, 7.

"Miner Brown Near A Shut-Out Game," *The Brooklyn Daily Eagle*, October 3, 1914, 18.

"Record $11,147 Series Paycheck for Every Giant," *The Sporting News*, October 13, 1954, 10.

"Shifts Uniforms After 16 Seasons," *The Sporting News*, November 22, 1928, 4.

"Superbas 20 Points Better Than At End Of Last Season," *The Brooklyn Daily Eagle*, September 21, 1914, 18.

Internet

http://www.baseball-reference.com/players/b/berrayo01.shtml
http://www.baseball-reference.com/players/b/broutda01.shtml
http://www.baseball-reference.com/players/b/brownmo01.shtml
http://www.baseball-reference.com/players/g/garagjo01.shtml
http://www.baseball-reference.com/players/l/lasorto01-pitch.shtml
http://www.baseball-reference.com/players/s/schalra01.shtml
http://www.baseball-reference.com/teams/BTT/
http://www.baseball-reference.com/teams/LAD/
http://www.baseball-reference.com/teams/NYM/
http://www.baseball-reference.com/teams/NYY/
http://www.baseball-reference.com/teams/SFG/
http://www.retrosheet.org/boxesetc/B/Pberry101.htm
http://www.retrosheet.org/boxesetc/B/Pbroud101.htm
http://www.retrosheet.org/boxesetc/B/Pbrowm102.htm
http://www.retrosheet.org/boxesetc/G/Pgaraj101.htm
http://www.retrosheet.org/boxesetc/L/Plasot101.htm
http://www.retrosheet.org/boxesetc/S/Pschar103.htm

Additional Sources

A. Bartlett Giamatti Research Center Clipping Files:
    Lawrence Peter (Yogi) Berra
    Dennis Joseph (Dan) Brouthers
    Mordecai Peter Centennial Brown
    Joseph Henry (Joe) Garagiola
    Thomas Charles (Tom) Lasorda
    Ray William Schalk

Los Cubanos in New York's October

An overview of Cubans in the postseason for New York-based clubs

Reynaldo Cruz Díaz

Playing in the postseason is high stress and tension-packed, bringing ballplayers to the edge, making them play harder and sometimes better, sometimes making mistakes along the way. The idea of reaching the postseason in New York City—the Capital of Baseball—brings an extra burden for players, even more with the hard-core rivalries like the New York Giants versus the Brooklyn Dodgers or the New York Yankees, or the Yankees versus the Dodgers. When the players come from small towns in the long-isolated island of Cuba and find themselves in crucial baseball games played in the Big Apple, the pressure is further magnified. Every move in New York is scrutinized by the media. And now we will scrutinize some of those players ourselves. from Adolfo Luque (known to fans stateside as Dolf Luque), the first ever Cuban to see postseason action in a New York uniform, to Yoenis Céspedes, the most recent. Whether in the spotlight with classy demeanor, appearing with one brilliant intervention, or withering their performance to oblivion, guys from the Greater of the Antilles have honored the Yankees, Mets, Dodgers, and Giants with postseason appearances.

Playing for Troy and the Mutuals of the National Association, Esteban Bellán was the first Latino to sign a contract for professional baseball in 1871. That also made him the first Cuban to play baseball for a New York-based club, even though the major leagues were not in existence yet, nor were playoffs/postseason as we know them today.

In 1917, in the twilight of an injury-plagued career that included a .317 batting average for the Cincinnati Reds in 1912 and a couple of adventures in the Federal League with the St. Louis Terriers, Armando Marsáns—one of the two first Cubans to don major league uniforms, along with Rafael Almeida—was traded by the St. Louis Browns to the New York Yankees. With that trade, the talented outfielder earned the distinction of being the first Cuban to play for the Yankees, although he was preceded to the city by Emilio Palmero and José Rodríguez (who debuted for the New York Giants in 1915 and 1916, respectively).

Marsáns's biggest distinction is that of being the top holder in hits among Cubans who have worn the pinstripes with 49.

But none of these three players made it to the playoffs while in New York. Marsáns played two seasons in which the American League pennant was won by the White Sox (1917) and the Red Sox (1918), both eventual World Series champions; Palmero's Giants finished last in 1915. Joined by Rodríguez in 1916, they finished 7 games behind the pennant-winning Dodgers. Rodríguez didn't see any Fall Classic action when his Giants lost to the White Sox in 1917, before finishing second—10½ games from the Cubs—in 1918.

Therefore, the first postseason appearance by a Cuban in the Big Apple was by none other than the aforementioned Adolfo Luque. Luque had been a successful pitcher for the Cincinnati Reds, and he was with them when they won the infamous 1919 World Series against the Chicago White Sox when eight (or fewer) players threw the World Series and became known as the Black Sox. While roaming the bullpen of the Polo Grounds for the Giants in the 1933 World Series against the Washington Senators, he was in the decline of a rather successful 20-year career in which he amassed 194 wins, including 27 in 1923 alone.

In the deciding game five, played on October 7 in Griffith Stadium, Luque came in to relieve Hal Schumacher in the sixth inning with two outs, after the Giants' starter had yielded a three-run shot to Fred Schulte, and two more singles that put runners on first and second. The Pride of Havana retired Luke Sewell on a grounder to second to end the inning, and allowed two hits (both to Joe Cronin in the eighth and the tenth) and two walks while striking out five Senators—three of them in the seventh frame. At the plate, he singled in his lone at bat, off Jack Russell in the top of the ninth. The run that decided it all came on a home run by Mel Ott off Russell in the top of the tenth inning. Luque's 4.1 innings of work made him the winning pitcher in the game.

Nineteen years would pass before another Cuban made the postseason, and it was with the other New

NATIONAL BASEBALL HALL OF FAME, COOPERSTOWN, NY

Adolfo Luque was the first Cuban player to play for a New York team in the World Series.

York franchise that would soon relocate to the West Coast. The year was 1952, and outfielder Edmundo Amorós (known in the States as Sandy) was wearing Dodger blue, playing for Brooklyn against the Yankees, appearing in just one game with no plate appearance.

On October 4, 1955, however, Sandy played a pivotal role in the Fall Classic when the Dodgers were taking on the Yankees. Writes SABR researcher Rory Costello, "His racing catch off Yogi Berra near the left-field line at Yankee Stadium saved the Bums' 2–0 lead in Game Seven of the World Series. Johnny Podres held on for the remaining three innings to bring Brooklyn its only title. The grab by Amorós still stands as one of the greatest in Series history, and it was the defining moment of the Cuban's career."[1]

The catch was indeed crucial for Brooklyn, but it was not Amorós's only feat that postseason. He went 4-for-12 at the plate, with three runs scored, a home run, three RBIs and four walks, for a 1.113 OPS. His plate prowess during that World Series was slightly overlooked because of the game-saving grab. Amorós was celebrated as a hero in Cuba, and over half a century later his crucial fielding is still remembered, even long after the Dodgers moved westward to Los Angeles.

Amorós was honored by a Day in his name in Brooklyn on June 20, 1992. Sadly, he never made that trip because he was hit by pneumonia on June 16 and died eleven days later. Amorós also holds the distinction in Cuba of being one of the first Afro-Cubans to gain "international exposure." As Costello writes about the sixth Central American and Caribbean Games in 1950 in Guatemala City, "Cuba won all seven of its games in the eight-team baseball tournament—led by Amorós, who hit .370 with six homers and 14 RBIs."[2]

The move to the Pacific Coast by the Giants (to San Francisco) and the Dodgers (to Los Angeles) caused a

drought of Cubans in the big city, as only the Yankees were left, and when the Mets came along in 1962 they were far from competitive. Their first Cuban player turned out to be Humberto "Chico" Fernández, who came mid-season from the Detroit Tigers in only the franchise's second season.

In 1998, long after Amorós had passed away, another player from the island nation made his way to the playoffs wearing a New York uniform, this time with the Yankees. Orlando Hernández, known to Cubans (and New Yorkers) as "El Duque," defected from the island following his brother Livan's defection and his own subsequent falling into disfavor with the Cuban authorities. One year earlier, Liván had won World Series Most Valuable Player plaudits while bringing the first title to the Florida Marlins as a rookie.

Without no appearance in the American League Division Series, El Duque started game four of the AL Championship Series on October 10 against the Cleveland Indians and went seven shutout innings, allowing only three hits, striking out six and walking only two. Then, in game two of the World Series against the San Diego Padres, the 32-year-old rookie threw seven frames with six hits, one earned run, seven strikeouts, and three walks, helping the pinstripes sweep the Fall Classic in four games.

Those turned out to be golden years for the Joe Torre-managed and Derek Jeter-led Yankees, as they won the World Series three consecutive seasons, from 1998 through 2000, and El Duque took part in all of them. He also went scoreless in his first ALDS game. Following his great success during the 1999 regular season, he was given the call in game one on October 5 and he went eight shutout frames, with only two hits, six walks, and four strikeouts against the Texas Rangers. In the ALCS he again got the game one nod against the Red Sox on October 13, but despite going eight strong innings of three runs (one unearned), seven hits, two walks, and four strikeouts, received a no-decision when the Yankees won, 4–3. In game five, played in Fenway Park five days later, Hernández threw seven-plus innings of one-run ball, allowing just five hits (including a round-tripper by Jason Varitek in the eighth) with four walks and nine batters fanned. Thanks to that performance, he was voted the ALCS most Valuable Player.

In the Fall Classic, on October 23 as the game one starter, he checked the box again, winning his lone game against the Atlanta Braves and eventual Hall of Famer Greg Maddux. As a starter, he had arguably his best postseason outing, pitching seven frames with one hit (Chipper Jones's home run in the fourth inning), one run, two walks and ten strikeouts.

Hernández had yet another convincing outing in the 2000 Division Series against the Oakland A's. He won game three by throwing seven strong frames with four hits, five walks, and four strikeouts, allowing two runs; and then got a hold on game five allowing one hit and getting one out. In the League Championship Series, he was not so dominant, as his ERA was 4.20 (seven earned runs in 15 innings), but he won both his starts against the Seattle Mariners, 7–1 and 9–7.

In the first Subway Series played in New York since the 1950s, El Duque had his last Fall Classic decision, losing his lone start against the Mets on October 24. In 7.1 innings of work, he gave up nine hits and four earned runs while walking three and striking out 12.

In each playoff series the following season, El Duque (having his worst regular season with the pinstripes, with a 4–7 record and 4.85 ERA) got a start and went 1–1, beating the A's in the ALDS, falling to the Mariners in the ALCS, and getting a no-decision in his last World Series start, in game four against the Arizona Diamondbacks, throwing 6.1 innings while yielding four hits, four walks, and one run (on a home run by Mark Grace), while plunking two batters. The Yankees would tie the game in the ninth inning thanks to a home run by Tino Martínez, and would walk the game off in the tenth frame with Derek Jeter's blast. However, the team all of America was rooting for—following the terrorist attacks against the World Trade Center on 9/11—lost the series in seven games on a ninth inning blown save by Mariano Rivera and a bases-loaded walk-off bloop single by Luis González, an outfielder with Cuban ancestry. That World Series also marked the end of the almost invincible Bronx Bombers, who ruled all of baseball under the helm of Joe Torre.

The crafty Cuban would make it to the postseason again in a Yankee uniform in 2002, but his performance was well past his best: he entered in the fourth inning of game two of the ALDS trailing by three runs against the Anaheim Angels and pitched four innings, but allowed two solo home runs and was charged with the loss, 8–6. In game four he threw 2.1 frames in relief, entering in the fifth with two outs, when New York was down by seven tallies.

After missing 2003 due to a rotator cuff injury in his shoulder that required surgery—he had been traded to the Montreal Expos in the offseason but returned to New York prior to Opening Day in 2004—El Duque had yet another postseason start, his last playoff game as a Yankee. This time he faced the Boston Red Sox in game four of the ALCS, played on

October 17 at Fenway Park. He left the game after five innings, allowing three runs and three hits, while walking five and striking out six. The Red Sox would tie the game in the ninth, avoid the sweep (the Yankees were ahead in the Series 3–0 at the time) and eventually put up the greatest comeback in postseason history, going on to win three more games as well as sweeping the St. Louis Cardinals in the Fall Classic.

Perhaps, what is most remarkable about Orlando Hernández was the fact that his major league debut came when he was already 32, and he managed to win nine postseason games and lose only three, all decisions as a Yankee. In 102 innings of postseason work, he struck out 101 opponents, gave 51 free passes and had an ERA of 2.65, whereas his WHIP was 1.245 in 17 games—14 starts. It is also important to note that he had a 2–1 record in four World Series, of which New York won three. Perhaps his ability of working well under pressure is explained in Peter C. Bjarkman's words about him and his half-brother, Liván Hernández: "One colorful rookie-season incident that has become legend has Hernández questioned by New York media about the pressures of first facing the Red Sox and Pedro Martínez in 'The House That Ruth Built.' [It would have been the game of September 14, in which Duque tossed a three-hit shutout.] El Duque is reported to have laughed off the question by responding that no pressure could compare to what he had already known pitching against rival Santiago de Cuba with 50,000 fanatics crammed into Havana's Latin American Stadium."[3]

While the former Industriales star—the Cuban League's all-time record holder in winning percentage—was shining in the Bronx, another Cuban was making his way in Queens, wowing the crowds with his glove, and reaching the postseason in 1999. It was no other than defensive-whiz shortstop Rey Ordóñez, who had the opportunity of becoming the first Cuban to play in the postseason for the New York Mets.

Sandy Amoros made a pivotal catch in the 1955 World Series, the definitive moment in his career and the lone championship for the Brooklyn Dodgers.

Orlando Hernandez had a big leg kick and a big impact on the winning ways of Joe Torre's Yankees.

Ordóñez, who had defected from the Cuban College Squad in Buffalo in 1993, came up as a weak-hitting, highly regarded defensive shortstop. He would be a three-time Gold Glove recipient with the Mets, and made his postseason debut on October 5. He would go on to play all games of the National League Division Series against Arizona and the National League Championship Series against the Atlanta Braves.

The Havana-born infielder participated in ten games, four in the NLDS and the other six in the NLCS, with five hits in 38 at bats, for a .132 batting average. He hit a double (his only postseason extra-base hit) and stole one base in game two against the D'Backs. He scored a run and had an RBI in game one of that series and drove in another one in game three. Against the Braves, he got only a single in 24 at bats, and his OPS for the entire postseason was a weak .289. But not much more can be expected from a guy who batted .246 for life with 12 career dingers in 973 games. He would miss the 2000 postseason, including the Subway Series, after a left arm fracture on May 29, which hampered his fielding for the rest of his career. There was another Cuban on that roster, who never saw action in the postseason: first baseman Jorge Luis Toca.

The Yankees would soon have another Cuban on the mound. Unlike El Duque, who relied on his crafty deliveries and wit, José Ariel Contreras—who defected at age 30 following the 2002 National Series season in Cuba—was considered the island's top pitcher at the time. Having achieved a status of nearly invincible in Cuba, the tall, black righty from Pinar del Río was usually given the ball by Team Cuba managers for do-or-die games, and he came through.

With the hope that success both in Cuba and the international arena—basically against pros—would translate into big-league success, the New York front office signed him and Contreras responded by going 7–2 with a 3.30 ERA in 71 innings of work that season. But management did not have enough confidence in him to let him start in the postseason, and he would pitch four relief games in the ALCS against the Boston Red Sox, losing one. In the World Series against the Florida Marlins, he also pitched four games out of the bullpen and also lost his only decision.

Contreras would not last long with the Yankees and parted ways with the team midseason in 2004. He wound up with the Chicago White Sox, and helped them—teaming up with El Duque—conquer the World Series in 2005, winning his lone start.

Then along came Yoenis Céspedes, the Granma outfielder who caught scouts' eyes while playing in the 2009 World Baseball Classic and then went on to set a single-season home run record in the Cuban National Series prior to his defection. Céspedes signed with the Oakland A's, making his major league debut in 2012. After being traded to the Boston Red Sox midseason in 2014, and then to the Detroit Tigers in that very offseason, the talented Cuban player moved to the New York Mets before the 2015 trade deadline. He instantly exploded and became a sensation, hitting 17 dingers in just 57 games, helping the club reach the postseason with his .942 OPS after the transaction.

With ten previous postseason games under his belt (all with Oakland), Céspedes had a lackluster start with the Mets in Dodger Stadium. His first game in the NLDS could not be more disastrous, as he went 0-for-4 with three strikeouts (two of them against Dodgers ace Clayton Kershaw). But he would hit a blast in the next game, and on October 12, his playoff home debut in Citi Field, he would prove to the Mets he was worth his money, going 3-for-5 with three runs and a three-run home run off reliever Alex Wood.

After getting a single in four at bats on October 13, Céspedes would have exactly the same outcome he had had in game one (zero hits in four at bats with three strikeouts), this time victimized by Zack Greinke, who in three times up fanned him twice. Two days later, the Mets took the series.

Against the Chicago Cubs in the NLCS, Céspedes had a particularly good performance in game three, getting three hits in five at bats, with a double, a run and two RBIs. He batted in the first Mets run in the top of the first inning, with a double off Kyle Hendricks that drove in David Wright. With the game tied, 2–2, he singled in the sixth frame, moved to second on a sacrifice bunt by Lucas Duda, stole third, and scored on a third-strike wild pitch by Trevor Cahill to Michael Conforto. Yoenis would then drive in the first of two insurance runs in the seventh, with a single that sent Wright to the plate.

He would get only three hits and an RBI in the five World Series games against the eventual champions, the Kansas City Royals. Céspedes's fielding doubts also helped Alcides Escobar get an inside-the-park home run in the first game—a game that would go to extra innings and would be won by the Royals.

In 2016, Céspedes had only one playoff game, this time the Wild Card game against the San Francisco Giants, who had Madison Bumgarner on the mound. The superior lefty would go the distance, blanking the Mets with only four hits and six strikeouts (two of them by the Cuban).

Yoenis has shown, the same as he did in Cuba, incredible performance deficits in the postseason.[4] His October numbers for the Mets are well below his proven quality: a .207/.217/.328 line with a meager .544 OPS, 19 strikeouts, 12 hits, and two home runs with eight RBIs are numbers he can actually improve in the near future. If the Mets starting rotation can stay impressive, the team could reach many postseasons in the coming years; Céspedes is under contract until 2020.

Another Cuban who is under contract for a New York-based club currently is Aroldis Chapman. The big lefty, whose fastball has been clocked at over 105 miles per hour, was credited with the win in the last game of the 2016 World Series for the Chicago Cubs, and then returned to the Yankees, this time on a deal that goes as far as 2021—although he may opt out after the 2019 campaign. The Bronx Bombers, out of the postseason since losing in the 2015 Wild Card game to Dallas Keuchel and the Houston Astros, have a young team and have been rebuilding the franchise, so the future looks bright for them and for Chapman.

Only the Mets have won a World Series among New York teams without a Cuban in their roster. The

NATIONAL BASEBALL HALL OF FAME, COOPERSTOWN, NY

Rey Ordoñez, a defensive whiz from Havana, was the first Cuban to play in the postseason for the New York Mets.

Giants and the Dodgers had indeed important interventions from Cubans in deciding games, and the Yankees had in Orlando Hernández arguably the best Cuban performer in the Big Apple. With his bat and his arm, Céspedes might reverse the trend that has haunted him and become the first Cuban to win the World Series with the Mets. ■

Sources
In addition to the sources cited in the notes, the author also consulted:
    Baseball-encyclopedia
    Baseball-Reference.com

Notes
1. Biography of Sandy Amorós: Rory Costello, edited by Len Levin, Bill Nowlin and Peter C. Bjarkman, *Cuban Baseball Legends: Baseball's Alternative Universe* (Society for American Baseball Research, 2016).
2. Idem.
3. Biography of Orlando Hernández and Liván Hernández: Peter C. Bjarkman, edited by Len Levin, Bill Nowlin and Peter C. Bjarkman, *Cuban Baseball Legends: Baseball's Alternative Universe* (Society for American Baseball Research, 2016).
4. The very same year in which he broke the single season home run record in Cuba's National Series, Yoenis Céspedes was completely silenced in the playoffs, which led to his team's eventual elimination before the finals (Author's note).

Contributors

MARTY APPEL is the author of 24 books including *Casey Stengel: Baseball's Greatest Character*, published by Doubleday in 2017.

JOHN J. BURBRIDGE, JR. is Professor Emeritus at Elon University where he was both a dean and professor. While at Elon he introduced and taught Baseball and Statistics. A native of Jersey City, he authored "The Brooklyn Dodgers in Jersey City" which appeared in the *Baseball Research Journal*, and has presented at SABR conventions and the Seymour meetings. He is a lifelong New York Giants baseball fan (he does acknowledge they moved to San Francisco). The greatest Giants-Dodgers game he attended was a 1–0 Giants' victory in Jersey City in 1956. (Yes, the Dodgers did play in Jersey City in 1956 and 1957.) John can be reached at burbridg@elon.edu.

PAUL BROWNE is the author of *The Coal Barons Played Cuban Giants: A History of Early Professional Baseball in Pennsylvania, 1886–1896* (McFarland). His article on the Cuban Giants' first victory over a major league team appears in *Inventing Baseball: The 100 Greatest Games of the Nineteenth Century*. Browne has been a member of SABR since the mid-1990s. He has contributed several player biographies to the SABR BioProject, a previous article in the 2013 *National Pastime*, McFarland's journal *Black Ball*, SABR's Nineteenth Century and Minor Leagues committees, as well as local newspapers. Browne is executive director of the Carbondale Technology Transfer Center.

ALAN COHEN has been a SABR member since 2011, serves as Vice President-Treasurer of the Connecticut Smoky Joe Wood Chapter, and is the datacaster (stringer) for the Hartford Yard Goats. He has written more than 35 biographies for the SABR BioProject, and has contributed to several SABR books. He has expanded his research into the Hearst Sandlot Classic (1946–65), the annual youth All-Star game which launched the careers of 88 major-league players. He graduated from Franklin and Marshall College with a degree in history. He has four children and six grandchildren and resides in West Hartford, Connecticut, with his wife Frances, one cat (Morty), and two dogs (Sam and Sheba).

REYNALDO CRUZ DÍAZ is the founder and head editor of the Cuban-based magazine *Universo Béisbol*, which is hosted in MLBlogs. He is a language graduate of the University of Holguin, in his hometown, and has been leading the aforementioned magazine since March 2010. A SABR member since the summer of 2014, he writes, translates, and photographs baseball and was in the first row of the Barack Obama game in Havana, shooting from the Tampa Bay Rays dugout. In spite of the rich history of Cuban baseball, his favorite player happens to be no other than Ichiro Suzuki, whom he hopes to meet and interview. A retro-ballpark lover, he envisions Fenway Park, Wrigley Field, Koshien Stadium, and Estadio Palmar de Junco as the can't-miss places in baseball.

ROB EDELMAN teaches film history courses at the University at Albany. He is the author of *Great Baseball Films* and *Baseball on the Web*, and is co-author (with his wife, Audrey Kupferberg) of *Meet the Mertzes*, a double biography of *I Love Lucy*'s Vivian Vance and fabled baseball fan William Frawley, and *Matthau: A Life*. He is a film commentator on WAMC (Northeast) Public Radio and a Contributing Editor of *Leonard Maltin's Movie Guide*. He is a frequent contributor to *Base Ball: A Journal of the Early Game* and has written for *Baseball and American Culture: Across the Diamond*; *Total Baseball*; *Baseball in the Classroom*; *Memories and Dreams*; and *NINE: A Journal of Baseball History and Culture*. His essay on early baseball films appears on the DVD *Reel Baseball: Baseball Films from the Silent Era, 1899–1926*, and he is an interviewee on the director's cut DVD of *The Natural*.

ED EDMONDS is Professor Emeritus of Law at the University of Notre Dame. He is the former law library director at William & Mary, Loyola New Orleans, St. Thomas (MN), and Notre Dame. He is a frequent speaker at the *NINE* Spring Training Conference and the Cooperstown Symposium. With Frank Houdek, he is the co-author of *Baseball Meets the Law* (McFarland 2007). He has taught a seminar on sports law for over 30 years and written numerous law review articles on the legal aspects of labor and antitrust law and baseball.

GORDON J. GATTIE serves as a human-systems integration engineer for the U.S. Navy. His baseball research interests involve ballparks, historical records, and statistical analysis. A SABR member since 1998, Gordon earned his Ph.D. from SUNY Buffalo, where he used baseball to investigate judgment/decision-making performance in complex dynamic environments. Originally from Buffalo, Gordon learned early the hardships associated with rooting for Buffalo sports teams. Ever the optimist, he also cheers for the Cleveland Indians and Washington Nationals. Lisa, his lovely bride who also enjoys baseball, continues to challenge him by supporting the Yankees. Gordon has contributed to multiple SABR publications.

STEVEN GLASSMAN has been a SABR member since 1994 and regularly makes presentations for the Connie Mack Chapter. "A Hall of Fame Cup of Coffee in New York" will be his fourth article in SABR's convention journal, *The National Pastime*. The Temple University graduate in Sport and Recreation Management is currently the Manor College Volunteer Director of Sports Information in Jenkintown, Pennsylvania. He has attended Phillies games since the 1970s. Steven serves as first base coach/scorekeeper for his summer league softball team. He currently resides in Warminster, Pennsylvania.

JOHN R. HARRIS is a writer, photographer and the Senior Producer of the B&H Photography Podcast. In addition to writing on baseball history, he has written extensively on photography and camera technology. His photographs have appeared in *The New York Times* and have been exhibited at the International Center of Photography, Museum of Modern Art, and Victoria and Albert Museum. A lifelong Indians fan, he had a short stint with the baseball team of his alma mater, Fordham University. John can be reached at harrisfoto@gmail.com or @jrockfoto10 on Twitter.

LESLIE HEAPHY is Associate Professor of history at Kent State at Stark. She is also the vice president of SABR—currently in her seventh year of SABR board service—and has chaired SABR's Women in Baseball committee since 1995.

FRANCIS KINLAW, as a youngster in North Carolina, listened to hundreds of broadcasts of baseball games on New York radio stations for enjoyment but also to overcome a lack of access to the big city's newspapers. A member of SABR since 1983, he resides in Greensboro, North Carolina, and writes extensively about baseball, football, and college basketball.

DAVID KRELL is the author of *Our Bums: The Brooklyn Dodgers in History, Memory and Popular Culture* (McFarland, 2015) and the co-editor of In the *Arena: A Sports Law Handbook* (New York State Bar Association, 2013). David has spoken at SABR's 19th Century Conference, Negro Leagues Conference, and Annual Convention. He has also spoken at the Cooperstown Symposium on Baseball and American Culture, Queens Baseball Convention, Mid-Atlantic Nostalgia Convention, and Hofstra University's New York Mets 50th Anniversary Conference. David's writing has appeared in *Black Ball: A Negro Leagues Journal*, *Base Ball: A Journal of the Early Game*, *The Baseball Research Journal*, *The National Pastime*, and the *New York State Bar Association's Entertainment, Arts and Sports Law Journal*, and thesportspost.com.

BOB MAYER is a retired bank executive from JPMorgan/Chase and Bankers Trust Co. A member of SABR since 2004, Bob collects vintage baseball artifacts and researches early baseball in the Westchester, Orange, Dutchess, Ulster and Putnam Counties in New York. He has spoken at many SABR and baseball historical conferences, produced the Old Timers Baseball Celebration in Peekskill (July 2012), and serves on the Board of Directors of the Middletown Historical Society. He is a trustee and former president of the Peekskill Museum.

TONY MORANTE, a SABR member since 1995, is the Director of Yankee Stadium Tours. He started working at Yankee Stadium in 1958 as an usher and came aboard full-time in 1973 in the Group/Season Sales Department. Morante, with the encouragement of then-principal owner, Mr. George M. Steinbrenner III, instituted the Yankee Stadium Tour program in 1985, bringing Yankees history to life for school children, visitors and employees' orientations. Morante served in the United States Navy and he is currently involved with the Wounded Warrior Project and the Special Operations Program through the New York Yankees. Tony is a graduate of Fordham University and he is currently Adjunct Professor there teaching "Baseball: The New York Game."

GARY SARNOFF is a historian, a published author and a long-time SABR member. He was written articles for SABR's BioProject and Games project, *Nats News*, *Minor League News*, *Base Ball: A journal of the early game* and SABR's 2009 edition of *The National Pastime*. In addition, he covered the Silver Spring-Takoma Thunderbolts of the Cal Ripken Sr. League from 2011–13, and has made several presentations about baseball, football, aviation and American History at historical societies and museums throughout the country.

DR. DEBRA A. SHATTUCK has been researching women baseball players since 1987. Her area of expertise is the nineteenth century and she recently published a first-of-its-kind history documenting the extent to which girls and women have played baseball from its earliest inception: *Bloomer Girls: Women Baseball Pioneers* (University of Illinois Press, 2017). Deb is a retired Air Force Colonel and a long-time SABR member. She is Provost and Associate Professor of History and Leadership at John Witherspoon College in Rapid City, South Dakota, and, though far from her roots in northern Ohio, is still a proud fan of all things Cleveland.

MARK SOUDER served as the US Congressman for northeastern Indiana 1995–2010. He was a senior staff member in the US House and Senate for a decade prior to being elected to Congress. He was one of the primary questioners in the hearings on steroids abuse in baseball. His article "Why did Wrigley, Lasker, and the Chicago Cubs Join a Presidential Campaign?" was published in the 2015 *The National Pastime*. "When Boston Dominated Baseball" was included in the 2016 SABR book *Boston's First Nine*. He has written articles that will appear in scheduled SABR books on Puerto Rican baseball and the Boston Beaneaters. The article on John Wildey in this magazine is an expanded version of his presentation at the 19th Century SABR Conference (the FRED) at Cooperstown in 2015. Souder is retired other than occasional political commentary and meddling. He lives in Fort Wayne with his wife Diane and his books.

JOHN THORN is the Official Historian for Major League Baseball. He is the author of too many books.

STEW THORNLEY is the author of *Land of the Giants: New York's Polo Grounds* and editor of a soon-to-be-published anthology of the Polo Grounds. He received the *USA Today Baseball Weekly* Award for best research presentation at the 1998 Society for American Baseball Research convention in San Francisco for a presentation on the Polo Grounds. Stew has been a SABR member since 1979.

DAN VANDEMORTEL became a Giants fan in Upstate New York and moved to San Francisco to follow the team more closely. He has written extensively on Northern Ireland political and legal affairs, and his Giants-related writing has appeared in San Francisco's *Nob Hill Gazette* and *The National Pastime*. An investigation into the shooting of a spectator at the Polo Grounds will be published in 2017 in a Polo Grounds anthology. He is currently writing a book and related articles on the 1971 Giants and welcomes feedback at giants1971@yahoo.com.

CORT VITTY resides in Maryland with his wife Mary Anne and their pet golden-doodle Sparkle. A New Jersey native, Vitty graduated from Seton Hall University and continues to root for the New York Yankees. He's been a SABR member (Bob Davids Chapter) since 1999 and his articles have been featured in both *The Baseball Research Journal* and *The National Pastime*. He has contributed to several SABR book projects and his work is also posted at Seamheads.com and PhiladelphiaAthletics.org.

BILL YOUNG of Hudson, Quebec, is a retired academic administrator from Quebec's Community College system. Throughout his life he has been fascinated by the game of baseball and its history, especially the baseball history of Quebec. In addition to numerous articles on this topic for SABR, seamheads.com, and other publications, he also co-authored (with colleague Danny Gallagher) two books on the Montreal Expos: *Remembering the Montreal Expos* (2005) and *Ecstasy to Agony: The 1994 Montreal Expos—how the best team in baseball ended up in Washington ten years later (2013)*.